장준성	링구아어학원
장현정	헤리티지영수학원
장혜진	용인필탑학원
장호진	홍수학영어입시학원
장효선	영어의품격
전성준	이든학원
전성훈	훈선생영어학원
전수빈	전문과외
전우정	안T영어학원
전주원	필압단과전문학원
전지애	고양국제고등학교
전지혜	위슬런학원
전호준	채움영어
정규빈	대치다다학원
정다움	카인드학원
정다은	전문과외
정미란	티앤씨학원
정병채	탁클래스영어수학학원
정선영	전문과외
정선영	코어플러스영어학원
정성은	JK영어수학전문학원
정성태	에이든영어학원
정소연	이투스 전홍철 연구실
정연우	최강학원
정연욱	인크쌤영어학원
정영선	시퀀스학원
정영훈	BS반석학원
정유진	전문과외
정지연	공부의정석 학원
정지영	이지학원
정하경	에듀플렉스
정희찬	파란영어학원
제정미	제이영어
조대웅	전문과외
조병희	이철영어학원
조승규	제이앤와이 어학원
조용원	이티엘영어교습소
조원웅	클라비스 영어
조은쌤	조은쌤장쌤영어학원
조재만	가평한샘기숙학원
조정화	유하이에듀 학원
조준모	에스라이팅
조춘화	뮤엠영어발곡학원
조현지	전문과외
조혜원	The 131
주지은	JIEUN ENGLISH CLASS
진남용	영어종결센터신봉학원
차안나	아이비스 영어학원
채희수	전문과외
채희연	전문과외
최광현	포인트학원
최명지	이천 청솔기숙
최민석	탑클래스기숙학원
최상이	엄마영어아빠수학학원
최성원	패스파인더
최세열	JS수학영어학원
최영임	국립중앙청소년디딤센터
최유나	전문과외
최은진	고래영어학원
최은희	공부에 강한 아이들
최인선	캐써린쌤의슈가영어교습소
최창식	조나단영어보습학원
최희연	채움영어학원
최희정	SJ클쌤영어

편광범	야탑고등학교
표호진	아너스영어전문학원
하사랑	덕계한셈학원
하수용	시흥 대성학원
한순현	동탄 SKY 비상학원
한예진	필탑학원
함수향	진심팩토리인재양성소
현윤아	중동그린타운해법영어교습소
홍승완	전문과외
홍은화	라라영어수학 학원
홍정우	정현영어학원
홍호영	닉고등입시학원
홍희섭	조이 영어공부방
홍희진	청평 한샘 학원
황다연	The study 꿈자람
황명덕	옥정 엠베스트
황서윤	공부방
황은진	더에듀영어수학학원
황일선	M&E

경남

강진원	T.O.P 에듀학원
고성관	T.O.P 에듀학원
권승구	더케이영어학원
권승미	전문과외
권장미	인서울영어학원
권지현	우리모두의 영수학원
김계영	성신학원
김국희	새라영어학원
김루	상승영수전문학원
김민경	창선고등학교
김민기	민쌤영어
김선우	진성학원
김신영	김가영어학원
김신현	세종학원
김용진	다락방 남양지점 학원
김주은	동상교일학원
김준	가우스 sme 전문학원
김지윤	에듀퍼스트
김지은	HNC영어전문학원
김진영	연세어학원
김형돌	통영여자고등학교
김화선	마산중앙고등학교
남유림	이루다영어교습소
노경지	전문과외
노수진	인피니티영수전문학원
박민정	더클래스수학영어학원
박선영	전문과외
박성용	박성용입시전문학원
박신영	GH영수전문학원
박영하	네오시스템영어학원
박재형	인투잉글리쉬어학원
박정아	전문과외
박제선	주식회사김은정교육그룹
박준권	박준권 개인과외
배승빈	에스영어전문학원
배종원	마산무학여자고등학교
배찬희	라하잉글리시신진주역점
신형섭	크림슨어학원
심동현	The오름 영수학원
안혜경	T.O.P Edu학원
양경화	봄영어
양기영	다니엘학원
원임미	링구아어학원
유인희	보듬영어과외교습소

이문식	리더스 아카데미학원
이수길	명성영수학원
이연홍	리즈(Rhee's) 영어연구소
이윤섭	창원경일여자고등학교
이인아	인잉글리쉬학원
임진희	어썸영어학원
장경출	야꿈영수학원
장은정	케이트학원
장재훈	메르센학원
정상락	비상잉글리시아이 영어교습소
정수연	Got Them
정수정	지탑영어
정희성	원스텝영수학원
최승관	창선고등학교
최지영	시퀀스영수학원
최현정	토킹스타영어학원
최환준	Jun English
최효정	인에이블영수학원
하동권	네오시스템영어학원
하수미	진동삼성영수학원
한지용	성민국영수학원
허민정	허달영어

경북

강민표	현일고등학교
강선우	EiE 고려대 국제 어학원
강유진	지니쌤영어
강은석	은석학원
강혜성	EiE 고려대 국제 어학원
고일영	영어의비법학원
김광현	전문과외
김귀숙	퀸영어교습소
김규남	경상북도 영양교육지원청
김도량	다이너마이트잉글리시
김도영	김도영영어
김민정	잇올초이스
김상호	전문과외
김윤채	포카학원
김으뜸	EIE학원 옥계캠퍼스
김정선	바투하이영어
김주훈	공터 영어학원
김지현	토피아 영어 교습소
김지훈	전문과외
김현우	창녕 대성고등학교
김형표	표쌤영어학원
문상헌	에이원영어
문홍민	메디컬영어학원
박경애	포항대성초이스학원
박계민	영광중학교
박규정	베네치아 영어 교습소
박령이	한뜻입시학원
박보성	문화고등학교
박예진	선주고등학교
박지수	포스코교육재단
배세왕	BK영수전문학원
성룡	미르어학원
손누리	이든샘영수학원
손희경	성균관아카데미 과학영어학원
유영선	아이비티주니어
유진욱	공부의힘 영수학원
윤재호	이상렬단과학원
이강정	이룸단과학원
이리나	제일영어놀이터
이민정	레이먼원어민어학원
이보라	전문과외

이상열	이상렬입시단과학원
이소연	전문과외
이주연	Rachel's English
이지연	전문과외
장미	잉글리시아이 원리학원
장정원	옥스포드영어학원
전영아	문일학원
정소연	YBM퍼펙트잉글리쉬
정현갑	구미여자고등학교
정현수	엠베스트se위닝학원
정호정	인지니어스
조효근	수학만영어도학원
최경주	전문과외
최미선	3030영어망청포은러닝센터
허우열	탑세븐입시

광주

강나검	스위치영어수학
곽해림	AMG 영어학원
김도엽	스카이영어학원
김도영	KOUM ENGLISH
김동익	전문과외
김명재	범지연영어학원
김병남	일등급수학위즈덤영어학원
김상연	우리어학원
김서현	전문과외
김수인	모조잉글리쉬
김유경	프라임 아카데미
김유진	위트니영어유타학원
김인화	김인화영어학원
김재곤	김재곤 중고등영어학원
김한결	상무외대어학원
김효은	청담아카데미학원
김효정	광주 메이드영어학원
문장엽	엠제이영어수학전문학원
박동훈	유캔영어
박정준	동아여자고등학교
박주형	본선동 한수위 국어 영어
박혜지	YBM잉글루 최강학원
배연주	본영수학원
봉병주	철수와영수
손아미	공감스터디학원
신지수	온에어영어학원
양신애	오름국어영어학원
오승리	이지스터디
오평안	지산한길어학원
우진일	블루페스 영어학원
유현주	U's유즈영어교습소
윤은주	아이비영어교실
이민정	롱맨어학원
이소민	더클래스영어전문학원
이영조	전문과외
이진희	이마스터
이현창	진월유앤아이어학원
전솔	서강고등학교
정세윤	아름드리학원
정지선	이지스터디
최연숙	엠베스트se공부학원
최현욱	최현욱 영어학원
최혜란	토킹클럽영어학원
한기석	이(E)영어교습소
한방엽	신통학원
현동욱	박철영어학원
황선미	함께가는영어

대구

구교찬	새롬영어
구범모	굿샘영어학원
구수진	전문과외
구현정	헬렌영어학원
권보현	씨즈더데이어학원
권익재	제이슨영어교습소
권하련	아너스이엠에스학원
김근아	블루힐영어학원
김기목	목샘영어교습소
김나래	더베스트영어학원
김미나	전문과외
김민재	열공열강 영어수학학원
김병훈	LU어
김상완	YEP영어학원
김수미	스펙마스터
김연정	유니티영어
김유환	대구 유신학원
김윤정	독쭝영어
김은혜	고등학원 중등관
김정혜	제니퍼영어 교습소
김종석	에이블영어학원
김준석	NOTION영어
김지영	김지영영어
김진호	강성영어
김철우	메라키 영어 교습소
김하나	전문과외
김현정	도우영수학원
김호연	KK 수학 영어
김희정	이선생영어학원
나기원	문광월성점
노태경	윙스잉글리쉬
문창육	지앤비(GnB)스페셜입시학원
민승규	민승규영어학원
박고은	스테듀입시학원
박라율	열공열강영어수학학원
박민지	소나무학원
박연희	좀다른영어
박예지	전문과외
박지환	전문과외
박희숙	열공열강영어수학학원
방성모	방성모영어학원
백수양	태학영어학원
백재민	에소테리카 영어학원
서상진	대진고등학교
서정인	서울입시학원
신경순	전문과외
신정식	넛지영어교습소
신혜경	외대어학원
심경아	Shim's English
안다영	일라영어학원
엄재경	하이엔드영어학원
오선연	전문과외
원현지	원샘영어교습소
위은령	대구 브릿지영어
유소영	YH영어교습소
윤원채	원잉글리쉬영어교습소
윤이강	카르페디엠 영어수학학원
이근성	헬렌영어학원
이동환	쌤마스터입시학원
이샛별	데카어학원
이소민	프라임영어학원
이수연	하이어영어
이수희	이온영어

이승민 전문과외	이원성 파스칼베스티안학원	이유림 유림영어교습소	김영미 WIN영어	성수하 전문과외
이승재 파머스어학원 침산캠퍼스	이유나 전문과외	이윤호 메트로 영어	김영삼 중계YS영어	성언형 대치AOP
이승현 대구 학문당입시학원	이재근 이재근영어수학학원	이은정 영어를ON하다	김윤선 쎌영어	송상종 에듀플러스 학원
이승희 독쫑영어학원	이진경 이룸학원	이재우 무한꿈터 동래캠퍼스	김은진 ACE영어 교습소	송정근 기정학원
이애진 한솔영어수학이쌤파워학원	이홍원 모티브에듀학원	이정윤 아벨영어	김종윤 가온에듀	송정은 이은재어학원
이정인 계성고등학교	장혜진 피어오름영어	이지은 Izzy English	김종현 김종현영어	송현우 양서중학교
이진영 전문과외	정동녘 에스오에스학원	이지현 Serena영어	김주혜 라온학원	송혜민 전문과외
이헌욱 이헌욱 영어학원	정동현 대성외국어	이진선 전문과외	김지영 강서고등학교	신경훈 제프영어
임형주 사범대단과학원	정라라 영어문화원 정라라 영어교습소	이혜정 로엠어학원	김진돈 중계세일학원	신동주 공감학원
장현진 고려대EIE어학원 현풍캠퍼스	정윤희 Alex's English	이희정 로엠영어 E&F English	김채원 정이조 영어학원	신연우 전문과외
전윤애 전문과외	정혜수 쌜리영어	장민지 탑클래스영어학원	김하나 전문과외	신정애 당산점 와와학습코칭학원
정대웅 유신학원	조영재 카이젠교육	전정은 전문과외	김현지 목동 하이스트 본원	신호현 아로새김
정승덕 JSD English	조현 시나브로학원	정영훈 J&C 영어전문학원	김형준 미래탐구 오목관	신희경 신쌤영어
정용회 에스피영어학원	진정회 코너스톤엘 상대학원	조은상 드림엔영어	김혜림 대치 청담학원	심건희 전문과외
조성애 조성애세움영어수학학원	채송은 위캔영어학원	조정훈 고려화 고등영어전문	김혜영 스터디원	심나현 성북메가스터디
조혜현 연쌤영수학원	최성호 에이스영어 교습소	채지영 리드앤톡영어도서관학원	나선아 전문과외	심민철 수능영어플러스+
주현지 E.T Betty	최현우 엠베스트SE엘리트학원	최우성 초이English&Pass	나영은 강남청솔기숙학원	심민혜 신일류수학학원
채유란 전문과외	한형식 서대전여자고등학교	최이내 일광IGSE 어학원	노은경 이은재어학원	심은지 연세YT어학원
최효진 너를 위한 영어		탁아진 에이블영어	노재순 씨투엠학원	안나연 전문과외
하해준 일라영어학원	**부산**	하현진 브릿츠영어	노종주 전문과외	안미영 스카이플러스학원
한정아 능인고등학교	고경원 남구감만한맥학원	한구상 전문과외	도선혜 중계동 영어 공부방	안성연 안스잉글리시학원
홍지수 홍글리시영어	김달용 Able 영어교습소	한영희 미래탐구	류기동 기동찬 영어학원	안웅희 이엔엠 영수전문학
황윤슬 사적인영어	김대영 나무와숲영어교습소	홍지안 에이블 어학원	맹혜선 휘경여자고등학교	안일훈 안일훈영어교습소
	김도담 도담한영어교실		명가은 명가은 영어학원	안현우 지니영어학원
대전	김도윤 코어영어교습소	**서울**	문명기 문명기영어학원	양세희 양세희수능영어학원
Tony Park Tony Park English	김동혁 코어국영수전문학원	Diana 위례광장 해법영어	문민아 다른학원	양하나 목동 씨앤씨
강태헌 끊어읽기영어	김동휘 장정호 영어전문학원	Simon뱅 에이플교육	문영선 키맨학원	어효주 이-베스트 영어학원
고우리 브릭스 영어학원	김미혜 더멘토영어	가혜림 목동종로학원	문지현 목동CNC	엄태열 대치 차오름학원
곽연우 유성고등학교	김병택 탑으로가는영어	강동수 일신학원	문진완 대원고등학교	염석민 은평1230
권현미 디디샘영어	김성미 다올영어	강민정 네오 과학학원	박광운 전문과외	오은경 전문과외
길민주 전문과외	김소연 전문과외	강성호 대원고등학교	박귀남 Stina+ English	용혜영 SWEET ENGLISH 영어전문 공부방
김경이 영어서당학원	김재경 탑클래스영어학원	강예린 TG 영어전문학원	박기철 한진연 입시전략연구소	우승희 우승희영어학원
김근범 딱쌤영어	김정화 센텀영어교습소	강인환 스터디코칭영어전문학원	박남규 알짜영어교습소	위정훈 앤트스터디 명품 대입관 학원
김기형 관저진학학원	김지애 전문과외	강정호 더(the)상승학원	박미애 명문지혜학원	유수연 인헌중학교
김수연 둔산 엠폴리어학원	김진규 의문을열다	공진 리더스	박민주 석선생 영어학원 중관	유현승 심슨어학원
김영철 전문과외	김현지 이헌 영수 학원 초량분원	구민모 키움학원	박병석 주영학원	윤나예 미래영재
김재원 중촌브레인학원	나유진 채움영어교습소	구지윤 전문과외	박선경 씨투엠학원	윤명원 이지수능교육원
김하나 김하나영어연구소	남경화 전문과외	권보현 대치 다원교육	박소영 JOY	윤상혁 전문과외
나규성 비전21입시학원	남재호 제니스학원	권영진 경동고등학교	박소하 전문과외	윤성 대치동 새움학원
남영종 엠베스트SE	류미향 류미향입시영어	권원주 권쌤영어	박소현 전문과외	윤은미 CnT영어학원
민지원 민쌤영어교습소	박문기 시너지학원	권재현 icu학원	박숭규 SK 영어연구소	윤정아 윤정아영어
박난정 제일학원	박미진 MJ영어학원	권혜령 전문과외	박예나 강북예일학원	이강희 시온영어학원
박성회 청담프라임학원	박수진 제이엔씨 영어전문학원	길수련 전문과외	박윤주 에이원 아카데미 보습학원	이계훈 이지영어학원
박신지 청명대입학원	박아름 빡스잉글리쉬	김경수 목동탑킴입시연구소	박은경 오늘영어 교습소	이광희 가온에듀 2관
박주형 전문과외	박아림 틔움영어교습소	김나결 레이쌤영어교습소	박인선 신촌 나교수어학원	이국재 이은재어학원
박진선 전문과외	박정희 학림학원	김다은 진인영어학원	박정호 전문과외	이남규 신정송현학원
박진주 아이린인스티튜트	박지우 영어를 ON하다	김라영 목동퀸즈영어학원	박정효 메가스터디학원	이동근 이지스아카데미학원
박현진 전문과외	박지은 박지은영어전문과외방	김명열 대치명인학원	박준용 은평 G1230	이명순 Top Class English
박효진 박효진 영어 교습소	배거용 배거용영어전문학원	김미경 정이조 영어학원	박지연 영어공부연구소	이미영 티엠하버드영어학원
백지수 플랫폼학원	배찬원 에이플러스영어	김미선 낸시영어교습소	박지영 전문과외	이석원 숭실중학교
서윤주 전문과외	서대광 서진단과학원	김미은 오늘도맑음 영어교습소	박진경 JAYz ENGLISH	이석호 교원더퍼스트캠퍼스 학원
송신근 일취월장학원	성장우 전문과외	김미정 아발론콘신내캠퍼스	박진아 사과나무학원	이성택 엠아이씨영어학원
심효령 삼부가람	손복건 대신종로학원	김민지 클라라영어교습소	박찬경 펜타곤영어학원	이소민 임팩트영어
안수정 궁극의 사고	손소희 안창모 특목수능영어	김보영 대치 다원교육	박효원 링크영어교습소	이소윤 늘품영수전문학원
양지현 청출어람	손지안 정관 아슬란학원	김상희 스카이플러스	박희삼 대치쿰인학원	이승미 금천정상어학원
오봉우 새미래영수학원	안영실 개금국제어학원	김새온 온클래스영어교습소	방요한 대치에스학원	이시현 YBM학원
오지현 영어의 꿈 & 영재의 꿈	안정희 GnB영어전문학원양성캠퍼스	김석주 올림포스학원	배수경 강일연세학원	이아진 에이제이 인스티튜트
우희진 전문과외	오세창 범천반석단과학원	김선경 마크영어	배수현 남다른 이해 학원	이영건 감탄교육
유정인 제니영어	오정안 장산역 우영어학원	김선영 압구정 플래티넘 아카데미	백주희 레인메이커학원	이운정 전문과외
윤영숙 스칼렛영어	유수진 전문과외	김세현 필오름영어	변지예 북두칠성학원	이유빈 채움학원
이고은 고은영어	윤지영 잉글리쉬 무무	김수진 리더스영어보습학원	서승희 대치동 함영원학원	이유정 지앤비우이캠퍼스
이길형 빌드업영어	윤혜은 링구아어학원 동래본원	김승환 Arnold English Class	서은조 용강중학교	이은정 전문과외
이대회 청명대입학원	이상석 상석영어	김아름 ABC학습방향연구소	선지혜 최선메이트 본사	이재연 대원여자고등학교
이성구 나린학원	이선영 매리쌤잉글리시	김여진 전문과외	성수빈 전문과외	이정경 더스터디 영수학원
이수미 둔산0505	이순실 CDK국제어학당	김연희 전문과외		

이정혜 서초고려학원
이종현 대원고등학교
이지연 석률학원
이지연 중계케이트영어학원
이지향 전문과외
이철웅 비상하는 또또학원
이태희 진학학원 고등관
이헌승 스탠다드학원
이현민 대원고등학교
이혜숙 사당대성보습학원
이혜정 이루리학원
이희진 씨앤씨학원
임서은 H&J 형설학원
임지효 전문과외
장근아 씨티에이정도학원
장민정 전문과외
장서영 전문과외
장서희 전문과외
장재원 전문과외
장혜민 에스클래스 영어전문학원
전다은 동화세상에듀코_와와센터
전보람 상명대학교사범대학부속고등학교
전성연 대성학원고척캠퍼스주식회사
전여진 진중고등영어
정가람 촘촘영어
정경록 미즈원어학원
정경아 정쌤영어교습소
정민혜 정민혜밀착영어학원
정성준 팁탑영어
정원경 대원고등학교
정유진 탑잉글리쉬매쓰학원
정윤하 전문과외
정은미 류헌규영어학원
정은아 헨리영어학원
정재욱 씨알학원
정해림 전문과외
조미영 튼튼영어마스터클럽구로학원
조민석 더원영수학원
조민정 정성학원
조봉현 조셉영어국어학원
조봉희 자이온엘연구소
조아라 강북청솔학원
조연아 전문과외
조용현 바른스터디학원
조윤나 오세용학원
조윤신 조이스 영어 교습소
조정현 동원중학교
조현미 조현미 영어 클래스
주정연 DYB최선어학원 마포캠퍼스
지현진 목동JSB영어학원
진수범 이상숙어학원
진영민 브로든영어학원
진주현 EMC
차주훈 트라인 영어 수학 학원
채민지 전문과외
채상우 클레어영어
채에스더 문래중학교
최민주 전문과외
최유리 아이디어스 아카데미
최윤정 잉글리쉬앤 매쓰매니저 학원
최정문 한성학원
최진 금천정상어학원
최현선 수재학원
최형미 전문과외

최혜선 디와이비최선어학원 마포캠퍼스
최희재 이주화어학원
하슬기 세종학원
한문진 이룸영어
한안미 한스잉글리시영어교습소
한인혜 레나잉글리쉬
함규민 클레어영어
허동녕 학림학원
허유정 YJ최강영어
홍대균 선덕고등학교 특강강사
홍영민 성북상상학원
홍제기 정상어학원
황규진 잉글리쉬잇업
황상희 어나더레벨 영어전문학원
황혜정 석선생영어학원
황혜진 이루다 영어

세종
강봉식 맥스터디학원
곽영우 연세국제영어
권은경 전문과외
김지원 도램14영어
박혜진 전문과외
방종영 세움학원
백승희 백승희 영어
손대령 강한영어학원
송지원 베이 영어 & 입시컨설팅
안성주 더타임학원
안초롱 21세기학원
윤정근 만점영어학원
이다솜 세종장영실고등학교
이민지 공부방 마스터잉글리쉬
이지영 세종중학교
장소영 상위권학원
지영주 제나쌤의 영어교실

울산
강상배 1%단과전문학원
김경수 핀포인트영어학원
김내경 박정민영어
김성희 1%단과전문학원
김윤정 전문과외
김한중 스마트영어전문학원
김해섭 에임하이학원
양혜정 양혜정영어
이서경 오선생학원
이수현 제이엘영어교습소
정은선 한국ESL어학원
조충일 YBM 울산언양제1학원
최나비 더오름 high-and 학원
한건수 한스영어
한아련 블루밍영어교습소
허부배 비즈단과학원

인천
강미현 로렌영어
곽소희 인명여자고등학교
구하라 동인천 종로 엠
김남주 전문과외
김미경 김선생 영어/수학교실
김서애 제이+영어
김선나 태풍영어학원
김성률 좋은나무학원
김영재 강화펜타스학원
김영태 에듀터학원
김영호 조주석 수학&영어 클리닉학원

김윤경 엠베스트SE학원
김재혁 토피아 어학원
김정형 연령도고등학교
김정훈 TNL 영어 교습소
김종만 문일여자고등학교
김지연 인천 송도탑영어학원
김지우 청담 에이프릴 어학원
김진용 학산학원
김태무 전문과외
김택수 부개제일학원
나일지 두드림 HIGH학원
문지현 전문과외
박나혜 TOP과외
박세웅 서인천고등학교
박소희 북인천SLP
박재형 들결영어교습소
박종근 유빅학원
박주현 Ashley's English Corner
박진영 인천외국어고등학교
신영진 엉끌쌤과외
신은주 명문학원
신현경 청라 미라클 어학원
안진용 Tiptop학원
안현정 진심이교육하는학원
양현진 지니어스영어
양희진 지니어스영어
오성택 소수정예 중고등영어
오희정 교습소
원준 전문과외
윤희영 세실영어
이가희 S&U영어
이금선 전문과외
이미선 고품격EM EDU
이슬 청라영썸영어학원
이윤주 Triple One
이은정 인천논현고등학교
이용제 숭덕여자고등학교
임현주 원소운과외
장승혁 지엘학원
전혜원 제일고등학교
정도영 대신학원
정수진 11월의 비상
정은혜 즐거운 정쌤 영어학원
정지웅 정지웅 영어교실
정춘기 올어바웃잉글리쉬
조윤정 원당중학교
최민지 빅뱅어학원
최윤정 BK영어전문학원
최지유 J(제이)영수전문학원
최지혜 유베스타 어학원
최창영 학산학원
한보륜 더뉴에버
한승완 청라하이츠영수학원
허대성 방과후1교시
홍덕창 송현학원 계양분원
홍승표 보스턴영어학원
홍정희 지성의 숲
황성현 인천외국어고등학교

전남
강용문 JK영어입시전문
강유미 목포남악정상영어학원
고경희 에이블잉글리쉬
김미선 여수영어교습
김수희 Irin영어

김아름 지앤비 어학원
김은정 BestnBest 영어전문
김지현 이써밋영수학원
김채연 전문과외
라희선 재스민영어 전문과외
류성준 타임영어학원
박동규 정상학원
박은유 함평월광기독학교
박팔주 하이탑학원
손성호 아름다운 11월 학원
심명희 SP에듀학원
양명승 엠에스 어학원
오은주 순천금당고
이상호 스카이입시학원
이영주 재키리 영어학원
조소을 수잉글리쉬
차형진 상아탑학원
황상윤 K&H 영어 전문학원

전북
강지훈 고려학원
길지만 비상잉글리시아이영어학원
김나은 애플영어학원
김나현 전문과외
김대환 엠베스트se
김설아 에듀캠프학원
김수정 베이스탑스터디
김숙 매딘원영어
김영해 피렌체 어학원
김종찬 부안최강학원
김태연 전문과외
김현영 하이어잉글리쉬 영어교습소
나종훈 와이엠에스입시전문학원
박욱현 군산외대어학원
박준근 이투스247
박차희 연세바움
배영섭 YMS 입시학원
서명원 군산 한림학원
신원섭 리종영어학원
심미연 호남고등학교
안지은 안지은영어학원
유영목 유영목영어전문
이경훈 리더스영수전문학원
이예진 고려대EIE 어학원
이윤경 코드영수전문학원
이지원 탄탄영어수학전문학원
이한결 DNA영어학원
이현준 전문과외
이효상 에임하이영수학원
장동욱 의치약한수학원
정방현 익산투탑영수학원
조형진 대니아빠앤디영어교습소
최석원 전주에듀캠프학원
최유화 순창 탑학원
허욱 YMS입시전문학원
홍진영 지니영어교습소

제주
강수빈 전문과외
고보경 제주여자고등학교
고승용 RNK 알앤케이 영어수학학원
김민정 제주낭만고등학교
김태형 Top Class Academy
김희 전문과외
박시연 에임하이학원

배동환 뿌리와샘
송미라 세렌디피티 영어과외 공부방
이지은 제주낭만고등학교
임정열 엑셀영어 전문과외
정승현 J's English
한동수 위드유 학원

충남
고유미 고유미영어
권선교 합덕토킹스타학원
김선영 어플라이드 영어학원
김인영 더오름영어
김일환 김일환어학원
김창식 서산 꿈의학교
김창현 타임영어학원
김현우 프렌잉글리시로엘입시전문학원
남궁선 공부의맵 학원
박아영 닥터윤 영어학원
박재영 로제타스톤 영어교실
박제희 대안학교 레드스쿨
박태웅 인디고학원
박희진 박쌤 과외
백일선 명사특강
설재윤 마스터입시학원
송수아 송수아 영어 교습소
심현정 홀리영어
오근혜 셀렌쌤영어
유정선 메가수학메가영어학원
이규현 글로벌학원
이사랑 오성GnB영어학원
이정찬 두빛나래영수학원
이종화 오름에듀
이지숙 마이티영어학원
이호영 이플러스학원
이황 천안강대학원
임한수 탑클래스학원
임혜지 전문과외
장성은 상승기류
장완기 장완기학원
장진아 종로엠스쿨
주희 천안 탑씨크리트영어학원
채은주 위너스학원
최용원 서일고등학교
허길 에듀플러스학원
허지수 전문과외

충북
강홍구 청주오창비상아이비츠학원
김도현 에스라이팅학원
마종수 새움다움학원
박광수 필립영어전문
박상하 상하영어
박수열 팍스잉글리쉬학원
신유정 비타민 영어클리닉 학원
연수지 탑클랜영수학원
우선규 우선규영어교습소
윤홍석 대학가는길학원
이경수 더에스에이티영수단과학원
이재욱 대학가는 길 학원
이재은 파머스영어와이즈톡학원
임용원 KGI의대학원
최철우 최쌤영어
최하나 라이트에듀영어교습소
최하나 전문과외
하선빈 어썸영어전문학원

GRAMMAR MASTER

MASTER

Level 1

WRITERS

정은정 서주희 류은정 김진아 홍석현 조은영 구미순 이천우 홍인혁 복나희 홍미정

STAFF

발행인 정선욱

퍼블리싱 총괄 남형주

개발 김태원 박하영

기획 · 디자인 · 마케팅 조비호 김정인 강윤정

유통 · 제작 서준성 신성철

Grammar Master Level 1 202205 제3판 1쇄 202408 제3판 5쇄

펴낸곳 이투스에듀(주) 서울시 서초구 남부순환로 2547

고객센터 1599-3225

등록번호 제2007-000035호

ISBN 979-11-389-0845-0 [53740]

문법을 공부하는 이유

Why do you study English grammar?

처음 영어를 배우던 때를 기억하세요?

알파벳을 배우고 원어민 발음을 따라 말하면서 재미있는 놀이로 영어를 배웠습니다.

낯선 단어의 철자를 하나하나 알게 되고 제법 긴 문장도 말할 수 있구요.

영어로 읽고 말하는 내가 정말 자랑스럽죠?

그런데 가끔 궁금할 때가 있지 않아요?

우리말로는 같은 뜻인데 영어로는 왜 각각 다르게 쓸까요?

I was a little boy.	나는 작은 소년이었다.
You were a little boy.	너는 작은 소년이었다.

많은 학생이 초등학교부터 영어를 배워 오면서 우리말의 규칙과 영어의 규칙이 다르다는
것을 어렴풋이 알고 있지만 그 규칙이 무엇인지는 정확하게 알고 있지 않습니다.

그런데 규칙을 알게 되면 처음 보는 문장도 규칙을 적용하여 쉽게 이해할 수 있게 됩니다.

그래서 규칙을 따로 배우게 되는데, 그게 바로 「문법」인 것이죠.

문법을 공부하면 단어만으로는 알 수 없었던 문장의 뜻을 명쾌하게 알게 되고

영어로 문장을 쓸 때도 아주 유용합니다.

영어 문장의 규칙을 발견하는 기쁨을 여러분 스스로 느껴 보시기 바랍니다. 준비되었나요?

이투스 Grammar Master가 여러분이 문법을 통달하는 데 든든한 동행이 되겠습니다.

Why don't you come with us?

Structures

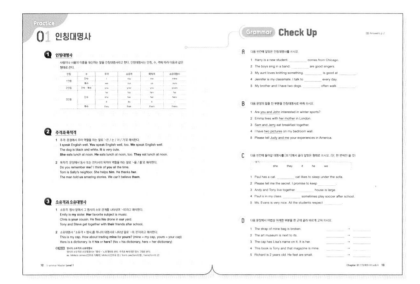

Grammar Practice

꼭 알아 두어야 할 문법 내용을 쉽게 핵심만 정리하였습니다. 학습에 가장 적절한 예문을 통해 문법 내용을 바로 확인해 볼 수 있습니다. 반드시 암기해야 하고, 짚고 넘어가야 할 내용은 ⊕ PLUS 로 제시했습니다.

Grammar Check Up

학습한 문법 내용을 적용해 볼 수 있는 다양한 형태의 문제를 제공합니다. 반복적으로 연습함으로써 문법 내용을 외우지 않아도 자연스럽게 학습이 되는 구조입니다.

Writing Exercise

다양한 유형의 쓰기 문제를 통해 학습한 문법 내용을 문장이나 글에서 자연스럽게 익힐 수 있으며, 더 나아가 스스로 영어로 글을 써 볼 수 있는 기본기를 다질 수 있습니다.

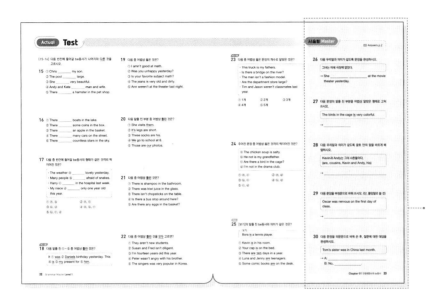

Actual Test

내신형 문제를 Chapter당 총 35문항으로 구성하여 충분한 연습이 되도록 하였습니다. 특히 최근 내신 빈출 유형과 서술형 문제의 비중을 높여 완벽한 내신 대비가 가능합니다. [내신 빈출]과 [고난도]를 표시하여 문제를 풀며 주요 객관식 문제를 확인할 수 있습니다.

서술형 Master

학교 내신 서술형 문제에 대비할 수 있는 문항들을 회별 10문항 수록하여 서술형 대비 학습을 마스터할 수 있습니다.

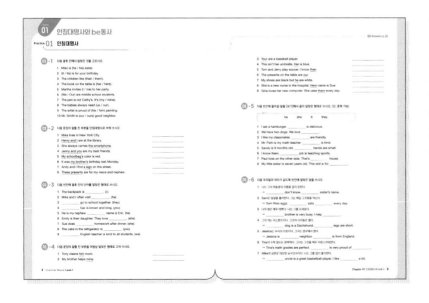

Workbook

본책보다 난이도가 조금 높은 문제들로 영작/서술형 대비 충분한 분량의 문제를 반복 학습함으로써 본책의 내용을 완벽히 체득하도록 하였습니다. 또한 Chapter Test로 내신형 문제를 한 번 더 풀며 단원을 마무리하도록 구성하였습니다.

Contents

01 문장의 구성 요소

문장을 이루는 기본 구성 요소에는 **주어, 동사, 목적어, 보어**가 있으며,
수식어는 기본 구성 요소를 꾸며 주는 역할을 한다.

주어
- 문장의 주인이 되는 말로 '누가, 무엇이'에 해당하며 주로 문장의 맨 앞에 온다.
- 주어가 될 수 있는 품사 : 명사, 대명사

> James runs.
> 주어(명사)
>
> He is a teacher.
> 주어(대명사)

동사
주어의 상태나 동작을 나타내는 말로 '~하다, ~이다'에 해당하며 주로 주어 뒤에 온다.

> The girl is pretty.
> 동사(상태)
>
> Sora walks to school.
> 동사(동작)

목적어
- 동사의 동작이 영향을 미치는 대상으로 '누구를, 무엇을'에 해당하며 주로 동사 뒤에 온다.
- 목적어가 될 수 있는 품사 : 명사, 대명사

> You drink milk.
> 목적어(명사)
>
> Mike likes her.
> 목적어(대명사)

보어
- 주어나 목적어를 보충 설명해 주는 말로 누구, 무엇, 어떠한에 해당하는 말이다. 주어를 설명해 주는 보어는 주로 동사 뒤에 오고, 목적어를 설명해 주는 보어는 주로 목적어 뒤에 온다.
- 보어가 될 수 있는 품사 : 명사, 대명사, 형용사

> My father is a doctor.
> 주격 보어(명사)
>
> The movie's leading actor is him[he].
> 주격 보어(대명사)
>
> My sister keeps her room clean.
> 목적격 보어(형용사)

수식어
- 문장의 기본 구성 요소(주어, 동사, 목적어, 보어)의 앞뒤에 붙어 꾸며 주는 말이다.
- 수식어로 쓰이는 품사 : 형용사(구), 부사(구)

> She became a famous designer.
> 형용사
>
> The sun rises in the east.
> 부사구

02 문장의 형식

문장의 기본 틀은 주어와 동사로 이루어지며, 동사는 종류에 따라 보어나 목적어를 필요로 한다. 문장에 보어나 목적어가 있는지 또는 없는지에 따라 **5가지 문장 형식**으로 나누어지는데, 모든 문형에는 꾸며 주는 말(수식어)이 포함될 수 있다.

목적어가 없는 문장

1형식 : 주어 + 동사

Chanho runs (very fast).
주어   동사

Jessica sings (on the stage).
주어   동사

• 주어와 동사만으로 완전한 문장을 이루며, 수식어로 부사(구)가 이어질 수 있다.

2형식 : 주어 + 동사 + 주격 보어

Betty is my friend.
주어 동사 주격 보어

John looks happy (today).
주어   동사   주격 보어

• 주어를 보충 설명해 주는 주격 보어가 있는 문장이다. 보어 자리에 부사를 쓸 수 없는 것에 유의한다.

목적어가 있는 문장

3형식 : 주어 + 동사 + 목적어

She has a brother.
주어 동사   목적어

Minho helps his teacher.
주어   동사   목적어

• 동사 뒤에 주어가 하는 동작의 대상이 되는 목적어가 있는 문장이다. 목적어는 우리말로 '~을/를'로 해석한다.

4형식 : 주어 + 동사 + 간접목적어 + 직접목적어

He gave the boy a book.
주어 동사   간접목적어   직접목적어

My mom made me potato pizza.
주어   동사 간접목적어   직접목적어

• 2개의 목적어가 있는 문장으로, 4형식에는 '~에게 …을 -(해) 주다'라는 뜻을 갖는 수여동사 (give, make, send, buy 등)가 쓰인다.

5형식 : 주어 + 동사 + 목적어 + 목적격 보어

She made her parents angry.
주어 동사   목적어   목적격 보어

They called the boy Kevin.
주어   동사   목적어   목적격 보어

• 목적어를 보충 설명해 주는 목적격 보어가 있는 문장이다. 주격 보어와 마찬가지로 목적격 보어 자리에 부사를 쓸 수 없는 것에 유의한다.

꼭 알아두어야 할 **불규칙 동사**

동사원형		과거형	동사원형		과거형
be	~이다/있다	was, were	let	~하게 하다	let
become	되다	became	lose	잃다, 지다	lost
begin	시작하다	began	make	만들다	made
bite	물다	bit	mean	의미하다	meant
blow	불다	blew	meet	만나다	met
break	깨뜨리다	broke	pay	지불하다	paid
bring	가지고 오다	brought	put	놓다	put
build	짓다	built	quit	그만두다	quit
buy	사다	bought	read	읽다	read
catch	잡다	caught	ride	(탈것을) 타다	rode
choose	선택하다	chose	ring	울리다	rang
come	오다	came	rise	오르다	rose
cut	자르다	cut	run	달리다	ran
deal	다루다	dealt	say	말하다	said
do	하다	did	see	보다	saw
draw	그리다	drew	sell	팔다	sold
drink	마시다	drank	send	보내다	sent
drive	운전하다	drove	set	놓다	set
eat	먹다	ate	shake	흔들다	shook
fall	떨어지다	fell	sing	노래하다	sang
feed	먹이다	fed	sink	가라앉다	sank
feel	느끼다	felt	sit	앉다	sat
fight	싸우다	fought	sleep	자다	slept
find	찾다	found	speak	말하다	spoke
fly	날다	flew	spend	소비하다	spent
forget	잊다	forgot	stand	서 있다	stood
get	얻다, 받다	got	steal	훔치다	stole
give	주다	gave	sweep	쓸다	swept
go	가다	went	swim	수영하다	swam
grow	자라다	grew	swing	흔들리다	swung
hang	매달다	hung	take	가지고 가다	took
have	가지고 있다	had	teach	가르치다	taught
hear	듣다	heard	tell	말하다	told
hide	숨다	hid	think	생각하다	thought
hit	치다	hit	throw	던지다	threw
hold	(손에) 쥐다	held	understand	이해하다	understood
keep	유지하다	kept	wake	깨우다	woke
know	알다	knew	wear	입다	wore
leave	떠나다	left	win	이기다	won
lend	빌려주다	lent	write	쓰다	wrote

Chapter

01

인칭대명사와 be동사

01 인칭대명사

1 인칭대명사

사람이나 사물의 이름을 대신하는 말을 인칭대명사라고 한다. 인칭대명사는 인칭, 수, 격에 따라 다음과 같은 형태로 쓴다.

인칭	수	주격	소유격	목적격	소유대명사
1인칭	단수	I	my	me	mine
	복수	we	our	us	ours
2인칭	단수 · 복수	you	your	you	yours
3인칭	단수	he	his	him	his
		she	her	her	hers
		it	its	it	–
	복수	they	their	them	theirs

2 주격과 목적격

1 **주격**: 문장에서 주어 역할을 하는 말로 '~은 / 는 / 이 / 가'로 해석한다.
I speak English well. **You** speak English well, too. **We** speak English well.
The dog is black and white. **It** is very cute.
She eats lunch at noon. **He** eats lunch at noon, too. **They** eat lunch at noon.

2 **목적격**: 문장에서 동사 또는 전치사의 목적어 역할을 하는 말로 '~을 / 를'로 해석한다.
Do you remember **me**? I think of **you** all the time.
Tom is Sally's neighbor. She helps **him**. He thanks **her**.
The man told **us** amazing stories. We can't believe **them**.

3 소유격과 소유대명사

1 **소유격**: 명사 앞에서 그 명사의 소유 관계를 나타내며 '~의'라고 해석한다.
Emily is **my** sister. **Her** favorite subject is music.
Chris is **your** cousin. He flies **his** drone in **our** yard.
Tony and Steve get together with **their** friends after school.

2 **소유대명사**: 「소유격 + 명사」를 하나의 대명사로 나타낸 말로 '~의 것'이라고 해석한다.
This is my cap. How about trading **mine** for **yours**? (mine = my cap, yours = your cap)
Here is a dictionary. Is it **his** or **hers**? (his = his dictionary, hers = her dictionary)

➕ **PLUS** 명사의 소유격과 소유대명사
명사의 소유격과 소유대명사는 「명사 + 's」의 형태로 쓴다. 주격과 목적격은 명사 그대로 쓴다.
ex. Minho's camera(민호의 카메라), Minho's(민호의 것) / Tom's pen(Tom의 펜), Tom's(Tom의 것)

A 다음 빈칸에 알맞은 인칭대명사를 쓰시오.

1 Harry is a new student. _____ comes from Chicago.

2 The boys sing in a band. _____ are good singers.

3 My aunt loves knitting something. _____ is good at _____ .

4 Jennifer is my classmate. I talk to _____ every day.

5 My brother and I have two dogs. _____ often walk _____ .

B 다음 문장의 밑줄 친 부분을 인칭대명사로 바꿔 쓰시오.

1 Are you and John interested in winter sports?

2 Emma lives with her mother in London.

3 Sam and Jerry eat breakfast together.

4 I have two pictures on my bedroom wall.

5 Please tell Judy and me your experiences in America.

C 다음 빈칸에 들어갈 대명사를 [보기]에서 골라 알맞은 형태로 쓰시오. (단, 한 번씩만 쓸 것)

보기
she   they   it   he   we

1 Paul has a cat. _____ cat likes to sleep under the sofa.

2 Please tell me the secret. I promise to keep _____ .

3 Andy and Tony live together. _____ house is large.

4 Paul is in my class. _____ sometimes play soccer after school.

5 Ms. Evans is very nice. All the students respect _____ .

D 다음 문장에서 어법상 어색한 부분을 한 군데 골라 바르게 고쳐 쓰시오.

1 The strap of mine bag is broken.　　_____ → _____

2 The art museum is next to its.　　_____ → _____

3 The cap has Lisa's name on it. It is her.　　_____ → _____

4 This book is Tony and that magazine is mine.　　_____ → _____

5 Richard is 2 years old. He feet are small.　　_____ → _____

02 be동사의 현재형과 과거형

1 be동사의 의미와 현재형

1 be동사는 뒤에 오는 말에 따라 '~이다', '~하다', '(~에) 있다'라는 의미를 갖는다.

be동사 + 명사	~이다	Seoul **is** *the capital city of Korea.*
be동사 + 형용사	~하다	She **is** *kind* and *outgoing.*
be동사 + 장소 부사(구)	(~에) 있다	The dancers **are** *on the stage* now.

2 be동사의 현재형은 주어의 인칭과 수에 따라 3가지 형태로 쓴다.

주어			be동사 현재형	「주어 + be동사」의 줄임말
단수	1인칭	I	am	I'm
	2인칭	You	are	You're
	3인칭	He / She / It	is	He's / She's / It's
복수	1 / 2 / 3인칭	We / You / They	are	We're / You're / They're

I **am** a soccer player. You **are** a soccer player, too. We **are** on the same team.

He **is** absent from school. She **is** absent from school, too. They **are** all sick in bed.

It **is** my childhood photo. They **are** Jason and Tim. We **are** still good friends.

⊕ **PLUS** 주어가 명사일 때의 **be동사**
주어가 명사일 경우는 모두 3인칭이므로 단수일 때는 is, 복수일 때는 are를 쓴다.
ex. A ball **is** round. Mangoes **are** sweet. Eddy and Joe **are** friends.

2 be동사의 과거형

주어의 인칭과 수에 따라 was, were를 쓰고, be동사의 과거형은 인칭대명사와 줄여 쓰지 않는다.

1 am, is의 과거형: was

I **was** an elementary school student last year.

It **was** very cold yesterday, so she **was** at home all day.

2 are의 과거형: were

You **were** in the school soccer team last year.

The books **were** on the table then.

3 There is / are

「There + be동사」는 '~이 있(었)다'라는 의미로, be동사 뒤에 오는 명사가 주어이므로 주어의 수에 따라 be동사를 맞춰 쓴다.

1 There is + 단수명사 / There are + 복수명사: ~이 있다

There is *a computer* in the room.

There are *fifty seats* in the hall.

2 There was + 단수명사 / There were + 복수명사: ~이 있었다

There was *a hotel* on the corner.

There were *some stores* around the park.

A 다음 괄호 안에서 알맞은 것을 고르시오.

1 The boys (is / are) on their way home.

2 The airport (is / are) crowded with many people.

3 You (are / were) late for school yesterday.

4 There is (a bird's nest / two birds) in the tree.

5 There (is / are) only ten people in the theater.

B 다음 빈칸에 알맞은 be동사의 현재형을 쓰시오.

1 I _____ a member of the book club.

2 The hospital _____ far from the subway station.

3 My brother has a cold so he _____ in bed.

4 Webtoons _____ very popular in Korea these days.

5 There _____ a bakery across the street.

C 다음 우리말과 의미가 같도록 빈칸에 알맞은 be동사를 쓰시오.

1 다음 주 화요일은 개교기념일이다.   → Next Tuesday _____ the school anniversary.

2 내 계획에 뭔가 문제가 있었다.   → Something _____ wrong with my plan.

3 런던은 한때 안개로 유명했다.   → London _____ once famous for its fogs.

4 나는 수학과 과학에 관심이 있다.   → I _____ interested in math and science.

5 그 군인들은 매우 강하고 용감했다.   → The soldiers _____ very strong and brave.

D 다음 문장의 밑줄 친 부분을 어법상 알맞은 형태로 고쳐 쓰시오.

1 There were a car by the side of the road.

2 There is many bright stars in the sky.

3 My neighbor is really noisy last night.

4 Mr. Bell and his students is on the playground.

5 We live in Seoul. We are in New York last month.

03 be동사의 부정문과 의문문

1 be동사 현재형의 부정문

be동사의 현재형(am / are / is) + not: ~가 아니다, ~하지 않다, (~에) 없다

주어	be동사 + not	줄임말	
I	am not	I'm not	I amn't (×)
We / You / They	are not	We're / You're / They're not	We / You / They aren't
He / She / It	is not	He's / She's / It's not	He / She / It isn't

I am a stranger. I **am not** familiar with this area.
You are brave. You **are not[aren't]** afraid of spiders.
Anna is in her room. She **is not[isn't]** in the kitchen.
There is an airplane in the sky. There **is not[isn't]** a cloud in the sky.

2 be동사 현재형의 의문문

be동사의 현재형(Am / Are / Is) + 주어 ~?: ~이니?, ~하니?, (~에) 있니?

주어	수	의문문	대답	
1인칭	단수	Am I ~?	Yes, you are.	No, you aren't.
	복수	Are we ~?	Yes, you / we are.	No, you / we aren't.
2인칭	단수	Are you ~?	Yes, I am.	No, I'm not.
	복수	Are you ~?	Yes, we are.	No, we aren't.
3인칭	단수	Is he / she / it ~?	Yes, he / she / it is.	No, he / she / it isn't.
	복수	Are they ~?	Yes, they are.	No, they aren't.

Are you a student at this school? – Yes, I am. / No, I'm not.
Is the ground wet from the rain? – Yes, it is. / No, it isn't.
Are Emma and Lisa in the same class? – Yes, they are. / No, they aren't.

3 be동사 과거형의 부정문과 의문문

부정문은 be동사의 과거형에 not을 붙여 만들고, 의문문은 be동사의 과거형을 주어 앞에 써서 만든다.

부정문	was not[wasn't] / were not[weren't]
의문문	Was + 주어 ~? / Were + 주어 ~? – Yes, 주어 + was[were]. / No, 주어 + wasn't[weren't].

부정문   I was thin last year. I **was not[wasn't]** overweight then.
        You were in Korea last year. You **were not[weren't]** in Japan.

의문문   **Was Eric** happy with his grades? - Yes, he was. / No, he wasn't.
        Were you present at the meeting? - Yes, I was. / No, I wasn't.

⊕ **PLUS**   **There is / are**의 의문문에 대한 대답
Is / Are there ~?에 대한 대답은 Yes, there is / are. 또는 No, there isn't / aren't.로 한다.
ex. **Is there** any cheese on the plate? – Yes, there is. / No, there isn't.

📖 Answers p.2

A 다음 문장을 부정문으로 바꿔 쓸 때, 빈칸에 알맞은 말을 쓰시오. (단, 줄임말로 쓸 것)

1 Ending of the movie is surprising. → Ending of the movie _____ surprising.

2 Jessi was nervous about the audition. → Jessi _____ nervous about the audition.

3 You are tall enough to reach the shelf. → You _____ tall enough to reach the shelf.

4 There are enough chairs in the hall. → There _____ enough chairs in the hall.

5 The eggs in the box were fresh. → The eggs in the box _____ fresh.

B 다음 질문에 대한 알맞은 대답을 완성하시오.

1 A: Are you and Tony ready to play soccer? B: Yes, _____ _____ .

2 A: Were you a student president in middle school? B: Yes, _____ _____ .

3 A: Was it hot in Jeju last week? B: No, _____ _____ .

4 A: Are these books on the table $3 each? B: No, _____ _____ .

5 A: Is there a bus stop around here? B: No, _____ _____ .

C 다음 우리말과 의미가 같도록 빈칸에 알맞은 말을 쓰시오.

1 나는 목이 마르지만 배고프지는 않다. → I am thirsty but I _____ _____ hungry.

2 내 신발은 그 개집 안에 없었다. → My shoe _____ _____ in the doghouse.

3 그 고대 도시에 대한 이야기는 사실이 아니다. → The story about the ancient city _____ true.

4 그 두 화가의 그림들이 비슷했니? → _____ the pictures of the two artists similar?

5 그 책은 지구 온난화에 관한 것이니? → _____ _____ _____ about global warming?

D 다음 문장의 밑줄 친 부분을 어법상 알맞은 형태로 고쳐 쓰시오.

1 The guidebook <u>weren't</u> helpful to me.

2 A few students <u>wasn't</u> quiet in class.

3 The bottle <u>not is</u> full of fresh milk.

4 Those are my shoes. They <u>isn't</u> comfortable.

5 <u>Were</u> your sister second in the 200-meter race?

A 다음 문장을 괄호 안의 지시대로 바꿔 쓰시오.

1 I am always busy in the morning. (I를 she로 바꿔서)

→ _____

2 My uncle is a famous director. (부정문)

→ _____

3 The band is popular with teenagers. (의문문)

→ _____

4 Tom and Jerry were born in the same year. (부정문)

→ _____

5 Dave was late for the movie again. (의문문)

→ _____

B 다음 우리말과 의미가 같도록 괄호 안의 말을 바르게 배열하시오.

1 이 채소들은 신선하다. (are, vegetables, fresh, these)

→ _____

2 그들은 초등학생들이 아니다. (aren't, students, they, elementary school)

→ _____

3 냉장고가 식품으로 가득 차 있니? (full of food, is, the refrigerator, ?)

→ _____

4 Einstein은 음악가가 아니었다. (was, a musician, Einstein, not)

→ _____

5 너는 어제 학교에 결석했니? (absent from school, were, yesterday, you, ?)

→ _____

C 다음 두 문장을 한 문장으로 나타낼 때 빈칸에 알맞은 인칭대명사와 be동사를 쓰시오.

1 Brian isn't American. Lisa isn't American, either.

→ _____ _____ American.

2 You are afraid of ghosts. Your sister is afraid of ghosts, too.

→ _____ _____ afraid of ghosts.

3 That white house is mine. It is my wife's house, too.

→ That white house _____ _____ house.

4 There is a desk in Hana's room. There is a closet in Hana's room.

→ There _____ a desk and a closet in _____ room.

5 Hyori's nickname is Dancing Queen. Sunny's nickname is Dancing Queen, too.

→ _____ nickname _____ Dancing Queen.

D 다음 괄호 안에 주어진 말을 이용하여 영작하시오.

1 3일 전에 날씨는 추웠니? (weather, cold)

→ _____

2 공항으로 가는 버스가 있습니까? (there, to the airport)

→ _____

3 어제 공원에 많은 사람들이 있었다. (there, many, at the park)

→ _____

4 그 과학 수업은 나에게 어렵지 않았다. (the science lesson, difficult for)

→ _____

5 그녀의 이름은 Jane이고, 그녀는 캐나다 출신이다. (be from)

→ _____

6 나는 요리를 잘하고, 그녀는 그림을 잘 그린다. (good at, cooking, drawing)

→ _____

01 다음 빈칸에 들어갈 말로 알맞은 것은?

> My brother and sister _____ in the living room now.

① am
② are
③ is
④ was
⑤ were

02 다음 빈칸에 공통으로 들어갈 말로 알맞은 것은?

> • I _____ a basketball player last year.
> • The weather _____ so cold last weekend.

① is
② am
③ are
④ was
⑤ were

03 다음 빈칸에 들어갈 말로 알맞은 것을 모두 고르면?

> There is _____ on the table.

① a cup
② flowers
③ some books
④ a loaf of bread
⑤ forks and knives

04 다음 빈칸에 들어갈 말로 알맞지 않은 것은?

> _____ are kind to other people.

① You
② His father
③ The doctors
④ My roommates
⑤ Ms. and Mr. Owen

05 다음 빈칸에 들어갈 말로 알맞지 않은 것을 모두 고르면?

> Was _____ at school all day?

① Tim
② you
③ the teacher
④ Sue and Bill
⑤ your mother

06 다음 빈칸에 들어갈 말로 알맞게 짝지어진 것은?

> • There _____ cookbooks on the top shelf.
> • There _____ a restaurant at the top of the building.

① is - is
② is - are
③ are - is
④ are - are
⑤ were - are

07 다음 (A), (B), (C)의 각 네모 안에서 어법에 맞는 것을 골라 바르게 짝지은 것은?

> • The garden (A) is / was very nice last month.
> • (B) Are / Were you at the library right now?
> • Anita and her family (C) are / were in Canada last winter.

	(A)		(B)		(C)
①	is	–	Are	–	are
②	was	–	Are	–	were
③	is	–	Are	–	were
④	was	–	Were	–	are
⑤	is	–	Were	–	are

08 밑줄 친 부분을 인칭대명사로 잘못 바꾼 것은?

① I like you and George.
　　　　→ you
② Do you know Bora's cousin?
　　　　　　→ hers
③ My husband and I have a new car.
　　　　→ We
④ The math problems are very easy.
　　　　→ They
⑤ Rita buys a magazine at the bookstore.
　　　　　　→ it

내신 빈출
09 다음 두 문장의 의미가 같도록 할 때, 빈칸에 들어갈 말로 알맞게 짝지어진 것은?

> These concert tickets are _____.
> = These are _____ concert tickets.

① my - me　　　　② her - her
③ him - his　　　　④ ours - our
⑤ their - theirs

10 다음 우리말을 영어로 바르게 옮긴 것은?

> 그는 그들의 주소를 안다.

① He knows they address.
② He knows their address.
③ His knows they address.
④ Him knows their address.
⑤ Him knows theirs address.

11 다음 질문에 대한 대답으로 알맞은 것은?

> Are those people your fans?

① Yes, she is.　　　　② Yes, it is.
③ No, they aren't.　　④ Yes, these are.
⑤ No, these aren't.

12 짝지어진 대화 중 어색한 것은?

① A: Is this her smartphone?
　 B: Yes, she is.
② A: Is there a pillow on the bed?
　 B: No, there isn't.
③ A: Are they your grandparents?
　 B: Yes, they are.
④ A: Was Tony sick yesterday?
　 B: Yes, he was.
⑤ A: Were you in the kitchen then?
　 B: No, I wasn't.

13 밑줄 친 부분을 줄임말로 바꾼 것 중 알맞지 않은 것은?

① They are not toy cars.
　　　→ aren't
② My puppy is not white.
　　　→ isn't
③ I am not a swimmer.
　　　→ amn't
④ The calendar was not on the desk.
　　　→ wasn't
⑤ There were not candles on the cake.
　　　→ weren't

고난도
14 다음 중 의문문으로 잘못 바꾼 것은?

① Judy is a good writer.
　　→ Is Judy a good writer?
② Your brothers are good at tennis.
　　→ Are your brothers good at tennis?
③ The weather was bad last summer.
　　→ Was the weather bad last summer?
④ There are many animals in the zoo.
　　→ Are many animals there in the zoo?
⑤ A few students were in the classroom.
　　→ Were a few students in the classroom?

[15-16] 다음 빈칸에 들어갈 be동사가 나머지와 <u>다른</u> 것을 고르시오.

15 ① Chris _____ my son.
② The pool _____ large.
③ She _____ very beautiful.
④ Andy and Kate _____ man and wife.
⑤ There _____ a hamster in the pet shop.

16 ① There _____ boats in the lake.
② There _____ some coins in the box.
③ There _____ an apple in the basket.
④ There _____ many cars on the street.
⑤ There _____ countless stars in the sky.

17 다음 중 빈칸에 들어갈 be동사의 형태가 같은 것끼리 짝지어진 것은?

> · The weather ⓐ _____ lovely yesterday.
> · Many people ⓑ _____ afraid of snakes.
> · Harry ⓒ _____ in the hospital last week.
> · My niece ⓓ _____ only one year old this year.

① ⓐ, ⓑ   ② ⓐ, ⓒ
③ ⓑ, ⓓ   ④ ⓐ, ⓑ, ⓒ
⑤ ⓑ, ⓒ, ⓓ

18 다음 밑줄 친 ①~⑤ 중 어법상 <u>틀린</u> 것은?

> It ① <u>was</u> ② <u>Daniels</u> birthday yesterday. This ③ <u>is</u> ④ <u>my</u> present for ⑤ <u>him</u>.

19 다음 중 어법상 옳은 것은?

① I amn't good at math.
② Was you unhappy yesterday?
③ Is your favorite subject math?
④ The jeans is very old and dirty.
⑤ Ann weren't at the theater last night.

20 다음 밑줄 친 부분 중 어법상 <u>틀린</u> 것은?

① She visits <u>them</u>.
② <u>It's</u> legs are short.
③ These socks are <u>his</u>.
④ <u>We</u> go to school at 8.
⑤ Those are <u>our</u> photos.

21 다음 중 어법상 <u>틀린</u> 것은?

① There is shampoo in the bathroom.
② There was kiwi juice in the glass.
③ There isn't chopsticks on the table.
④ Is there a bus stop around here?
⑤ Are there any eggs in the basket?

22 다음 중 어법상 <u>틀린</u> 것을 <u>모두</u> 고르면?

① They aren't new students.
② Susan and Fred isn't diligent.
③ I'm fourteen years old this year.
④ Peter wasn't angry with his brother.
⑤ The singers was very popular in Korea.

내신 빈출

23 다음 중 어법상 옳은 문장의 개수로 알맞은 것은?

> · This truck is my fathers.
> · Is there a bridge on the river?
> · The man isn't a fashion model.
> · Are the department store large?
> · Tim and Jason weren't classmates last
> year.

① 1개   ② 2개   ③ 3개
④ 4개   ⑤ 5개

24 주어진 문장 중 어법상 옳은 것끼리 짝지어진 것은?

> ⓐ The chicken soup is salty.
> ⓑ He not is my grandfather.
> ⓒ Are there a bird in the cage?
> ⓓ I'm not in the drama club.

① ⓐ, ⓒ   ② ⓐ, ⓓ
③ ⓑ, ⓒ   ④ ⓑ, ⓓ
⑤ ⓒ, ⓓ

고난도

25 [보기]의 밑줄 친 be동사와 의미가 같은 것은?

> ┌ 보기 ┐
> Bora <u>is</u> a tennis player.

① Kevin <u>is</u> in his room.
② Your cap <u>is</u> on the bed.
③ There <u>are</u> 365 days in a year.
④ Luna and Jenny <u>are</u> teenagers.
⑤ Some comic books <u>are</u> on the desk.

26 다음 우리말과 의미가 같도록 문장을 완성하시오.

> 그녀는 어제 극장에 없었다.

→ She _____ _____ at the movie
theater yesterday.

27 다음 문장의 밑줄 친 부분을 어법상 알맞은 형태로 고쳐
쓰시오.

> The birds in the cage <u>is</u> very colorful.

→ _____

28 다음 우리말과 의미가 같도록 괄호 안의 말을 바르게 배
열하시오.

> Kevin과 Andy는 그의 사촌이다.
> (are, cousins, Kevin and Andy, his)

→ _____

29 다음 문장을 부정문으로 바꿔 쓰시오. (단, 줄임말로 쓸 것)

> Oscar was nervous on the first day of
> class.

→ _____

30 다음 문장을 의문문으로 바꿔 쓴 후, 질문에 대한 대답을
완성하시오.

> Tom's sister was in China last month.

→ A: _____
    B: No, _____.

31 다음 문장에서 어법상 틀린 부분을 찾아 바르게 고쳐 쓰시오.

> There is twenty-six letters in the English alphabet.

_____ → _____

32 다음 우리말과 의미가 같도록 괄호 안의 말을 이용하여 문장을 완성하시오.

> 내 것 옆에 있는 John의 자전거는 빨간색이다.
> (bicycle)

→ _____ _____ next to _____ is red.

33 다음 그림을 보고, 빈칸 ⓐ ~ ⓒ에 들어갈 말을 [보기]에서 골라 알맞은 형태로 쓰시오. (단, 영어 숫자 표현을 포함할 것)

보기

cake   girl   candle

There ⓐ _____ in the room.
There ⓑ _____ on the table.
There ⓒ _____ in the cake.

34 다음 대화의 빈칸 ⓐ ~ ⓒ에 들어갈 be동사의 알맞은 형태를 쓰시오.

> A : ⓐ _____ you alone yesterday?
> B: No, I ⓑ _____ . I ⓒ _____
>   with my parents.

35 다음 우리말과 의미가 같도록 [조건]에 맞게 문장을 완성하시오.

> 나는 작년에 학교에서 인기가 많았다.
>
> 조건
> 1. popular at school을 이용할 것
> 2. 필요시 단어를 추가할 것

→ _____ last year.

Chapter

02

일반동사

01 일반동사의 현재형

1 일반동사의 의미

일반동사는 be동사와 조동사를 제외한 동사를 가리키며, 주어의 동작이나 상태를 나타낸다.

be동사	am, are, is, was, were
조동사	can, may, must, should 등
일반동사	go, want, like, eat, have, run 등

Ricky **is** in his room. His room **is** very dirty.
Students **must** follow the school rules.
I often **write** short stories. Ann **likes** to read them.

2 일반동사의 현재형 1 - 주어가 3인칭 단수가 아닐 때

1 현재형은 현재의 사실이나 반복되는 습관을 나타낼 때 사용한다.
Sally and Mike **work** at the same office. (현재의 사실)
I **drink** a glass of milk every morning. (반복되는 습관)

2 일반동사의 현재형은 주어가 1인칭, 2인칭, 복수일 때 동사원형을 쓴다.
I **meet** my friends on the weekend.
You often **play** computer games after dinner.
The girls **take** ballet lessons at 3:30 p.m.
My grandparents **visit** us every other week.

3 일반동사의 현재형 2 - 주어가 3인칭 단수일 때

일반동사의 3인칭 단수 현재형은 보통 동사원형에 -(e)s를 붙여서 만든다.

대부분의 동사	+ -s	come → comes make → makes	know → knows feel → feels	walk → walks meet → meets
-o, -s, -x, -sh, -ch로 끝나는 동사	+ -es	do → does wash → washes	pass → passes teach → teaches	fix → fixes touch → touches
「자음 + y」로 끝나는 동사	-y → -ies	cry → cries	study → studies	try → tries
예외	have → has			

My brother **walks** 10 kilometers a day.
Somi always **brushes** her teeth after meals.
The student **studies** hard to get better grades.
The library **has** a wide range of books.

➕ PLUS 「모음 + y」로 끝나는 동사의 3인칭 단수 현재형
「자음 + y」로 끝나는 동사와 달리 끝에 -s를 붙여서 만든다.
ex. buy → buy**s**, enjoy → enjoy**s**, play → play**s**, say → say**s** 등

A 다음 괄호 안에 주어진 말을 이용하여 문장을 완성하시오. (단, 현재형으로 쓸 것)

1 Her baby often _____ at night. (cry)

2 Paul often _____ cornflakes for breakfast. (have)

3 The art museum _____ at 9 o'clock. (open)

4 My mother _____ the drama from 8 o'clock. (watch)

5 We _____ English three times a week. (learn)

B 다음 밑줄 친 부분을 괄호 안에 주어진 말로 바꿔 문장을 다시 쓰시오.

1 I always run in the marathon. (Sally) → _____

2 We listen to the teacher. (the student) → _____

3 You spend too much time on sport. (the boy) → _____

4 They go to a ball park on weekends. (my uncle) → _____

5 Many people buy things on the Internet. (he) → _____

C 다음 빈칸에 알맞은 단어를 [보기]에서 골라 현재형 문장을 완성하시오. (단, 한 번씩만 쓸 것)

보기				
walk	come	live	make	study

1 Martha _____ to school in time.

2 Dave _____ a quiet life in a small city.

3 Laura _____ her dog twice every day.

4 Andy _____ English without a dictionary.

5 You often _____ a mistake in calculation.

D 다음 문장의 밑줄 친 부분을 어법상 알맞은 형태로 고쳐 쓰시오. (단, 현재형으로 쓸 것)

1 Emma practice the violin every day.

2 I knows her name and phone number.

3 Students borrows books from the library.

4 The ship carrys more than 500 passengers at a time.

5 Ms. Hunt teachs music at the art school.

02 일반동사의 과거형

1 동사의 과거형

과거의 일을 나타낼 때 be동사나 일반동사의 과거형을 사용하며 과거를 나타내는 부사(구)와 자주 쓰인다.

It **was** very cold outside this morning.

I **bought** a pair of jeans and Lisa **bought** a couple of T-shirts yesterday.

2 일반동사의 과거형 1 - 규칙 변화

일반동사의 과거형은 보통 동사원형에 -(e)d를 붙여서 만든다.

대부분의 동사	+ -ed	help → helped	start → started	want → wanted
-e로 끝나는 동사	+ -d	decide → decided	live → lived	move → moved
「단모음 + 단자음」으로 끝나는 동사	자음 추가 + -ed	jog → jogged	plan → planned	drop → dropped
「자음 + y」로 끝나는 동사	-y → -ied	cry → cried	study → studied	worry → worried

The TV show **started** twenty minutes ago.

The bakery **decided** to close for two weeks.

The audience **clapped** after her performance.

Two people **carried** the sofas and the table upstairs.

⊕ PLUS 「모음 + y」로 끝나는 동사의 과거형
「자음 + y」로 끝나는 동사와 달리 끝에 -ed를 붙여서 만든다.
ex. enjoy → enjoy**ed**, play → play**ed**, stay → stay**ed** 등

3 일반동사의 과거형 2 - 불규칙 변화

일반동사의 과거형이 동사원형과 같거나 철자가 바뀌는 경우가 있다.

동사원형과 같은 경우	cut → cut	put → put	hit → hit	read → read	set → set
철자가 바뀌는 경우	do → did fly → flew sit → sat go → went tell → told feed → fed get → got	eat → ate run → ran see → saw ride → rode win → won find → found send → sent	meet → met have → had give → gave sing → sang wear → wore drive → drove write → wrote	come → came buy → bought drink → drank make → made begin → began catch → caught teach → taught	

Ann **read** an exciting article in the newspaper.

The girls **made** a loud noise in the library.

My family **went** camping and **had** a great time last weekend.

A 다음 괄호 안에서 알맞은 것을 고르시오.

1 The teacher (tells / telled / told) some funny stories to us last time.

2 A lot of animals (sleep / sleeped / slept) during winter.

3 Many children (use / used / ussed) smartphones these days.

4 I (buy / buyed / bought) a few old stamps at the flea market last weekend.

5 Julie (takes / taked / took) a lot of selfies in front of the Eiffel Tower yesterday.

B 다음 괄호 안에 주어진 말을 이용하여 문장을 완성하시오. (단, 과거형으로 쓸 것)

1 We _____ a small campfire last night. (have)

2 The boy _____ his ice cream on the floor. (drop)

3 My parents and I _____ in a big hotel by the river. (stay)

4 The journalist _____ an article about global warming. (write)

5 Junho _____ the world record at the last Olympics. (break)

C 다음 빈칸에 알맞은 단어를 [보기]에서 골라 과거형 문장을 완성하시오. (단, 한 번씩만 쓸 것)

보기				
set	sew	begin	pick	dry

1 My mom was busy, so I _____ the table for her.

2 It _____ to rain in the late afternoon.

3 She _____ her hair in front of the mirror.

4 The child _____ some flowers from the garden.

5 I _____ the badge to my uniform jacket.

D 다음 문장의 밑줄 친 부분을 어법상 알맞은 형태로 고쳐 쓰시오.

1 I <u>cutted</u> the cake into six pieces a few minutes ago.

2 Sumin <u>graduates</u> from elementary school in 2016.

3 We <u>spended</u> a whole week in London last winter.

4 Jenny and Bora <u>studyed</u> science together yesterday.

5 A famous architect <u>design</u> the church a hundred years ago.

03 일반동사의 부정문과 의문문

1 일반동사 현재형의 부정문

주어의 인칭과 수에 따라 do나 does를 이용하여 부정문을 만든다.

주어	부정문
1인칭 / 2인칭 / 복수 (I / We / You / They)	do not[don't] + 동사원형
3인칭 단수 (He / She / It)	does not[doesn't] + 동사원형

I know Tony's phone number, but I **do not[don't] know** his address.
Public libraries usually **do not[don't] open** on holidays.
She **does not[doesn't] want** ice cream for dessert.
This lemon tea **does not[doesn't] taste** sour at all.

2 일반동사 현재형의 의문문

주어의 인칭과 수에 따라 do나 does를 주어 앞에 써서 의문문을 만든다. 의문문에 대한 대답에서 주어는 인칭 대명사로 써야 한다.

주어	의문문	대답
1인칭 / 2인칭 / 복수	Do + 주어 + 동사원형 ~?	Yes, 주어 + do. / No, 주어 + don't.
3인칭 단수	Does + 주어 + 동사원형 ~?	Yes, 주어 + does. / No, 주어 + doesn't.

Do you usually **have** six classes a day?
- Yes, I do. / No, I don't.
Does Brenda clean her room every day?
- Yes, she does. / No, she doesn't.

⊕ PLUS do의 다양한 쓰임
(1) 일반동사 do: '~하다'라는 뜻
    ex. We **do** volunteer work once a month.
(2) 조동사 do: 일반동사의 부정문과 의문문을 만들 때 사용
    ex. Harry **does** not join a reading club. / **Do** you like fantasy novels?

3 일반동사 과거형의 부정문과 의문문

주어의 인칭과 수에 상관없이 did를 이용하여 부정문과 의문문을 만든다.

부정문	did not[didn't] + 동사원형
의문문	Did + 주어 + 동사원형 ~? – Yes, 주어 + did. / No, 주어 + didn't.

I **did not[didn't] send** a text message to you.
Jason **did not[didn't] keep** a promise with his father.
Did the students **go** to the aquarium by bus?
- Yes, they did. / No, they didn't.

Grammar Check Up

A 다음 문장을 부정문으로 바꿔 쓸 때, 빈칸에 알맞은 말을 쓰시오. (단, 줄임말로 쓸 것)

1 My dog barks at strangers. → My dog ＿＿＿＿＿＿ at strangers.

2 Lisa forgot her parents' anniversary. → Lisa ＿＿＿＿＿＿ her parents' anniversary.

3 People laughed at the comedian's joke. → People ＿＿＿＿＿＿ at the comedian's joke.

4 Ron found his keys in his pocket. → Ron ＿＿＿＿＿＿ his keys in his pocket.

5 My father goes to work by subway. → My father ＿＿＿＿＿＿ to work by subway.

B 다음 질문에 대한 알맞은 대답을 완성하시오.

1 A: Do you wear a school uniform? B: Yes, ＿＿＿＿＿ ＿＿＿＿＿.

2 A: Did the train arrive on time? B: No, ＿＿＿＿＿ ＿＿＿＿＿.

3 A: Did he get along with his friends? B: Yes, ＿＿＿＿＿ ＿＿＿＿＿.

4 A: Does your sister eat spaghetti with chopsticks? B: No, ＿＿＿＿＿ ＿＿＿＿＿.

C 다음 우리말과 의미가 같도록 괄호 안의 단어를 이용하여 문장을 완성하시오. (단, 부정문은 줄임말로 쓸 것)

1 나는 오늘 밤에 해야 할 숙제가 없다. (have)

→ I ＿＿＿＿＿ ＿＿＿＿＿ any homework to do tonight.

2 너는 저녁 식사 전에 손을 씻지 않았다. (wash)

→ You ＿＿＿＿＿ ＿＿＿＿＿ your hands before dinner.

3 그 회사는 바다에 쓰레기를 버리니? (throw)

→ ＿＿＿＿＿ the company ＿＿＿＿＿ waste into the sea?

4 그는 수학 경시대회에서 우승을 했니? (win)

→ ＿＿＿＿＿ he ＿＿＿＿＿ first prize in the math contest?

D 다음 문장의 밑줄 친 부분을 어법상 알맞은 형태로 고쳐 쓰시오.

1 Some people <u>not like</u> the taste of this food.

2 Water doesn't <u>boils</u> below 100 degrees Celsius.

3 It did not <u>rained</u> in Seoul yesterday.

4 <u>Were</u> you feed the cats yesterday?

5 Did you <u>met</u> new friends in the train?

A 다음 우리말과 의미가 같도록 [보기]의 단어를 이용하여 문장을 완성하시오.

┌ 보기 ┐
need   buy   want   exercise   bring

1 그녀는 요리에 관한 책을 원한다.

→ She _____ a book about cooking.

2 엄마는 나에게 쿠키와 우유를 가져다주셨다.

→ Mom _____ me cookies and milk.

3 이 식물은 너무 많은 물을 필요로 하지 않는다.

→ This plant _____ _____ too much water.

4 내 남동생은 아침에 운동을 하지만, 나는 운동을 하지 않는다.

→ My brother _____ in the morning, but I _____ _____ .

5 David는 그 백화점에서 아무것도 사지 않았다.

→ David _____ _____ anything at the department store.

B 다음 문장을 괄호 안의 지시대로 바꿔 쓰시오. (단, 부정문은 줄임말로 쓸 것)

1 The tourist lost his passport in Italy. (부정문)

→ _____

2 The library opens from 6 a.m. every morning. (의문문)

→ _____

3 Nancy goes camping during her vacation. (과거형)

→ _____

4 I made a cake for her birthday. (부정문)

→ _____

5 The Korean national soccer team won the game. (의문문)

→ _____

C 다음 문장에서 어법상 <u>어색한</u> 부분을 고쳐 문장을 다시 쓰시오. (단, 부정문은 줄임말로 쓸 것)

1 The player haves a strong spirit and a strong body.

→ _____

2 She doesn't cuts the sandwiches into rectangles.

→ _____

3 Most people not knew the value of the painting.

→ _____

4 The restaurant offerred good food at cheap prices.

→ _____

5 Does Jason makes a model plane in his free time?

→ _____

6 Do Ann and Kevin climbed the mountain yesterday?

→ _____

D 다음 괄호 안에 주어진 말을 이용하여 영작하시오.

1 Sam은 매일 아침 7시 30분에 일어난다. (wake up, every morning)

→ _____

2 그는 방과 후에 산책을 하지 않는다. (take a walk)

→ _____

3 나의 할머니는 나를 위해 스웨터를 떠 주셨다. (knit a sweater)

→ _____

4 나는 햇빛 때문에 선글라스를 썼다. (wear, because of, the sunlight)

→ _____

5 너는 일주일에 한 번 패스트푸드를 먹니? (eat fast food, once a week)

→ _____

6 그들은 지난 주말에 그들의 조부모님을 찾아뵙지 않았다. (visit, last weekend)

→ _____

01 동사의 3인칭 단수 현재형이 잘못 짝지어진 것을 모두 고르면?

① fix – fixs   ② pay – pays

③ copy – copys   ④ miss – misses

⑤ finish – finishes

02 동사의 과거형이 잘못 짝지어진 것을 모두 고르면?

① bake – baked   ② drop – droped

③ reply – replied   ④ bring – brought

⑤ begin – begined

03 다음 빈칸에 들어갈 말로 알맞은 것은?

Susan _____ a text message to him.

① send   ② sends

③ sendes   ④ is send

⑤ does sends

04 다음 빈칸에 들어갈 말로 알맞지 않은 것을 모두 고르면?

_____ go to bed after 10:00 p.m.

① I   ② Steve

③ My sister   ④ My roommates

⑤ Ms. and Mr. Owen

05 다음 빈칸에 들어갈 말로 알맞지 않은 것은?

Daniel _____ yesterday.

① went hiking   ② read a book

③ walked his dog   ④ cleaned his room

⑤ watches a movie

06 다음 빈칸에 공통으로 들어갈 말로 알맞은 것은?

· I _____ not like vegetables in my childhood.

· _____ you visit the new restaurant yesterday?

① do[Do]   ② did[Did]

③ was[Was]   ④ does[Does]

⑤ were[Were]

07 다음 빈칸에 들어갈 말로 알맞게 짝지어진 것은?

· Did Ms. Lee _____ music last year?

· Mom _____ *gimbap* for me last night.

① teach – make   ② teach – made

③ teach – makes   ④ taught – made

⑤ teaches – made

내신 빈출
08 다음 (A), (B), (C)의 각 네모 안에서 어법에 맞는 것을 골라 바르게 짝지은 것은?

· (A) Does / Did the vacation start last weekend?

· (B) Do / Does Tony and Steve know each other?

· Linda (C) doesn't / didn't touch the painting then.

	(A)	(B)	(C)
①	Does	– Do	– doesn't
②	Did	– Do	– didn't
③	Does	– Does	– didn't
④	Did	– Does	– didn't
⑤	Did	– Do	– doesn't

09 다음 우리말을 어법에 알맞게 영작할 때 빈칸 ⓐ에 들어갈 말로 알맞은 것은?

> · Cathy는 수업 시간에 내 옆에 앉지 않는다.
> → Cathy _____ ⓐ _____
>   _____ _____ in class.

① to
② me
③ sit
④ next
⑤ doesn't

10 다음 우리말을 어법에 알맞게 영작한 것은?

> 그 콘서트는 10시에 끝났니?

① Do the concert end at ten?
② Did the concert end at ten?
③ Does the concert end at ten?
④ Do the concert ended at ten?
⑤ Did the concert ended at ten?

11 다음 중 부정문으로 잘못 바꾼 것은?

① They go to the same school.
→ They don't go to the same school.
② She left her umbrella on the subway.
→ She didn't leave her umbrella on the subway.
③ My cousin plays the ukulele well.
→ My cousin doesn't play the ukulele well.
④ I have a lot of homework today.
→ I doesn't have a lot of homework today.
⑤ The girl cried loudly last night.
→ The girl didn't cry loudly last night.

12 다음 중 의문문으로 잘못 바꾼 것은?

① The bus stops here.
→ Does the bus stop here?
② Susan and Blair like K-pop.
→ Do Susan and Blair like K-pop?
③ Andy wants chocolate for dessert.
→ Do Andy wants chocolate for dessert?
④ She had a headache last night.
→ Did she have a headache last night?
⑤ They went to an amusement park last Sunday.
→ Did they go to an amusement park last Sunday?

13 다음 질문에 대한 대답으로 알맞은 것은?

> Does he have English class on Friday?

① Yes, he is.
② No, he isn't.
③ Yes, he does.
④ Yes, he have.
⑤ No, he don't.

14 짝지어진 대화 중 어색한 것은?

① A: Does Mina have curly hair?
   B: Yes, she does.
② A: Does your uncle grow vegetables?
   B: No, he isn't.
③ A: Do you and Tom study English hard?
   B: Yes, we do.
④ A: Did the kids ride the roller coaster?
   B: No, they didn't.
⑤ A: Did you take piano lessons last month?
   B: Yes, I did.

15 다음 빈칸에 들어갈 말이 나머지와 <u>다른</u> 것은?
(단, 대·소문자 무시할 것)

① I _____ not write Christmas cards.

② _____ they meet Susie at the park?

③ We _____ not know the boy's name.

④ _____ there lockers in the classroom?

⑤ _____ you put sugar and milk in your coffee?

16 다음 중 빈칸에 들어갈 말이 같은 것끼리 짝지어진 것은?
(단, 대·소문자 무시할 것)

· The bus ⓐ _____ stop here anymore.

· I ⓑ _____ not like horror movies.

· ⓒ _____ the firefighters wear helmets?

· ⓓ _____ he play the piano well?

① ⓐ, ⓑ   ② ⓐ, ⓒ

③ ⓑ, ⓒ   ④ ⓐ, ⓑ, ⓒ

⑤ ⓐ, ⓑ, ⓓ

17 다음 밑줄 친 ①~⑤ 중 어법상 틀린 것은?

Then, the mayor ① <u>didn't</u> ② <u>cutted</u> the ribbon ③ <u>with</u> a ④ <u>pair</u> of ⑤ <u>scissors</u>.

18 다음 중 어법상 <u>틀린</u> 것은?

① They don't take a taxi.

② People look at the full moon.

③ Does the child like ice cream?

④ Alice isn't know his phone number.

⑤ He practices *taekwondo* after school.

19 다음 중 밑줄 친 부분을 어법에 맞게 고친 것으로 알맞지 <u>않은</u> 것은?

① Tim <u>carryed</u> heavy boxes. → carried

② <u>Was</u> you borrow David's bike? → Were

③ She <u>comed</u> to my birthday party. → came

④ Does Mr. Hanks <u>has</u> much money? → have

⑤ The singer doesn't <u>danced</u> on the stage. → dance

20 다음 밑줄 친 부분 중 어법상 옳은 것은?

① My brother <u>hate</u> math.

② Mom <u>mixes</u> flour and milk.

③ <u>Do you helps</u> your grandparents?

④ Jenny <u>doesn't goes</u> to school today.

⑤ <u>Do she has</u> an apple in the morning?

21 다음 중 어법상 옳은 것을 <u>모두</u> 고르면?

① She didn't buys new clothes.

② Did he turn off his computer?

③ I clean the bathroom an hour ago.

④ You took photos with a smartphone.

⑤ Mr. Swift catched a big fish yesterday.

22 다음 중 어법상 옳은 문장의 개수는?

· Does the man works here?

· Did your father repair the fan?

· Some people don't like raw fish.

· Brian doesn't miss the school bus yesterday.

· Do the people take pictures of the landscape?

① 1개   ② 2개   ③ 3개

④ 4개   ⑤ 5개

고난도
23 다음 중 어법상 옳은 것으로 알맞게 짝지어진 것은?

> ⓐ Brian didn't answer my letter.
> ⓑ Do the store sells doughnuts?
> ⓒ Did Joan told the truth to you?
> ⓓ The girl doesn't pick up the trash.
> ⓔ We readed some comic books yesterday.

① ⓐ, ⓒ   ② ⓐ, ⓓ
③ ⓑ, ⓓ   ④ ⓐ, ⓑ, ⓓ
⑤ ⓑ, ⓒ, ⓔ

고난도
24 다음 중 밑줄 친 부분의 쓰임이 나머지와 다른 것은?

① Do you often go to the movies?
② Wendy does not like cloudy days.
③ The baby did not take a nap today.
④ I do exercise for an hour every morning.
⑤ Did Mr. Evans teach science at your school?

고난도
25 [보기]의 밑줄 친 부분과 쓰임이 같은 것은?

┌ 보기 ┐
Dad does the dishes after dinner.
└────┘

① Does Tyler speak Korean well?
② The girl does not eat ice cream.
③ The chefs do not wear an apron.
④ Do you wash your hair every day?
⑤ He sometimes doesn't do his homework.

26 다음 밑줄 친 부분을 어법에 알맞게 고쳐 쓰시오.

> He water the flowers every other day.

→ _____

27 다음 우리말과 의미가 같도록 괄호 안의 말을 이용하여 영작하시오.

> 너는 매일 책을 읽니? (read a book)

→ _____

28 다음 우리말과 의미가 같도록 괄호 안의 말을 바르게 배열하시오.

> 그녀는 그녀의 여동생을 돌보지 않았다.
> (care, sister, of, she, take, didn't, her)

→ _____

29 다음 문장에서 어법상 틀린 부분을 찾아 알맞게 고쳐 쓰시오.

> Did you waited in line for concert tickets?

_____ → _____

30 다음 문장을 부정문으로 바꿔 쓰시오. (단, 줄임말로 쓸 것)

> Tony wants a new digital camera.

→ _____

31 다음 문장을 의문문으로 바꿔 쓴 후, 질문에 대한 대답을 완성하시오.

> Julian misses his hometown.

→ A: _____

  B: Yes, _____.

32 다음 대화의 빈칸 ⓐ와 ⓑ에 들어갈 like의 알맞은 형태를 각각 쓰시오.

> A: Do bears ⓐ _____ bananas?
> B: No, they don't. They ⓑ _____ honey and fish.

33 다음 그림을 보고, 괄호 안의 말을 이용하여 문장을 완성하시오. (단, 과거형으로 쓸 것)

(1) A boy _____ the window. (close)

(2) A girl _____ something on the blackboard. (write)

34 다음 우리말과 의미가 같도록 [조건]에 맞게 문장을 완성하시오.

> 나는 어제 네 컴퓨터를 사용하지 않았다.

| 조건 |
1. use your computer를 이용할 것
2. 필요시 단어를 추가할 것

→ _____ yesterday.

35 다음 그림을 보고, 각 빈칸에 들어갈 말을 [보기]에서 골라 알맞은 형태로 쓰시오.

| 9:00 | 10:00 | 11:00 | 12:00 |

| 보기 |
    walk   meet   eat   get up

  Yesterday was Sunday. I _____ at 9:00 and I _____ breakfast at 10:00. I _____ my dog in the park at 11:00. I _____ Alice there at noon.

Chapter

03

시제

01 현재시제, 과거시제

1 현재시제

현재의 사실이나 상태, 현재의 습관이나 반복적으로 하는 일, 변하지 않는 사실이나 진리, 속담, 격언 등을 나타낼 때 사용하는 시제이다.

1 현재의 사실이나 상태
Tyler **is** an entertainer and he **lives** in Seoul.
There **are** five more stops to City Hall.
My brother **likes** action movies and detective movies.

2 현재의 습관이나 반복적으로 하는 일
I usually **clean** my room on Saturday afternoon.
She **goes** to the traditional market once a week.
We **take** a pop quiz in math class every week.

3 변하지 않는 사실, 진리, 속담, 격언
Water **freezes** at 0°C and **boils** at 100°C.
The sun **rises** in the east and **sets** in the west.
A bad workman **blames** his tools.

2 과거시제

과거에 일어난 일이나 동작, 과거의 상태, 역사적 사실을 나타낼 때 사용하는 시제이다.

1 과거에 일어난 일이나 동작, 과거의 상태
He **won** the Nobel Prize in Literature in 2000.
Did Ms. Parker talk about the science project?
There **was** a big department store on 5th street.

2 역사적 사실
King Sejong **invented** Hangeul in 1443.
Beethoven **composed** nine symphonies all his life.
Van Gogh **painted** "The Starry Night" in 1889.

⊕ PLUS 현재시제 부사(구) vs. 과거시제 부사(구)
• 현재시제와 자주 쓰이는 부사(구): now, every ~, on weekends[Mondays / Tuesdays ...], these days, nowadays, 빈도부사 (always, usually, often, sometimes, never ...) 등
• 과거시제와 자주 쓰이는 부사(구): then, yesterday, last ~, ~ ago, before, in + 과거연도, those days 등

A 다음 괄호 안에서 알맞은 것을 고르시오.

1 She (has / had) two cats and two dogs now.

2 One rotten apple (spoils / spoiled) the whole barrel.

3 Morgan (moves / moved) to San Francisco last week.

4 Alexander Graham Bell (invents / invented) the telephone.

B 다음 빈칸에 괄호 안의 단어를 알맞은 형태로 쓰시오.

1 The weather in Paris _____ very good last week. (be)

2 The English Channel _____ England from France. (divide)

3 Jenny _____ the guitar for an hour every day. (practice)

4 Many people _____ camping these days. (enjoy)

5 Kim Yuna _____ the gold medal at the Vancouver Olympics. (win)

C 다음 우리말과 의미가 같도록 [보기]에서 알맞은 단어를 골라 문장을 완성하시오.

보기
stay   buy   take   visit

1 그들은 그 가게에서 몇몇 기념품들을 샀다.

→ They _____ some souvenirs at the shop.

2 Alex는 주말마다 유기견 보호 센터를 방문한다.

→ Alex _____ the dog shelter on weekends.

3 미나는 일주일에 세 번 요가 수업을 받는다.

→ Mina _____ yoga classes three times a week.

4 나는 축구 경기를 보느라 밤늦게까지 깨어 있었다.

→ I _____ up until late at night watching a soccer game.

D 다음 문장의 밑줄 친 부분을 어법상 알맞은 형태로 고쳐 쓰시오.

1 Plants <u>needed</u> sunlight and water to grow.

2 She <u>breaks</u> her leg playing soccer three days ago.

3 Wild pandas <u>lived</u> up to 15 years on average.

4 We <u>go</u> sightseeing on a tour bus yesterday.

5 Many people <u>make</u> a donation to the charity last time.

02 진행시제

1 동사의 -ing형 만들기

동사의 -ing형은 보통 동사원형에 -ing를 붙여서 만든다.

대부분의 동사	+ -ing	go → going	play → playing	cook → cooking
-e로 끝나는 동사	-e → -ing	live → living	take → taking	come → coming
-ie로 끝나는 동사	-ie → -ying	lie → lying	tie → tying	die → dying
「단모음 + 단자음」으로 끝나는 동사	자음 추가 + -ing	sit → sitting	run → running	get → getting

2 현재진행형과 과거진행형

진행형은 '~하고 있다', '~하고 있었다'라는 뜻으로 현재 또는 과거에 진행 중인 동작을 나타낸다.

현재진행형	am / are / is + 동사원형-ing	~하고 있다, ~하고 있는 중이다
과거진행형	was / were + 동사원형-ing	~하고 있었다, ~하고 있는 중이었다

현재진행형

I **am going** to the concert by bus.
A girl **is walking** down the street.
A few cars **are running** on the road.

과거진행형

I **was going** to the concert by bus.
A girl **was walking** down the street.
A few cars **were running** on the road.

➕ PLUS 현재시제 vs. 현재진행형
- Luna **performs** at the theater every day. (현재시제 — 현재 반복적으로 하는 일)
- Luna **is performing** at the theater now. (현재진행형 — 현재 하고 있는 일)

3 진행형의 부정문과 의문문

1 현재진행형의 부정문과 의문문

부정문	am[are / is] + not + 동사원형-ing
의문문	Am[Are / Is] + 주어 + 동사원형-ing ~? – Yes, 주어 + am[are / is]. / No, 주어 + am not[aren't / isn't].

Julie **is not[isn't] waiting** for Jerry now. She is waiting for her cousin.
Are you **looking** for a book about Italy? – No, I'm not. I'm looking for a book about Greece.

2 과거진행형의 부정문과 의문문

부정문	was[were] + not + 동사원형-ing
의문문	Was[Were] + 주어 + 동사원형-ing ~? – Yes, 주어 + was[were]. / No, 주어 + wasn't[weren't].

Mike **was not[wasn't] playing** computer games. He was doing his homework.
Was she **cooking** food? – Yes, she was. She enjoys cooking.

➕ PLUS 진행형을 쓸 수 없는 동사
have, like, want, know, see, hear, smell, taste 등 소유, 감정, 인식, 지각 등 상태를 나타내는 동사는 진행형으로 쓸 수 없다.
cf. have가 '먹다(eat)'라는 뜻일 때는 진행형으로 쓸 수 있다. ex. We **are having[eating]** lunch now.

A 다음 괄호 안에 주어진 말을 이용하여 진행시제 문장을 완성하시오.

1 Boys and girls _____ to music on the stage now. (dance)

2 Dave _____ the basketball game now. (not, watch)

3 The police officers _____ after the thief then. (run)

4 _____ you _____ jeans and a sweatshirt then? (wear)

5 I _____ to the stationery store to buy a ruler now. (go)

B 다음 문장을 진행시제로 바꿔 쓸 때, 빈칸에 알맞은 말을 쓰시오. (단, 부정문은 줄임말로 쓸 것)

1 My grandmother tells me a very scary story.

→ My grandmother _____ me a very scary story.

2 You do your best to solve the math problem.

→ You _____ your best to solve the math problem.

3 The teacher waited for an answer to her question.

→ The teacher _____ for an answer to her question.

4 Tony didn't use an old computer in the classroom.

→ Tony _____ an old computer in the classroom.

5 Do they build a tunnel through the mountain?

→ _____ a tunnel through the mountain?

C 다음 괄호 안에 주어진 단어를 이용하여 대화를 완성하시오.

1 A: Is she _____ out the window? (look) B: Yes, she _____ .

2 A: _____ the dog _____ a hole? (dig) B: No, it wasn't.

3 A: Were the children _____ the road? (cross) B: Yes, they _____ .

4 A: _____ you _____ for your trip to Europe? (prepare) B: No, I'm not.

D 다음 문장의 밑줄 친 부분을 어법상 알맞은 형태로 고쳐 쓰시오.

1 My dog was <u>barks</u> at the stranger then.

2 Emma <u>weren't</u> looking out of the window.

3 I <u>am knowing</u> Jason Jones. He's in my class.

4 <u>Do</u> they having a barbecue in the yard?

5 Pam and Jason <u>were decorating</u> the Christmas tree now.

03 미래시제

1 미래시제

앞으로 일어날 일이나 계획을 나타낼 때 사용하는 시제이며, 조동사 will 또는 be going to로 표현한다.

현재	Laura **goes** to middle school.
과거	Laura **went** to middle school last year.
미래	Laura **will[is going to] go to** middle school next year.

2 will

1 will + 동사원형: '~할 것이다', '~하겠다'의 뜻으로 미래에 대한 예측이나 계획, 의지를 나타낸다.
I **will wait** for you at home tomorrow.
My father **will retire** from his job next month.

2 부정문: will not[won't] + 동사원형
I **will not[won't] eat** sweets and chocolate again.
She **will not[won't] take** a bus to the airport.

3 의문문: Will + 주어 + 동사원형 ~? – Yes, 주어 + will. / No, 주어 + won't.
Will they **sell** used toys and books? – Yes, they will. / No, they won't.

⊕ **PLUS** 조동사 will의 특징
• will은 조동사이므로 주어에 따라 형태가 변하지 않으며 뒤에 항상 동사원형이 온다.
• 인칭대명사와 will은 줄여 쓸 수 있다. ex. I'll, you'll, she'll, he'll, it'll, we'll, they'll

3 be going to

1 be going to + 동사원형: '~할 계획이다', '~할 것이다'의 뜻으로 예정된 미래의 일이나 예측을 나타내며, be동사는 주어에 따라 달라진다.
They **are going to construct** a hospital in the town.
Korea **is going to play** a match against Japan tonight.

2 부정문: be동사 + not going to + 동사원형
I **am not going to change** my plan to visit the museum.
Harry **is not[isn't] going to make** a speech in front of people.

3 의문문: Be동사 + 주어 + going to + 동사원형 ~? – Yes, 주어 + be동사. / No, 주어 + be동사 + not.
Are you **going to learn** Chinese next term? – Yes, I am. / No, I'm not.

⊕ **PLUS** 「be going to + 동사원형」 vs. 「be going to + 명사」
• be going to + 동사원형: ~할 것이다 (미래시제)
• be going to + 명사: ~에 가고 있다[있었다] (진행시제) – 여기에서 to는 전치사

A 다음 괄호 안에서 알맞은 것을 고르시오.

1 Sue (will / wills) fly to Madrid to visit her aunt.

2 The guide will (take / to take) us around the city tomorrow.

3 I (not will / will not) show my childhood photos to you.

4 He is going (stay / to stay) at his uncle's house this weekend.

5 Ken and Beth (will / are) going to open a restaurant together.

B 다음 괄호 안의 말과 be going to를 이용하여 문장을 완성하시오.

1 They _____ the class president. (elect)

2 The students _____ on a field trip to Jejudo. (go)

3 Steve _____ some exercise to keep healthy. (do)

4 _____ it _____ a lot this weekend? (rain)

5 I _____ my time any more. (not, waste)

C 다음 밑줄 친 부분을 괄호 안의 말로 바꿔 문장을 다시 쓰시오. (단, will을 사용할 것)

1 Hurricanes hit the area last month. (next month)

   → _____

2 Jangho took a math exam last Friday. (next Friday)

   → _____

3 Emma returned some books to the library last week. (next week)

   → _____

4 Did your father fix the bathtub yesterday? (tomorrow)

   → _____

D 다음 문장의 밑줄 친 부분을 어법상 알맞은 형태로 고쳐 쓰시오.

1 Dry weather will to continue for the whole week.

2 The man will swims across the Han River next year.

3 The plane to Busan doesn't will depart at 2 p.m.

4 I be going to wear a black jacket and jeans tomorrow.

5 Will the country going to host the next Olympics?

A 다음 우리말과 의미가 같도록 [보기]에서 알맞은 단어를 골라 문장을 완성하시오.

보기
| fix | spoil | close | do | draw |

1 요리사가 너무 많으면 수프를 망친다.

→ Too many cooks _____ the broth.

2 그 동물원은 월요일마다 일찍 문을 닫는다.

→ The zoo _____ early on Mondays.

3 Blair는 작년에 이 그림을 그렸다.

→ Blair _____ this picture last year.

4 그 남자는 세탁기를 수리하고 있다.

→ The man _____ the washing machine.

5 미래에는 로봇들이 사람들을 위해 많은 것들을 할 것이다.

→ Robots _____ lots of things for people in the future.

B 다음 우리말과 의미가 같도록 괄호 안의 말을 이용하여 문장을 완성하시오.

1 Tony는 그의 친구와 싸우지 않을 것이다. (will, fight with)

→ Tony _____ his friend.

2 그녀는 내년에 일본어를 배울 계획이다. (be going to, learn)

→ _____ Japanese next year.

3 Joe는 헬멧 없이 스쿠터를 타고 있니? (Joe, ride)

→ _____ a scooter without a helmet?

4 강아지들이 공을 가지고 놀고 있었다. (play with)

→ Puppies _____ a ball.

5 그들은 지금 텔레비전을 보고 있지 않다. (watch, television)

→ They _____ now.

C 다음 주어진 동사를 이용하여 문장을 완성하시오.

1 go

→ Daisy _____ hiking with her friends on weekends.

→ Daisy _____ hiking with her friends last weekend.

→ Daisy _____ hiking with her friends next weekend.

2 pay

→ Students _____ attention to their teacher in class.

→ Students _____ attention to their teacher in class yesterday.

→ Students _____ attention to their teacher in class tomorrow.

3 donate

→ The singer _____ some money every month.

→ The singer _____ some money last month.

→ The singer _____ some money next month.

D 다음 괄호 안에 주어진 말을 이용하여 영작하시오.

1 Susan은 아침 식사로 달걀 2개를 삶고 있다. (boil, for breakfast)

→ _____

2 Ted는 나의 잡지를 돌려주지 않았다. (return, magazine)

→ _____

3 너는 어젯밤에 피아노를 치고 있었니? (play the piano)

→ _____

4 그 여자는 그때 새로운 소설을 쓰고 있었다. (write a new novel, at that time)

→ _____

5 우리는 다음 달에 호주로 이민을 갈 것이다. (be going to, immigrate, Australia)

→ _____

6 너는 내 질문을 이해하지 못할 것이다. (will, understand, question)

→ _____

01 다음 중 동사와 현재분사형이 <u>잘못</u> 짝지어진 것은?

① fix – fixing ② tie – tying
③ sit – siting ④ live – living
⑤ cry – crying

02 다음 빈칸에 들어갈 말로 알맞은 것은?

My uncle _____ a used car last year.

① buys ② bought
③ will buy ④ is buying
⑤ is going to buy

03 다음 빈칸에 들어갈 말로 알맞은 것을 <u>모두</u> 고르면?

I _____ a motorcycle someday.

① rides ② riding
③ rode ④ will ride
⑤ am going to ride

04 다음 빈칸에 들어갈 말로 알맞지 <u>않은</u> 것은?

You _____ yesterday.

① weren't late ② stayed home
③ joined the club ④ won't watch TV
⑤ went to the hospital

05 다음 빈칸에 들어갈 말로 알맞지 <u>않은</u> 것을 <u>모두</u> 고르면?

Hana will go shopping _____ .

① soon ② yesterday
③ last week ④ next Saturday
⑤ this afternoon

06 다음 빈칸에 공통으로 들어갈 말로 알맞은 것은?

- My sister _____ eight years old this year.
- Daniel _____ feeding rabbits on the farm.
- He _____ going to clean the refrigerator.

① is ② be
③ do ④ does
⑤ will

07 다음 빈칸에 들어갈 말로 알맞게 짝지어진 것은?

- He _____ in the library then.
- She _____ a cooking class next week.

① studies – takes ② studied – took
③ studies – will take ④ studied – will take
⑤ was studying – took

08 다음 (A), (B), (C)의 각 네모 안에서 어법에 맞는 것을 골라 바르게 짝지은 것은?

- The child is (A) drink / drinking mango juice.
- Alice (B) is / was driving to the post office then.
- (C) Does / Will Amy pass the audition tomorrow?

	(A)	(B)	(C)
①	drink	– is	– Does
②	drink	– was	– Will
③	drinking	– is	– Will
④	drinking	– was	– Does
⑤	drinking	– was	– Will

09 다음 질문에 대한 대답으로 알맞은 것은?

> Are you going to climb the mountain next week?

① Yes, I do.　　② Yes, I will.
③ No, I don't.　　④ No, I won't.
⑤ No, I'm not.

10 다음 우리말을 어법에 알맞게 영작할 때 빈칸 ⓐ에 들어갈 말로 알맞은 것은?

> • 나는 네 비밀을 그에게 영원히 말하지 않을 거야.
> → I _____ ⓐ _____
> _____ _____ to him forever.

① tell　　② will　　③ not
④ your　　⑤ secret

11 다음 우리말을 어법에 알맞게 영작한 것은?

> Randy는 칠판을 닦고 있는 중이니?

① Will Randy clean the blackboard?
② Is Randy cleaning the blackboard?
③ Does Randy clean the blackboard?
④ Was Randy cleaning the blackboard?
⑤ Is Randy going to clean the blackboard?

12 다음 중 부정문으로 잘못 바꾼 것은?

① They will move to Cheonan.
　→ They won't move to Cheonan.
② Anne is washing the dishes.
　→ Anne isn't washing the dishes.
③ Jerry wants new sneakers.
　→ Jerry doesn't want new sneakers.
④ He was going to Busan by airplane.
　→ He didn't be going to Busan by airplane.
⑤ I'm going to order ice cream for dessert.
　→ I'm not going to order ice cream for dessert.

13 다음 문장을 의문문으로 바르게 바꾼 것은?

> The company is going to employ Mike.

① Did the company employ Mike?
② Is the company employing Mike?
③ Does the company employ Mike?
④ Was the company employing Mike?
⑤ Is the company going to employ Mike?

14 다음 빈칸에 들어갈 말이 나머지와 다른 것은?

① I _____ eating a large pizza then.
② Betty _____ playing the flute now.
③ The baby _____ sleeping at that time.
④ Mark _____ living alone in Mexico last year.
⑤ My mother _____ baking cookies an hour ago.

15 밑줄 친 부분을 will로 바꿔 쓸 수 없는 것은?

① I am going to go on a diet.
② Ted is going to play with his dog.
③ We are going to the rock concert.
④ They are going to have a garage sale.
⑤ She is going to read a fashion magazine.

16 다음 문장과 의미가 같은 것은?

> I will attend Brian's wedding.

① I attended Brian's wedding.
② I am going to Brian's wedding.
③ I was attending Brian's wedding.
④ I am going to attend Brian's wedding.
⑤ I was going to attend Brian's wedding.

고난도

17 다음 중 빈칸에 들어갈 말이 같은 것끼리 짝지어진 것은? (단, 대·소문자 무시할 것)

> - It will ⓐ _____ very foggy tomorrow.
> - The man ⓑ _____ waiting for a train then.
> - The movie ⓒ _____ going to be over by 3:00.
> - ⓓ _____ Alex taking a picture of koalas now?

① ⓐ, ⓑ   ② ⓑ, ⓒ

③ ⓒ, ⓓ   ④ ⓐ, ⓑ, ⓒ

⑤ ⓑ, ⓒ, ⓓ

18 다음 대화의 밑줄 친 ①~⑤ 중 어법상 틀린 것은?

> A: What are you ① doing now?
> B: I am ② watching TV on the sofa.
> A: ③ Does your sister watching TV, too?
> B: No, she ④ isn't. She ⑤ is playing with dolls.

19 다음 중 어법상 틀린 것은?

① You are lying to me again.

② My dad is taking a shower.

③ Mary was chating with her friends.

④ Was she cleaning the window then?

⑤ The waves were crashing on the sand.

20 다음 중 어법상 틀린 것을 모두 고르면?

① Water boils at 100°C.

② Edison invents the light bulb.

③ My brother is reading my diary now.

④ Steve Jobs had a lot of creative ideas.

⑤ One rotten apple spoiled the whole barrel.

내신 빈출

21 다음 중 밑줄 친 부분을 어법에 맞게 고친 것으로 알맞지 않은 것은?

① Will it is sunny tomorrow? → be

② Be she going to make *bulgogi*? → Does

③ I be going to solve the problems. → am

④ We don't going to miss the school bus.
　→ aren't

⑤ He wills be a famous cartoonist in the future.
　→ will

22 다음 중 어법상 옳은 것을 모두 고르면?

① Dave isn't flying a kite then.

② Nick always jogs before breakfast.

③ The earth traveled around the sun.

④ Columbus discovers America in 1492.

⑤ I'm going to borrow some books today.

고난도

23 다음 중 어법상 옳은 문장의 개수는?

> · Actions spoke louder than words.
> · A man is coming out of the house.
> · Eric won't cleans his room tomorrow.
> · Will you going to learn Spanish next year?
> · Were you looking for your dog last night?

① 1개　　　　② 2개　　　　③ 3개
④ 4개　　　　⑤ 5개

고난도

24 다음 중 어법상 옳은 것으로 알맞게 짝지어진 것은?

> ⓐ The ostrich is a bird but can't fly.
> ⓑ An electric car will reduce air pollution.
> ⓒ Do you collecting old CDs these days?
> ⓓ Some children were playing hide-and-seek.
> ⓔ The Industrial Revolution is in the nineteenth century.

① ⓐ, ⓒ　　　　　　② ⓐ, ⓑ, ⓓ
③ ⓐ, ⓒ, ⓓ　　　　④ ⓑ, ⓓ, ⓔ
⑤ ⓑ, ⓒ, ⓓ, ⓔ

내신 빈출

25 다음 중 밑줄 친 부분의 쓰임이 나머지와 다른 것은?

① The child is <u>going</u> to skip rope.
② Peter is <u>going</u> to paint the walls.
③ I'm <u>going</u> to play computer games.
④ Beth is <u>going</u> to the hospital to visit Sally.
⑤ We're <u>going</u> to spend Christmas in New York.

26 다음 밑줄 친 부분을 어법에 알맞게 고쳐 쓰시오.

> Mike <u>calls</u> his grandmother tomorrow.

→ _____

27 다음 우리말과 의미가 같도록 괄호 안의 말을 바르게 배열하시오.

> 그 아이들은 공원에서 달리고 있었니?
> (running, were, in the park, the children, ?)

→ _____

28 다음 빈칸에 공통으로 들어갈 알맞은 말을 쓰시오.

> · Mike is _____ to the amusement park.
> · We are _____ to ride the merry-go-round.

→ _____

29 다음 두 문장의 의미가 같도록 빈칸에 들어갈 알맞은 말을 쓰시오.

> He won't tell a lie to his parents.
>
> = He _____ _____ _____
> _____ a lie to his parents.

30 다음 문장을 괄호 안의 지시대로 바꿔 쓰시오.

> The wind was blowing very hard.

(부정문)
→ _____

(의문문)
→ _____

31 다음 우리말과 의미가 같도록 [조건]에 맞게 문장을 완성하시오.

> 나는 내년에 규칙적으로 운동할 것이다.

─┤ 조건 ├─
1. exercise regularly를 이용할 것
2. 필요시 단어를 추가할 것

→ I _____ next year.

32 다음 대화의 빈칸 ⓐ와 ⓑ에 들어갈 알맞은 말을 쓰시오.

> A: ⓐ _____ the students taking a test now?
> B: No, they ⓑ _____. They already finished it.

33 다음 그림을 보고, 괄호 안의 말을 이용하여 문장을 완성하시오.

> Judy and Alex _____ (play) tennis now. They _____ (study) in the library in an hour.

34 다음 글에서 어법상 틀린 부분을 2개 찾아 알맞게 고쳐 쓰시오.

> My parents and I do volunteer work every month. We will visit an abandoned dog center this weekend. We have a dog named Bamton, but we won't take her there. She was sick now. My sister will take care of her. I will feed the dogs at the center. Mom will washes the dogs. Will Dad wash the dogs, too? No, he won't. He will clean their houses.

(1) _____ → _____

(2) _____ → _____

35 다음 Tim의 여행 일정표를 보고, 빈칸 ⓐ ~ ⓒ에 들어갈 알맞은 말을 쓰시오.

Yesterday	visit the British Museum
Today	walk along the Thames River
Tomorrow	ride the London Eye

> Tim ⓐ _____ the British Museum yesterday. He ⓑ _____ along the Thames River now. He ⓒ _____ the London Eye tomorrow.

Chapter

04

조동사

01 can, may

1 can

1 능력, 가능: ~할 수 있다 (= be able to)

I **can** play the guitar very well.

The girl **cannot[can't]** reach the top shelf.

Can you stand on your head? – Yes, I can. / No, I can't.

2 허가: ~해도 된다 (= may)

You **can** eat or drink in the theater.

Can I hand in my homework tomorrow? – Yes, you can. / No, you can't.

평서문	can + 동사원형	~할 수 있다 / ~해도 된다
부정문	cannot[can't] + 동사원형	~할 수 없다 / ~해서는 안 된다
의문문	Can + 주어 + 동사원형 ~?	~할 수 있니? / ~해도 되니?

⊕ PLUS 조동사의 특징
- 주어에 따라 형태가 변하지 않으며 뒤에 항상 동사원형이 온다.
- 「조동사 + 조동사」의 형태로 쓸 수 없다. ex. You **will can** meet her again. (×)

2 be able to

'~할 수 있다'의 뜻으로 can과 같은 의미이며, be동사는 주어에 따라 변하고 뒤에 동사원형이 온다.

The figure skater **is able to** spin on the ice.

A newborn baby **isn't able to** walk.

Are you **able to** prepare a meal alone? – Yes, I am. / No, I'm not.

⊕ PLUS can vs. be able to
- 허가의 can은 be able to로 바꿔 쓸 수 없다.
- can의 과거형은 could이고, be able to의 과거형은 was[were] able to이다.
- can은 미래시제로 쓸 수 없지만, be able to의 미래시제는 will be able to이다.

3 may

1 허가: ~해도 된다 (= can)

You **may** sleep over at your friend's house.

May I park my car here for a while? – Yes, you may. / No, you may not.

2 추측: ~일지도 모른다

It **may** be cold and cloudy tomorrow.

The country **may not** win the World Cup this time.

평서문	may + 동사원형	~해도 된다 / ~일지도 모른다
부정문	may not + 동사원형	~해서는 안 된다 / ~이 아닐지도 모른다
의문문	May + 주어 + 동사원형 ~?	~해도 되니? / ~일까?

Grammar Check Up

A 다음 문장에서 밑줄 친 부분의 의미로 알맞은 것을 [보기]에서 골라 쓰시오.

보기
능력   허가   추측

1 James <u>may</u> know her secret. → _____

2 You <u>can</u> go out and play outside. → _____

3 <u>May</u> I use your phone for a while? → _____

4 The parrot <u>can</u> speak just like a person. → _____

B 다음 두 문장의 의미가 같도록 빈칸에 알맞은 조동사를 쓰시오.

1 You can use my scissors if you want.

= You _____ use my scissors if you want.

2 May I see your passport and ticket?

= _____ I see your passport and ticket?

3 He is able to run 100 meters in 11 seconds.

= He _____ run 100 meters in 11 seconds.

4 The player wasn't able to win the gold medal in the Olympics.

= The player _____ win the gold medal in the Olympics.

C 다음 우리말과 의미가 같도록 괄호 안의 말과 can 또는 may를 이용하여 문장을 완성하시오.

1 당신은 그것을 신용카드로 지불하셔도 됩니다. (pay)

→ You _____ for it with a credit card.

2 이 제품은 우리의 환경에 해로울지도 모른다. (be)

→ This product _____ harmful to our environment.

3 너는 도서관에서 책을 몇 권 빌릴 수 있다. (borrow)

→ You _____ some books from the library.

4 우리는 그를 오랫동안 기다릴 수 없었다. (wait)

→ We _____ for him for a long time.

D 다음 문장의 밑줄 친 부분을 어법상 알맞은 형태로 고쳐 쓰시오.

1 The purse <u>doesn't may</u> be Jessica's.

2 She <u>mays</u> not have a talent for singing.

3 You will <u>can</u> see her in three months.

4 You can't <u>to enter</u> the temple in shorts.

02 must, have to, should

1 must

1 의무: ~해야 한다 (= have to)

You **must** stop at a red traffic light.

You **must not[mustn't]** throw trash out of the window.

Must we go to the stadium early to get good seats?

2 강한 추측: ~임에 틀림없다

The boy **must** be so smart to solve the problem.

cf. '~일 리가 없다'는 뜻의 강한 부정의 추측은 must not이 아닌 can't를 쓴다.

Brad is a vegetarian. He **can't** like meat.

평서문	must + 동사원형	~해야 한다 / ~임에 틀림없다
부정문	must not[mustn't] + 동사원형	~해서는 안 된다
의문문	Must + 주어 + 동사원형 ~?	~해야 하니?

⊕ PLUS must의 과거와 미래 표현

must는 과거형이 없으므로 의무를 나타낼 경우 have to의 과거형 had to를 사용하고, 미래시제는 will have to로 쓴다.

ex. I **had to** clean my room yesterday. (과거)

You **will have to** water the plant every day. (미래)

2 have to

1 '~해야 한다'의 뜻으로 must와 같은 의미이며, have동사는 주어에 따라 형태가 바뀐다.

She **has to** arrive at the airport by 4:30 p.m.

We **have to** share information with each other.

2 부정문: don't[doesn't] have to의 형태로 쓰며 '~할 필요가 없다'라는 불필요의 의미이다.

Sally **doesn't have to** clean her room today.

You **don't have to** run to catch the bus.

⊕ PLUS must not vs. don't[doesn't] have to

must not은 '~해서는 안 된다'라는 금지의 의미이고, don't[doesn't] have to는 '~할 필요가 없다'라는 불필요의 의미이므로 잘 구별
해서 써야 한다.

3 should

'~해야 한다'의 뜻으로 의무를 나타내며 주로 충고, 조언, 제안의 의미로 사용된다.

You **should** be polite to your neighbor.

You **should not[shouldn't]** spend too much time on the computer.

Should I give you a hint for the problem?

Grammar Check Up

Answers p.8

A 다음 괄호 안에서 알맞은 것을 고르시오.

1 You (had to bow / must bowed) to your teacher.

2 They should (leave / to leave) home at 1 o'clock.

3 Wendy has (book / to book) a seat for Chicago in advance.

4 We (don't must / must not) destroy nature anymore.

B 다음 문장에서 밑줄 친 부분의 의미로 알맞은 것을 [보기]에서 골라 쓰시오.

보기			
의무	금지	불필요	추측

1 You should follow the school rules. → _____

2 Laura doesn't have to lose weight. → _____

3 You must not fight with your friends. → _____

4 Many people must be pleased to hear the news. → _____

C 다음 우리말과 의미가 같도록 괄호 안의 말과 must 또는 have to를 이용하여 문장을 완성하시오.

1 그 선수들은 지금 피곤함에 틀림없다. (be)

→ The players _____ tired right now.

2 학생들은 시험에서 부정행위를 해서는 안 된다. (cheat)

→ Students _____ on the test.

3 너는 이 문제에 대해 다시 생각해야 한다. (think)

→ You _____ again about this problem.

4 그녀는 서울역에 가기 위해 버스를 갈아탈 필요가 없다. (change)

→ She _____ buses to go to Seoul Station.

D 다음 문장의 밑줄 친 부분을 어법상 알맞은 형태로 고쳐 쓰시오.

1 You don't have wait in line to buy tickets.

2 Kate should does her best to improve her English.

3 Eric won first place. He has to be happy.

4 You don't must cross the street at a red light.

A 다음 빈칸에 들어갈 알맞은 말을 [보기]에서 골라 괄호 안의 단어를 이용하여 대화를 완성하시오.

보기

| have to | don't have to | mustn't | can | can't |

1 A: It's too cold. _____ (turn on) the heater?

   B: Of course, you can.

2 A: Can you come to the Club Festival?

   B: I'm afraid, I can't. I _____ (go) to the dentist.

3 A: I _____ (play) basketball.

   B: Don't worry. I'll teach you.

4 A: Let's cross the street here.

   B: No, we _____ (cross) the street here. We must cross at the crosswalk.

5 A: The museum is free today. You _____ (pay) to get in.

   B: Oh, really? That sounds great.

B 다음 우리말과 의미가 같도록 괄호 안의 말을 바르게 배열하시오.

1 제가 이 그림의 사진을 찍어도 되나요? (take, may, a photo, I)

   → _____ of this picture?

2 너는 이번 주말에 내 차를 사용해도 된다. (my car, use, you, can)

   → _____ this weekend.

3 Jessie는 그 테니스 경기를 이길 수 없었다. (to, was, Jessie, win, able, not)

   → _____ the tennis match.

4 너는 온라인 게임하는 데 많은 시간을 보내면 안 된다. (not, you, spend, should)

   → _____ lots of time playing online games.

5 Tyler는 세계에서 유명한 음악가임에 틀림없다. (be, a famous musician, must, Tyler)

   → _____ in the world.

C 다음 두 문장의 의미가 같도록 [보기]의 말을 이용하여 문장을 완성하시오. (단, 중복 이용 가능)

| 보기 |
| may   must   have to   be able to |

1 You have to spell the words correctly.

= You _____ spell the words correctly.

2 Can I come in an hour late tomorrow morning?

= _____ I come in an hour late tomorrow morning?

3 You don't need to worry about making mistakes.

= You _____ _____ _____ worry about making mistakes.

4 I can hold my breath for more than a minute.

= I _____ _____ _____ hold my breath for more than a minute.

5 You must drive a car on the right side in England.

= You _____ _____ drive a car on the right side in England.

D 다음 괄호 안에 주어진 말을 이용하여 문장을 완성하시오. (단, 조동사를 이용할 것)

1 제가 제 친구에게 사과해야 하나요? (apologize)

→ _____ to my friend?

2 너는 서울로 가는 마지막 버스를 놓칠지도 모른다. (miss)

→ _____ to Seoul.

3 너는 박물관에서 사진을 찍어서는 안 된다. (take pictures)

→ _____ in the museum.

4 제가 파티에 제 여동생을 데려가도 되나요? (bring)

→ _____ along to the party?

5 너는 밤에 운전할 때 조심해야 한다. (be)

→ _____ when you drive at night.

6 우리는 로마에서 하룻밤 더 머무를 수 있었다. (stay)

→ _____ in Rome.

01 다음 빈칸에 들어갈 말로 알맞은 것은?

> This problem is very easy for me. I _____ solve it.

① may
② can
③ mustn't
④ shouldn't
⑤ am not able to

02 다음 빈칸에 들어갈 말로 알맞은 것을 <u>모두</u> 고르면?

> Alex will _____ to a dentist soon.

① may go
② must go
③ should go
④ have to go
⑤ be able to go

03 다음 빈칸에 들어갈 말로 알맞지 <u>않은</u> 것은?

> Can you _____?

① climb this tree
② take pictures well
③ wait for me outside
④ able to read Chinese
⑤ swim across the river

04 다음 빈칸에 공통으로 들어갈 말로 알맞은 것은?

> · _____ you cook well?
> · I'm thirsty. _____ I drink this water?

① Can
② May
③ Must
④ Should
⑤ Have to

05 다음 중 빈칸에 must가 들어갈 수 <u>없는</u> 것은?

① You _____ be home by 9:00.
② I _____ get up early yesterday.
③ We _____ buy some vegetables.
④ Students _____ obey their teachers.
⑤ You _____ not watch too much TV.

06 다음 우리말과 의미가 같도록 빈칸에 들어갈 말로 알맞은 것은?

> · 나의 오빠는 내 생일을 기억하고 있을 리가 없다.
>   → My brother _____ remember my birthday.

① can't
② must not
③ is able to
④ should not
⑤ doesn't have to

07 다음 빈칸에 들어갈 말로 알맞게 짝지어진 것은?

> · The rumors _____ not be true.
> · You look very tired. You _____ take a rest.

① will - shouldn't
② may - should
③ should - can't
④ can - don't have to
⑤ must - aren't able to

08 다음 중 문맥이 자연스럽지 <u>않은</u> 것은?

① We can watch many stars at night.
② You should wash your hands often.
③ They have to hurry to catch the train.
④ Brian doesn't have to take your umbrella.
⑤ You mustn't wear your seat belt for your safety.

09 다음 문장을 부정문으로 바르게 바꾼 것은?

> The man may be a basketball player.

① The man may be not a basketball player.
② The man may not be a basketball player.
③ The man not may be a basketball player.
④ The man may doesn't be a basketball player.
⑤ The man doesn't may be a basketball player.

내신 빈출
10 다음 문장을 의문문으로 바르게 바꾼 것은?

> The robot is able to save people's lives.

① Is able the robot to save people's lives?
② Is the robot able to save people's lives?
③ Be the robot able to save people's lives?
④ Do the robot is able to save people's lives?
⑤ Does the robot be able to save people's lives?

11 다음 우리말을 어법에 알맞게 영작한 것은?

> 네 안경은 소파 밑에 있을지도 모른다.

① Your glasses can be under the sofa.
② Your glasses may be under the sofa.
③ Your glasses must be under the sofa.
④ Your glasses should be under the sofa.
⑤ Your glasses are able to be under the sofa.

12 다음 우리말과 의미가 같도록 괄호 안의 말을 배열할 때, 세 번째로 오는 단어는?

> 엘리베이터가 고장 났음에 틀림없다.
> (must, be, out, of, order, the, elevator)

① of   ② be   ③ out
④ must   ⑤ order

내신 빈출
13 다음 문장과 의미가 같은 것은?

> You can use my office for a month.

① You will use my office for a month.
② You may use my office for a month.
③ You might use my office for a month.
④ You should use my office for a month.
⑤ You have to use my office for a month.

14 다음 빈칸에 들어갈 말로 알맞은 것은?

> Kate could read at the age of five.
> = Kate _____ read at the age of five.

① might   ② has to
③ had to   ④ is able to
⑤ was able to

15 다음 중 짝지어진 두 문장의 의미가 같지 <u>않은</u> 것은?

① May I borrow this book?
   = Can I borrow this book?
② Cats can see in the dark.
   = Cats are able to see in the dark.
③ You must not sit on the chair.
   = You shouldn't sit on the chair.
④ She must come home early today.
   = She has to come home early today.
⑤ You must have the wrong number.
   = You have to have the wrong number.

내신 빈출

16 다음 밑줄 친 ①~⑤ 중 어법상 틀린 것은?

> Emma ① doesn't ② has ③ to ④ bring ⑤ her lunch box.

고난도

20 다음 중 어법상 옳은 것으로 알맞게 짝지어진 것은?

> ⓐ You shouldn't walk alone at night.
> ⓑ Lisa don't has to get up early today.
> ⓒ You must watch out for falling rocks.
> ⓓ I may can get some information here.
> ⓔ Jason has to takes care of his brother.

① ⓐ, ⓑ   ② ⓐ, ⓒ
③ ⓒ, ⓓ   ④ ⓐ, ⓑ, ⓓ
⑤ ⓑ, ⓒ, ⓔ

[17~18] 다음 밑줄 친 부분 중 어법상 틀린 것을 고르시오.

17 ① Sally may not win first prize.
② You shouldn't use plastic bags.
③ You have not to jog every day.
④ You mustn't drive a car at night.
⑤ The girl can't be Ms. Brown's child.

고난도

21 다음 중 어법상 옳은 문장의 개수는?

> · Can you fix the computer?
> · Sally shoulds speak more loudly.
> · The chair may be not comfortable.
> · Children must not eat too much chocolate.
> · I was not able to attend the meeting yesterday.

① 1개   ② 2개   ③ 3개
④ 4개   ⑤ 5개

18 ① Does the dog able to sing?
② Should she put on sunscreen?
③ May I borrow your car tomorrow?
④ Do they have to eat fresh vegetables?
⑤ Can the boy draw a picture with his feet?

19 다음 중 어법상 옳은 것은?
① It may be very cold tomorrow.
② Amy musts be a good student.
③ Ted doesn't have buy the book.
④ You don't should overeat at night.
⑤ Jennifer can makes dolls with paper.

22 다음 중 의도하는 바가 나머지와 다른 하나는?
① Don't waste time and money.
② You mustn't waste time and money.
③ You may not waste time and money.
④ You shouldn't waste time and money.
⑤ You don't have to waste time and money.

23 다음 중 밑줄 친 부분의 의미가 나머지와 <u>다른</u> 하나는?

① We <u>must</u> protect our environment.

② You <u>must</u> be polite to the teachers.

③ The sneakers are dirty. You <u>must</u> wash them.

④ Tom isn't at home. He <u>must</u> be in the gym now.

⑤ It's raining outside. You <u>must</u> take an umbrella.

24 [보기]의 밑줄 친 부분과 의미가 같은 것은?

┌ 보기 ┐
Sue <u>may</u> be late for school again.
└────┘

① You <u>may</u> leave a message.

② <u>May</u> I have some cold water?

③ You <u>may</u> ride my bike tomorrow.

④ You <u>may</u> take the medicine before meals.

⑤ The weather <u>may</u> be cloudy this afternoon.

고난도
25 다음 중 밑줄 친 부분의 의미가 같은 것끼리 짝지어진 것은?

ⓐ You <u>can</u> use my eraser.

ⓑ Pam <u>can</u> play the violin.

ⓒ You <u>can</u> open the window.

ⓓ My grandmother <u>can</u> use the Internet.

ⓔ The comedian <u>can</u> imitate many people.

① ⓐ, ⓑ   ② ⓐ, ⓒ

③ ⓒ, ⓓ   ④ ⓐ, ⓑ, ⓓ

⑤ ⓑ, ⓒ, ⓔ

26 다음 우리말과 의미가 같도록 밑줄 친 부분을 어법에 알맞게 고쳐 쓰시오.

┌─────────────────────────┐
You <u>are able to</u> turn on the air conditioner.
(너는 에어컨을 켜도 된다.)
└─────────────────────────┘

→ _____

27 다음 우리말과 의미가 같도록 괄호 안의 말을 바르게 배열하시오.

┌─────────────────────────┐
너는 실내에서 신발을 벗을 필요가 없다.
(take off, to, your shoes, have, don't)
└─────────────────────────┘

→ You _____ indoors.

28 다음 빈칸에 공통으로 들어갈 알맞은 말을 쓰시오.

┌─────────────────────────┐
· These pens _____ be Megan's.

· You _____ turn off your cell phone in the theater.
└─────────────────────────┘

→ _____

29 다음 두 문장의 의미가 같도록 빈칸에 들어갈 알맞은 말을 쓰시오.

┌─────────────────────────┐
Kevin can ride a bike with one hand.
└─────────────────────────┘

= Kevin is _____ _____ _____ a bike with one hand.

30 다음 문장을 부정문으로 바꿔 쓰시오.

┌─────────────────────────┐
You have to worry about your health.
└─────────────────────────┘

→ _____

31 다음 괄호 안의 단어와 조동사를 이용하여 문맥에 맞게 문장을 완성하시오.

> I broke my leg last summer. I _____ in bed for two weeks. (stay)

32 다음 대화의 빈칸 ⓐ와 ⓑ에 들어갈 알맞은 말을 쓰시오.

> A: ⓐ _____ you help me with my math homework?
> B: No, I ⓑ _____. I'm poor at math.

33 다음 표지판들을 보고, 조동사 must를 이용하여 문장을 완성하시오.

(1)   (2)   (3)

(1) You _____ _____ _____ in the hall.
(2) You _____ _____ _____ in this lake.
(3) You _____ _____ _____ in front of the entrance.

34 다음 우리말과 의미가 같도록 [조건]에 맞게 문장을 완성하시오.

> 너는 그에게 사실을 말해서는 안 된다.

조건
1. should, tell the truth를 이용할 것
2. 필요시 단어를 추가할 것

→ You _____ to him.

35 다음 빈칸 ⓐ ~ ⓒ에 들어갈 알맞은 말을 [A]와 [B]에서 각각 골라 글을 완성하시오.

> [A] have to   can   must not

> [B] go   talk   pay

> You ⓐ _____ to each other during the test. You ⓑ _____ attention to the test. You ⓒ _____ home early after the test.

Chapter

05

명사와 관사

01 명사

1 셀 수 있는 명사

1 '하나, 둘, 셋 …'처럼 수를 셀 수 있는 명사를 가리키며, 하나는 단수형으로 나타내고, 둘 이상은 복수형으로 나타낸다. 단수형 앞에는 부정관사 a(n)를 쓰고, 복수형은 주로 명사 끝에 -(e)s를 붙인다.

I prepared *a* **teddy bear** and *two* **toy cars**.
I ate *an* **orange** and my sister ate *two* **oranges**.

2 셀 수 있는 명사의 복수형

규칙 변화	대부분의 명사	+ -s	girls, books, eggs, dogs, houses, desks
	-(s)s, -x, -ch, -sh, -o로 끝나는 명사	+ -es	buses, dresses, boxes, benches, brushes, potatoes (예외: pianos, photos, radios)
	「자음 + y」로 끝나는 명사	-y → -ies	baby → babies, candy → candies, story → stories
	-f, -fe로 끝나는 명사	-f(e) → -ves	leaf → leaves, knife → knives (예외: roofs, proofs)
불규칙 변화	man → men, woman → women, foot → feet, tooth → teeth, child → children, mouse → mice, ox → oxen, goose → geese		
	단수·복수 형태가 같은 경우: fish → fish, sheep → sheep, deer → deer		

⊕ PLUS 항상 복수로 쓰는 명사
'장갑, 안경' 등 두 개가 짝을 이루는 명사는 항상 복수형으로 쓰며, a pair of ~의 형태로 수를 셀 수 있다.
ex. gloves, pants, jeans, scissors, shoes, socks, glasses, earrings 등

2 셀 수 없는 명사

1 일정한 형태가 없는 것(물질명사), 눈에 보이지 않는 것(추상명사), 사람이나 장소 등 고유한 것의 이름(고유명사)을 나타내는 명사를 가리킨다. 셀 수 없는 명사 앞에는 a(n)를 붙일 수 없고, 복수형이 없다.

I saved **money** to buy a new smartphone.
I have some important **information** for you.

2 물질명사는 용기나 단위를 이용하여 셀 수 있으며, 용기나 단위를 이용하여 복수를 나타낸다.

용기 / 단위	물질명사	용기 / 단위	물질명사
a cup of	coffee, tea	**a piece of**	paper, pizza, bread, cheese, cake, furniture
a glass of	milk, water, wine, juice, cola	**a slice of**	bread, cheese, cake, ham, meat
a bottle of		**a sheet of**	paper
a bowl of	soup, rice, cereal	**a loaf of**	bread, meat
a spoonful of	sugar, salt	**a jar of**	jam, honey

She drinks **a glass of milk** in the morning.
She drinks **two glasses of milk** every day.

⊕ PLUS 셀 수 없는 명사의 종류
• 물질명사: water, milk, money, salt, flour, paper, coffee, shampoo, snow, rain, furniture 등
• 추상명사: love, luck, health, friendship, advice, hope, homework, math, music 등
• 고유명사: Tom, Kate, Seoul, Korea, Monday, Christmas, *Chuseok* 등

Grammar Check Up

A 다음 괄호 안에서 알맞은 것을 고르시오.

1 The chairman spoke for (hour / an hour) at the meeting.

2 I'm going to donate some (money / moneys).

3 (Maria / A Maria) sang her favorite song in the audition.

4 There are eight (childs / children) in the playground.

5 I need some (match / matches) to light the candles.

B 다음 괄호 안에 주어진 단어를 알맞은 형태로 빈칸에 쓰시오. (단, 주어진 단어 순서대로 쓸 것)

1 This book is full of much useful _____. (information)

2 A spider has eight _____ and eight _____. (leg, foot)

3 There are many _____ and many _____ in the park. (tree, bench)

4 Beth took a pair of _____ to cut two sheets of _____. (scissor, paper)

5 The magician pulled a _____ and two _____ out of his hat. (dove, rabbit)

C 다음 괄호 안의 단어와 [보기]의 단어를 이용하여 문장을 완성하시오. (단, [보기]는 한 번씩만 쓸 것)

보기			
pair	spoonful	bowl	piece

1 Minho ate two _____ for dinner. (rice)

2 Draw a circle on a _____. (paper)

3 I bought two _____ for my twin boys. (sneaker)

4 You should take a _____ after a meal. (medicine)

D 다음 문장의 밑줄 친 부분을 어법상 알맞은 형태로 고쳐 쓰시오.

1 The child spilled some <u>milks</u> on the table.

2 Many <u>tourist</u> visit the ski resort every winter.

3 They bought some <u>furnitures</u> for their apartment.

4 Eric finished off two <u>bowl</u> of noodle soup in no time.

5 I want three slices of <u>cheeses</u> and a loaf of bread.

02 관사

1 부정관사 a / an

셀 수 있는 명사의 단수형 앞에 쓰며 자음 소리로 시작하는 명사 앞에는 a, 모음 소리로 시작하는 명사 앞에는 an을 쓴다.

1 불특정한 하나를 나타낼 때

We will stay at **a** very nice *hotel* in Seoul.

2 '하나(one)'의 의미를 나타낼 때

Boil **an** *egg* and **a** *potato* for 20 minutes.

3 '~마다, ~당(per)'의 의미를 나타낼 때

The trains to London come six times **a** *day*.

⊕ **PLUS** 철자와 발음이 다른 경우의 **a, an** 구별

모음 철자, 자음 발음: a uniform, a university 등 / 자음 철자, 모음 발음: an hour, an MP3 player 등

2 정관사 the

부정관사와 다르게 특정한 대상 앞에 쓰며, 단수명사와 복수명사 앞에 모두 쓸 수 있다.

1 앞에 언급되었거나 상황으로 알 수 있는 대상을 가리킬 때

I bought *a book* for you. **The** *book* is about wild animals.

Excuse me. Where is **the** *restroom*?

2 관용적으로 사용되는 경우

세상에 유일한 것	the earth, the sun, the moon, the sky, the world 등
악기 이름 (play와 함께)	play the piano, play the violin 등
방향을 나타내는 말	the east, the west, the south, the north 등
매체를 나타내는 말	the Internet, the movie, the radio, the theater 등 (예외: watch TV)

The *moon* is the only satellite of **the** *earth*.

Mark plays **the** *drums* in a school band.

3 관사를 쓰지 않는 경우

식사	breakfast, lunch, dinner 등	본래 목적의 장소	go to school, go to bed 등
운동 경기	soccer, baseball, tennis 등	by + 교통수단	by car, by bus, by subway 등
과목	math, science, music 등	고유명사	Seoul, Minsu, March 등

A lot of students like to play soccer after **school**.

My family decided to travel across Europe by **car**.

⊕ **PLUS** 하루의 때를 나타내는 표현

in the morning, at noon, in the afternoon, in the evening, at night, at midnight

Grammar **Check Up**

A 다음 괄호 안에서 알맞은 것을 고르시오.

1 Please pass me (a / the) napkin on the table.

2 (A / The) flower in that vase is beautiful.

3 (A / An) honest person has a lot of friends.

4 They are building (a / an) new bridge across the river.

B 다음 빈칸에 a, an, the 중 알맞은 것을 쓰시오. (단, 필요 없는 경우 ×표)

1 _____ sofa in the living room is very old.

2 _____ Australia is the world's smallest continent.

3 Dark clouds floated across _____ moon.

4 He can't play _____ tennis because of a sore elbow.

5 This morning I bought a magazine. _____ magazine is in my bag.

C 다음 우리말과 의미가 같도록 괄호 안의 말을 이용하여 문장을 완성하시오.

1 일본까지 비행기로 얼마나 걸리나요? (airplane)

→ How long does it take to Japan by _____?

2 나는 정보를 찾기 위해 인터넷을 검색했다. (Internet)

→ I searched on _____ to find information.

3 우리는 많은 것들을 배우기 위해 학교에 간다. (school)

→ We go to _____ to learn a lot of things.

4 우리는 한 달에 한 번 고아원에서 자원봉사를 한다. (month)

→ We do volunteer work at an orphanage once _____.

D 다음 문장의 밑줄 친 부분을 어법상 알맞은 형태로 고쳐 쓰시오.

1 The lighthouse on the hill flashes at the night.

2 My sister is interested in a German literature.

3 She usually sleeps about eight hours the day.

4 There is a carpet in my room. A carpet is round.

5 We always have the dinner at the same time every day.

A 다음 우리말과 의미가 같도록 괄호 안의 단어를 이용하여 문장을 완성하시오.

1 나는 지난 학기에 화학에서 A 학점을 받았다. (chemistry)

→ I got an A in _____ last semester.

2 나는 하루에 세 시간 TV를 본다. (day)

→ I watch TV three hours _____.

3 엄마는 가구 두 점을 사셨다. (piece, furniture)

→ Mom bought _____.

4 Alex는 저녁 식사 전에 숙제를 해야 한다. (homework)

→ Alex must do his _____ before dinner.

5 수연이는 지하철을 타고 할머니 댁에 갔다. (subway)

→ Suyeon went to her grandmother's house _____.

B 다음 우리말과 의미가 같도록 괄호 안의 말을 바르게 배열하시오.

1 그들은 금요일마다 다섯 개의 수업이 있다. (five, they, classes, have)

→ _____ on Fridays.

2 우리는 그 식당에서 저녁을 먹는다. (dinner, restaurant, at, have, the)

→ We _____.

3 나는 커피에 설탕 두 숟가락을 넣는다. (of, two, I, sugar, spoonfuls, put)

→ _____ in my coffee.

4 그 아이들은 동물원에서 늑대 세 마리를 보았다. (wolves, the kids, three, saw)

→ _____ at the zoo.

5 Vanessa는 동영상을 보고 피아노 치는 법을 배웠다. (the, play, learned, piano, to)

→ Vanessa _____ by watching a video.

C 다음 문장에서 어법상 <u>어색한</u> 부분을 고쳐 문장을 다시 쓰시오.

1 A laughter is the best medicine.

→ _____

2 My nephew lost two baby tooth yesterday.

→ _____

3 She will buy long ruler on her way to school.

→ _____

4 The bird on the branch has beautiful wing.

→ _____

5 I spread butter on four thick slice of bread.

→ _____

D 다음 괄호 안에 주어진 말을 이용하여 영작하시오. (단, 필요한 것만 이용할 것)

1 Clara는 양말 다섯 켤레를 샀다. (buy, sock, pair, piece)

→ _____

2 Brad는 배우로서 많은 돈을 번다. (earn, a lot of, a, an, the, actor)

→ _____

3 그 남자들은 황소 10마리와 양 5마리를 갖고 있다. (a, the, man, ox, sheep)

→ _____

4 태양은 우주에 있는 별들 중 하나이다. (one of, star, in, universe, a, the)

→ _____

5 너는 그 식물에 한 달에 한 번 물을 줘야 한다. (should, water, plant, once, a, an, the)

→ _____

6 나는 아침 식사로 사과 한 개와 우유 한 잔을 먹었다. (have, a, an, the, breakfast)

→ _____

01 다음 [보기]에서 셀 수 <u>없는</u> 명사의 개수로 알맞은 것은?

| 보기 |
| furniture   love   friend   oil |
| China   city   computer   fish |

① 없음　　　② 2개　　　③ 4개

④ 6개　　　⑤ 7개

02 다음 중 명사의 복수형이 <u>잘못</u> 짝지어진 것은?

① a box – many boxes

② a goose – five geese

③ a thief – three thiefs

④ a puppy – four puppies

⑤ a woman – two women

03 다음 중 표현이 <u>잘못된</u> 것은?

① a slice of juice

② a loaf of bread

③ a bowl of soup

④ a bottle of beer

⑤ a sheet of paper

04 다음 빈칸에 들어갈 말로 알맞은 것은?

Jessica is looking for _____ .

① cap　　　　　② bicycle

③ milk　　　　　④ smartphone

⑤ photo album

05 다음 빈칸에 들어갈 말로 알맞은 것을 <u>모두</u> 고르면?

My aunt sent a _____ to me.

① scarf　　　　② email

③ honey　　　　④ money

⑤ package

06 다음 빈칸에 들어갈 말로 알맞지 <u>않은</u> 것은?

There was a _____ in his yard.

① pond　　　　② horse

③ bench　　　　④ furniture

⑤ palm tree

07 다음 빈칸에 들어갈 말로 알맞지 <u>않은</u> 것을 <u>모두</u> 고르면?

Megan put _____ in the box.

① doll　　　　② candies

③ pencil case　④ some butter

⑤ twenty potatoes

08 다음 빈칸에 들어갈 말로 알맞게 짝지어진 것은?

· I brush my teeth three times _____ day.
· We have a car. _____ car is very old.

① a – A　　　　② a – The

③ an – The　　　④ the – A

⑤ the – The

09 다음 빈칸에 공통으로 들어갈 말로 알맞은 것은?

> · The cook cut two _____ of cheese.
> · Let me give you some _____ of advice.
> · She gave me ten _____ of paper.

① cups   ② pieces
③ loaves   ④ slices
⑤ bottles

10 다음 대화의 빈칸에 들어갈 말로 알맞지 <u>않은</u> 것은?

> A: Did you buy a pen?
> B: No, I didn't. I bought a _____.

① ruler   ② eraser
③ pencil   ④ notebook
⑤ paintbrush

11 다음 우리말과 의미가 같도록 빈칸에 들어갈 말로 알맞은 것은?

> · 그 여자는 물 한 잔을 원했다.
>   → The woman wanted a _____ of water.

① pair   ② loaf
③ slice   ④ glass
⑤ piece

12 다음 우리말을 어법에 알맞게 영작할 때 빈칸 ⓐ에 들어갈 말로 알맞은 것은?

> · 그 곰은 한 번에 꿀 세 병을 먹었다.
>   → The bear _____ _____ ⓐ _____
>   _____ _____ at a time.

① of   ② ate   ③ three
④ honey   ⑤ bottles

13 다음 우리말을 어법에 알맞게 영작한 것은?

> 그들은 자주 기차를 타고 여행을 한다.

① They often travel by train.
② They often travel by trains.
③ They often travel by a train.
④ They often travel by an train.
⑤ They often travel by the train.

14 다음 빈칸 ⓐ~ⓔ에 들어갈 말이 <u>잘못</u> 짝지어진 것은?

> In ⓐ _____, spring begins in ⓑ _____.
> Many ⓒ _____ come up in this season.
> In summer, it's hot. Many people swim in
> ⓓ _____. In fall, ⓔ _____ turn red
> and yellow. In winter, it's cold.

① ⓐ: Korea   ② ⓑ: a March
③ ⓒ: flowers   ④ ⓓ: the sea
⑤ ⓔ: the leaves

15 다음 (A), (B), (C)의 각 네모 안에서 어법에 맞는 것을 골라 바르게 짝지은 것은?

> · I went to (A) a / an bakery to buy bread.
> · The suspect has short brown (B) hair / hairs.
> · We can see many stars in (C) a / the sky at night.

	(A)		(B)		(C)
①	a	–	hair	–	a
②	an	–	hairs	–	a
③	a	–	hairs	–	the
④	an	–	hair	–	the
⑤	a	–	hair	–	the

16 다음 밑줄 친 ①~⑤ 중 어법상 틀린 것은?

They ① had ② a great adventure ③ in ④ an Africa ⑤ last winter.

17 다음 밑줄 친 부분 중 어법상 틀린 것은?

① The boy has sore feet.

② The child is using the scissors.

③ The shoes are too small for him.

④ There are many cars on the road.

⑤ Sheeps are eating grass on the field.

18 다음 중 어법상 틀린 것은?

① Barbara wants a pair of earring.

② I bought two kilograms of tomatoes.

③ He drank a cup of coffee after dinner.

④ Give me three sheets of paper, please.

⑤ Could you buy two bottles of orange juice?

19 다음 중 어법상 옳은 것은?

① We need two kilogram of salt.

② The waiter gave glass of milk to me.

③ The boys ordered three piece of pizza.

④ She bought two bag of flours for the cake.

⑤ We made thirty bowls of soup for elderly people.

20 다음 중 어법상 옳은 것으로 알맞게 짝지어진 것은?

ⓐ Please pass me the ruler.

ⓑ There is a mirror on the wall.

ⓒ A health is very important to us.

ⓓ A camel is a useful animal in a desert.

ⓔ He listens to radio on the way to school.

① ⓐ, ⓑ   ② ⓐ, ⓒ   ③ ⓒ, ⓓ

④ ⓐ, ⓑ, ⓓ   ⑤ ⓑ, ⓒ, ⓔ

21 다음 중 어법상 옳은 문장의 개수는?

· Mike is good at the math.

· I need three loaf of bread.

· The baby only has four tooth.

· James has two pairs of sneakers.

· Chuseok is August 15 on the lunar calendar.

① 1개   ② 2개   ③ 3개

④ 4개   ⑤ 5개

22 다음 중 빈칸에 the가 들어갈 수 없는 것은?

① We should protect _____ earth.

② The eagles are flying in _____ sky.

③ Put your socks in _____ washing machine.

④ My dad cleans the garden in _____ morning.

⑤ Minho and I play _____ basketball after school.

내신 빈출

23 다음 중 빈칸에 들어갈 관사가 나머지와 다른 것은?

① Hana has _____ little brother.

② A 3D printer is _____ useful tool.

③ She is _____ middle school student.

④ Mary plays _____ trumpet very well.

⑤ There are twelve months in _____ year.

24 [보기]의 밑줄 친 부분과 의미가 같은 것은?

┌─ 보기 ─────────────────────┐
│ Jenny eats out once a week. │
└────────────────────────────┘

① I feed my puppy twice a day.

② A chimpanzee is a clever animal.

③ The boy wants an ice cream cone.

④ Henry drinks a glass of wine at night.

⑤ There are a fork and a knife on the plate.

25 다음 중 밑줄 친 부분의 의미가 나머지와 다른 것은?

① David made a kite for me.

② We are going to buy a yacht.

③ Ann reads five books a month.

④ There is a potato in the basket.

⑤ A panda is sleeping under the tree.

26 다음 괄호 안의 단어를 이용하여 문장을 완성하시오.

┌─────────────────────────────────┐
│ The cat caught five _____. (mouse) │
└─────────────────────────────────┘

27 다음 우리말과 의미가 같도록 괄호 안의 말을 이용하여 문장을 완성하시오.

┌─────────────────────────────────┐
│ 지구는 태양으로부터 세 번째에 있는 행성이다. │
│ (earth, sun)   │
└─────────────────────────────────┘

→ _____ is the third planet from

_____ .

28 다음 빈칸에 공통으로 들어갈 알맞은 말을 쓰시오.

┌─────────────────────────────────┐
│ · The wind is blowing from _____ south. │
│ · The girl is playing _____ violin on the │
│   stage.   │
└─────────────────────────────────┘

→ _____

29 다음 우리말과 의미가 같도록 빈칸에 들어갈 알맞은 말을 쓰시오.

┌─────────────────────────────────┐
│ John은 후식으로 케이크 두 조각을 먹었다. │
└─────────────────────────────────┘

→ John ate _____ _____ _____

_____ for dessert.

30 다음 문장에서 어법상 틀린 부분을 찾아 알맞게 고쳐 쓰시오.

┌─────────────────────────────────┐
│ I bought an air cleaner last month. An air │
│ cleaner is broken.   │
└─────────────────────────────────┘

_____ → _____

📖 Answers p.10

31 다음 우리말과 의미가 같도록 괄호 안의 말을 바르게 배열하시오.

> 그들은 1년에 두 번 해외여행을 간다.
> (a, abroad, year, travel, twice)

→ They _____.

32 다음 [보기]의 말을 이용하여 빈칸 ⓐ~ⓒ에 들어갈 알맞은 말을 쓰시오.

> | 보기 |
> bottle   lunch   sandwich

> A: Let's have ⓐ _____.
> B: OK. Here are three ⓑ _____ and
>   two ⓒ _____ of orange juice.

33 다음 그림을 보고, 빈칸 ⓐ~ⓒ에 알맞은 말을 [보기]에서 골라 쓰시오. (단, 필요한 경우 관사와 함께 쓸 것)

> | 보기 |
> guitar   sun   badminton

> ⓐ _____ is shining brightly.
> Two boys are playing ⓑ _____
> on the playground. A girl is playing
> ⓒ _____ under the tree. They
> look happy.

34 다음 우리말과 의미가 같도록 [조건]에 맞게 문장을 완성하시오.

> 나는 주말마다 극장에 가는 것을 좋아한다.

> | 조건 |
> 1. go, theater를 이용할 것
> 2. 필요시 단어를 추가할 것

→ I like to _____ on weekends.

35 다음 빈칸 ⓐ~ⓔ에 a, an, the 중 알맞은 것을 쓰시오. (단, 필요 없는 경우 ×표)

> My mother is ⓐ _____ English teacher
> and my father is ⓑ _____ pilot. I'm
> ⓒ _____ middle school student. We live
> in ⓓ _____ Seoul. We go camping once
> ⓔ _____ week.

Chapter

06

대명사

01 지시대명사, 비인칭 주어 it

1 지시대명사 this, these

1 this는 '이것, 이 사람'이라는 뜻으로 가까이 있는 사물이나 사람을 가리킬 때 사용하는 대명사이며, 복수형은 these(이것들, 이 사람들)이다.

This is a photo of my family. We took **this** last year.
These are my textbooks. I'll put **these** into my locker.

2 지시형용사 this, these: 뒤에 오는 명사를 꾸며 주며 '이 ~(들)'의 의미이다.

This *movie* tells about the first moon landing.
These *foods* are good for your brain. Help yourself.

2 지시대명사 that, those

1 that은 '저것, 저 사람'이라는 뜻으로 멀리 있는 사물이나 사람을 가리킬 때 사용하는 대명사이며, 복수형은 those(저것들, 저 사람들)이다.

That is my favorite picture. I received **that** as a present.
Those are old stamps. Some people collect **those**.

2 지시형용사 that, those: 뒤에 오는 명사를 꾸며 주며 '저 ~(들)'의 의미이다.

That *city* is famous for its beautiful buildings.
I paid 100 dollars for **those** *baseball tickets*.

⊕ PLUS 지시형용사와 명사의 수
「this / that + 단수명사」, 「these / those + 복수명사」의 형태로 써야 한다.

3 비인칭 주어 it

1 시간, 요일, 날짜, 날씨, 계절, 거리, 명암 등을 나타낼 때 비인칭 주어 it을 쓰는데, 이때의 it은 해석하지 않는다.

It is seven thirty now (시간)   **It** was Saturday yesterday. (요일)
It is December 25th today. (날짜)   **It** wasn't warm yesterday. (날씨)
It is spring now. (계절)   **It** is 10 kilometers from here to LA. (거리)

2 시간, 요일, 날짜, 날씨, 계절, 거리 등을 묻는 말을 함께 알아둔다.

What time is **it**? (시간)   What day is **it**? (요일)
What's the date? (날짜)   What's the weather like? / How is the weather? (날씨)
What season is **it**? (계절)   How far is **it**? (거리)

⊕ PLUS 인칭대명사 it
'그것'이라는 뜻의 3인칭 단수 대명사로 앞에 언급된 단수명사를 대신하는 말이다. 복수형은 they이다.
ex. I have *a cap*. **It** is green. / There are *books* on the desk. **They** are Sumi's.

Grammar **Check Up**

A 다음 괄호 안에서 알맞은 것을 고르시오.

1 Look at (that / those) birds on the roof.

2 (This / These) are the only Spanish books in the library.

3 Do you know (that / those) person at the back of the room?

4 Happy birthday! (This / These) ticket is a present for you.

5 (It / That) is sunny today. You should wear (this / these) sunglasses.

B 다음 문장에서 밑줄 친 부분의 역할로 알맞은 것에 표시(✔) 하시오.

	인칭대명사	비인칭 주어
1 You should read this story. It is so touching.	☐	☐
2 It is a little hot even in winter in Hawaii.	☐	☐
3 How far is it from here to Seoul Station?	☐	☐
4 Try this *gimchi*. It is good for your health.	☐	☐
5 It takes about 20 minutes to walk to school.	☐	☐

C 다음 대화의 빈칸에 알맞은 말을 쓰시오.

1 A: What _____ is it tomorrow?　　　　B: _____ is Friday.

2 A: What _____ is it now in Australia?　　B: _____ is summer.

3 A: What's the _____ like in the polar region?　B: _____ is extremely cold.

4 A: What was the _____ of the concert?　　B: _____ was February 8th.

5 A: How _____ will it take to get to the airport?　B: _____ will take an hour and a half.

D 다음 문장의 밑줄 친 부분을 어법상 알맞은 형태로 고쳐 쓰시오.

1 What time is it now? – This is 5:30.

2 These K-pop band is very popular in the world.

3 What is the final destination of those bus?

4 My dog made this dirty marks on my new shoes.

5 Those is a great opportunity to improve your English.

02 부정대명사, 재귀대명사

1 부정대명사 one

1 앞에 나온 명사와 '종류는 같지만 불특정한 대상'을 가리키는 대명사로 복수형은 ones이다.

I missed the 8:30 train. I'll take a next **one**. (one = a train)

My colored pencils are too short. I want to buy new **ones**. (ones = colored pencils)

2 one과 it: one은 같은 종류의 불특정한 대상을 가리키지만 it은 앞에 언급된 바로 그 대상을 가리킨다.

My neighbor's dog always barks at me. I'm afraid of **it**. (it = the dog)

This mobile game doesn't look so interesting. I want to try another **one**. (one = a mobile game)

2 부정대명사 some, any

some과 any는 둘 다 '약간(의), 몇 개(의)'라는 뜻으로 대명사와 형용사로 모두 쓰인다.

1 some: 긍정문, 권유 및 부탁의 의문문에 사용

The magician performed several magic tricks. **Some** were unbelievable.

(Some = Some magic tricks)

We bought **some** tropical fruits at the street market. (긍정문)

Why don't you take **some** medicine? (권유의 의문문)

2 any: 부정문, 의문문에 사용

I didn't make **any** New Year's resolutions. Did you make **any**? (any = any resolutions)

There are not **any** restaurants near here. (부정문)

Do you do **any** special family activities? (의문문)

3 재귀대명사

1 '~ 자신'이라는 뜻으로 인칭대명사의 소유격이나 목적격에 -self(단수), -selves(복수)를 붙여 쓴다.

	1인칭	2인칭	3인칭		
단수	myself	yourself	himself	herself	itself
복수	ourselves	yourselves	themselves		

2 용법

재귀 용법	목적어가 주어와 같을 때 목적어 자리에 재귀대명사 사용	생략 불가능
강조 용법	문장의 주어, 목적어를 강조할 때	생략 가능

Mark likes to look at **himself** in the mirror. (재귀 용법)

I can't do the science project **myself**. (강조 용법)

⊕ **PLUS** 재귀대명사의 관용 표현

by oneself 홀로(= alone), for oneself 혼자 힘으로, of oneself 저절로

help oneself to ~을 마음껏 먹다, make oneself at home 편히 있다, enjoy oneself 즐기다

A 다음 괄호 안에서 알맞은 것을 고르시오.

1 You must take good care of (you / yourself).

2 They didn't pick up (some / any) trash in the park.

3 Do you want a square rug or a round (one / ones)?

4 We need to separate glass bottles and plastic (one / ones / it) for recycling.

5 There are (some / any) interesting magazines in the exhibition.

6 Don't throw away the old sweater. You can recycle (one / ones / it).

B 다음 빈칸에 one, ones, it 중 알맞은 것을 쓰시오.

1 My uncle lost his camera. He is looking for _____ .

2 The towel in the bathroom is dirty. Can I have a clean _____ ?

3 You should not mix the colored clothes with the white _____ .

4 I ordered a ham and cheese sandwich. This is a different _____ .

5 Where's your car? – I parked _____ in the parking lot behind the building.

C 다음 빈칸에 some 또는 any 중 알맞은 것을 쓰시오.

1 Would you like _____ ice in your drink?

2 There aren't even _____ clouds in the sky today.

3 The man inherited _____ money from his grandfather.

4 He went to the library to borrow _____ books.

5 Do you have _____ advice for young soccer players?

D 다음 빈칸에 괄호 안의 단어를 알맞은 형태로 바꿔 쓰시오.

1 The singer introduced _____ to the fans in Korea. (he)

2 We cut the grass _____ every spring. (we)

3 You have to clean all this mess _____ . (you, 단수)

4 Most people sometimes talk to _____ . (they)

5 The old lady can't go up the subway stairs by _____ . (she)

A 다음 우리말과 의미가 같도록 빈칸에 알맞은 말을 쓰시오.

1 너는 이 젓가락들을 사용해도 된다.

→ You may use _____ chopsticks.

2 내일 서울에는 비가 올 것이다.

→ _____ will rain in Seoul tomorrow.

3 Mary는 혼자서 조각 그림 맞추기를 끝냈다.

→ Mary finished the jigsaw puzzle by _____.

4 이것은 그녀의 손수건이고, 저것은 나의 것이다.

→ _____ is her handkerchief, and _____ is mine.

5 Tony는 때때로 직접 자신의 운동화를 세탁한다.

→ Tony sometimes washes his sneakers _____.

B 다음 우리말과 의미가 같도록 괄호 안의 말을 바르게 배열하시오.

1 오늘은 토요일이다. (today, Saturday, is, it)

→ _____

2 Paul은 신문에서 기사 몇 개를 읽었다. (articles, in the newspaper, read, some)

→ Paul _____ .

3 나는 초가 하나 필요해. 내가 하나 빌려도 되니? (I, one, borrow, can, ?)

→ I need a candle. _____

4 나의 개는 거울 속의 자신에게 짖어댔다. (at, barked, itself, my dog)

→ _____ in the mirror.

5 저 요리사는 15분 안에 스파게티를 만들 수 있다. (can, chef, spaghetti, that, make)

→ _____ in fifteen minutes.

○────────○ 目目 Answers p.12

C 다음 문장에서 어법상 <u>어색한</u> 부분을 고쳐 문장을 다시 쓰시오.

1 Drink warm water and get any sleep.

→ _____

2 May I use these computer for a while?

→ _____

3 Do you have some ideas for the project?

→ _____

4 These apples are rotten. I want a fresh one.

→ _____

5 We have to protect the environment for us.

→ _____

6 Can you build that big structures in the desert?

→ _____

D 다음 괄호 안에 주어진 말을 이용하여 영작하시오. (단, 필요한 것만 이용할 것)

1 이 방 안은 매우 밝다. (it, this, that, very, bright, in)

→ _____

2 그 낡은 책들은 그 상자 안에 있다. 새것들은 선반 위에 있다. (on the shelf, one, ones)

→ _____

3 너는 이 문장을 영어로 번역할 수 있니? (translate, this, that, into English, sentence)

→ _____

4 어떤 만화책들은 학생들에게 좋다. (some, any, comic book, be good for)

→ _____

5 우리는 어떤 새로운 가구도 살 필요가 없다. (have, to, some, any, furniture)

→ _____

6 그녀의 아이들은 그들 스스로 빨래를 한다. (do the laundry, by, them, themselves)

→ _____

01 다음 빈칸에 들어갈 말로 알맞은 것은?

> _____ is about two kilometers from here to the airport.

① It　　　　　　② One
③ This　　　　　④ That
⑤ They

02 다음 빈칸에 들어갈 말로 알맞은 것을 <u>모두</u> 고르면?

> _____ trees only grow in cold climates.

① It　　　　　　② This
③ That　　　　　④ These
⑤ Those

03 다음 대화의 빈칸에 들어갈 말로 알맞은 것은?

> A: Is there a bookstore near here?
> B: Sure. There is _____ behind your school.

① it　　　　　　② one
③ that　　　　　④ ones
⑤ them

04 다음 빈칸에 들어갈 말로 알맞지 <u>않은</u> 것은?

> This _____ is for children over six.

① pool　　　　　② game
③ blocks　　　　④ TV show
⑤ medicine

05 다음 빈칸에 공통으로 들어갈 말로 알맞은 것은?

> · Are you reading _____ books now?
> · Nick didn't listen to _____ advice from the doctor.

① it　　　　　　② one
③ any　　　　　④ some
⑤ others

06 다음 빈칸에 들어갈 말로 알맞게 짝지어진 것은?

> · I don't like small cars. I like big _____.
> · Jerry borrowed a book last week. He must return _____ today.

① it – it　　　　② one – it
③ it – one　　　④ ones – it
⑤ ones – ones

07 다음 중 빈칸에 some[Some]이 들어갈 수 <u>없는</u> 것은?

① Is there _____ food for me?
② _____ dancers wear blue jeans.
③ Can I have _____ more coffee?
④ Daniel has _____ friends in Seoul.
⑤ I bought _____ butter at the farmer's market.

08 다음 우리말과 의미가 같도록 빈칸에 들어갈 말로 알맞은 것은?

> · 탁자 위에 있는 어떤 사진도 만지지 마라.
>   → Don't touch _____ on the table.

① any photo　　　② any photos
③ some photo　　④ some photos
⑤ a few photos

09 다음 우리말을 어법에 알맞게 영작한 것은?

> 이 치킨 수프는 좀 짜다.

① Its chicken soup is a bit salty.
② This chicken soup is a bit salty.
③ That chicken soup is a bit salty.
④ These chicken soup is a bit salty.
⑤ Those chicken soup is a bit salty.

10 다음 우리말을 어법에 알맞게 영작할 때 빈칸 ⓐ에 들어갈 말로 알맞은 것은?

> · 나는 그 전시회의 어떤 그림도 맘에 들지 않는다.
> → I don't like ___ ⓐ ___ _____
>
> _____ _____ _____ .

① in
② the
③ any
④ paintings
⑤ exhibition

11 다음 밑줄 친 부분 중 생략할 수 없는 것은?

① Jinho cleaned his room himself.
② Tina writes all her songs herself.
③ I make my puppy's clothes myself.
④ Kevin repaired his computer himself.
⑤ They enjoyed themselves on the beach.

12 다음 밑줄 친 부분 중 생략할 수 있는 것은?

① Watch out! You'll hurt yourself.
② Linda carried all the boxes herself.
③ We learned the song by ourselves.
④ I made a delicious sandwich for myself.
⑤ Sam blamed himself about the accident.

13 다음 (A), (B), (C)의 각 네모 안에서 어법에 맞는 것을 골라 바르게 짝지은 것은?

> · My grandfather lives by (A) him / himself .
> · I may not have (B) any / some special talent.
> · (C) It / That will be snowy and cold tomorrow.

	(A)		(B)		(C)
①	him	–	any	–	It
②	him	–	some	–	That
③	himself	–	any	–	That
④	himself	–	some	–	It
⑤	himself	–	any	–	It

14 다음 중 빈칸에 들어갈 말이 나머지와 <u>다른</u> 것은?

① My phone is broken. I'll buy a new _____.
② Judy lost her wallet. She has to find _____.
③ This cake was nice. I want to have another _____.
④ This T-shirt is too small. Please show me a larger _____.
⑤ There are many pens in the pencil case. I need _____.

15 [보기]의 밑줄 친 부분과 쓰임이 <u>다른</u> 것은?

> ┌ 보기 ┐
> What time was <u>it</u> then?

① <u>It</u> will be May 1 tomorrow.
② <u>It</u> rained all day long yesterday.
③ <u>It</u> will be 20% off during the sale.
④ <u>It</u> is very dark in the movie theater.
⑤ <u>It</u> is about 300 meters to the bus stop.

16 다음 밑줄 친 ①~⑤ 중 어법상 틀린 것은?

> Jason and I ① don't ② have ③ some ④ plans ⑤ for this weekend.

17 다음 중 어법상 틀린 것은?

① That bike is a new model.
② Look at those gray clouds.
③ This is my teacher, Ms. Park.
④ This scissors aren't very sharp.
⑤ These are tickets for Bora and Hana.

내신 빈출
18 다음 중 밑줄 친 부분을 어법에 맞게 고친 것으로 알맞지 않은 것은?

① That is getting hot these days. → It
② Mary baked the bread her. → herself
③ Please help yourself to any *galbi*. → some
④ You don't have to prepare some food.
　　→ any
⑤ The king took part in the battle themselves.
　　→ him

19 다음 중 어법상 옳은 것은?

① Knowing myself isn't easy.
② Would you like any cookies?
③ This sofa is new. I like one.
④ She baked the cupcakes by her.
⑤ My pants are too old. I need new one.

고난도
20 다음 대화의 밑줄 친 ①~⑤ 중 어법상 틀린 것은?

> A: It is Sunday! ① How is the weather?
> B: ② This is sunny and warm. Let's go hiking.
> A: I don't like hiking. How about going shopping instead?
> B: Why not? Look at ③ that cap. ④ It is too old. I need a new ⑤ one.
> A: That's right. And I need new sneakers.

21 다음 중 어법상 옳은 것으로 알맞게 짝지어진 것은?

> ⓐ I cut me on a knife.
> ⓑ That sunset is really beautiful.
> ⓒ Is those your bike behind the tree?
> ⓓ Do you have any books about the earth?
> ⓔ We visited some interesting places in Korea.

① ⓐ, ⓑ　　　　　　② ⓐ, ⓒ
③ ⓒ, ⓓ　　　　　　④ ⓐ, ⓑ, ⓒ
⑤ ⓑ, ⓓ, ⓔ

고난도
22 다음 중 어법상 옳은 문장의 개수는?

> · Alice cut her hair herself.
> · That is fifteen past twelve now.
> · Is there any milk in the refrigerator?
> · I like this jacket. Do you have red ones?
> · I bought this cap yesterday. Does it look nice?

① 1개　　　　② 2개　　　　③ 3개
④ 4개　　　　⑤ 5개

내신 빈출

23 다음 중 밑줄 친 부분의 쓰임이 나머지와 <u>다른</u> 것은?

① <u>It</u> is five thirty.

② <u>It</u> is Linda's cushion.

③ What day is <u>it</u> today?

④ <u>It</u> is dark in the forest.

⑤ <u>It</u> is sunny and very hot today.

24 다음 중 빈칸에 들어갈 말이 같은 것끼리 짝지어진 것은?

- Yesterday ⓐ _____ was very hot and humid.
- Do you want these shoes or those ⓑ _____ ?
- Math is difficult for me. I don't like ⓒ _____ .
- There are two cats. The black ⓓ _____ is mine.

① ⓐ, ⓑ   ② ⓐ, ⓒ

③ ⓑ, ⓒ   ④ ⓐ, ⓑ, ⓓ

⑤ ⓑ, ⓒ, ⓓ

고난도

25 다음 중 밑줄 친 부분의 쓰임이 같은 것끼리 짝지어진 것은?

ⓐ <u>It</u> is my parents' anniversary.

ⓑ <u>It</u> is my brother's cell phone.

ⓒ <u>It</u> was so dark in the basement.

ⓓ <u>It</u> is a great documentary movie.

ⓔ <u>It</u> snows a lot in winter in the country.

① ⓐ, ⓑ   ② ⓑ, ⓔ

③ ⓒ, ⓓ   ④ ⓐ, ⓒ, ⓔ

⑤ ⓑ, ⓒ, ⓓ

26 다음 밑줄 친 부분이 가리키는 바를 영어로 쓰시오.

I have some teddy bears. I'll give you a cute <u>one</u>.

→ _____

27 다음 우리말과 의미가 같도록 괄호 안의 말을 바르게 배열하시오.

이 동물은 그것의 새끼들을 위해 사자와 싸운다.

(this, fights with, animal, for its babies, a lion)

→ _____

28 다음 빈칸에 공통으로 들어갈 알맞은 말을 쓰시오.

- My uncle washed his car for _____ hour.
- I don't like this bag. Will you show me another _____ ?

→ _____

29 다음 우리말과 의미가 같도록 문장을 완성하시오.

서울은 지금 무슨 계절인가?

→ _____ _____ _____

_____ now in Seoul?

30 다음 문장에서 어법상 <u>틀린</u> 부분을 찾아 바르게 고쳐 쓰시오.

Can the boy tie his shoes by him?

_____ → _____

31 다음 빈칸에 들어갈 알맞은 대명사를 쓰시오.

> We have to focus on small goals instead of big _____.

32 다음 대화의 빈칸 ⓐ와 ⓑ에 들어갈 알맞은 말을 [보기]에서 골라 쓰시오.

> ┌ 보기 ┐
> any   some

> A: Let's make ⓐ _____ omelet for breakfast.
> B: Sorry. There aren't ⓑ _____ eggs left.

33 다음 그림을 보고, 괄호 안의 말을 이용하여 문장을 완성하시오.

> The girl is drawing _____ on the paper. (she)

34 다음 3일간의 일기예보를 보고, [보기]에서 알맞은 말을 골라 문장을 완성하시오.

Yesterday	Today	Tomorrow

> ┌ 보기 ┐
> sunny   cloudy   rainy

(1) _____ yesterday.
(2) _____ today.
(3) _____ tomorrow.

35 다음 밑줄 친 ⓐ ~ ⓓ 중 어법상 틀린 것을 3개 찾아 그 기호를 쓰고 어법에 맞게 고쳐 쓰시오.

> Did you hear about a ghost house? There is ⓐ <u>one</u> in my town. It is on the hill. ⓑ <u>That</u> is dark inside. There aren't ⓒ <u>some</u> people in the house. ⓓ <u>Any</u> brave children play in the yard of the house.

(1) _____ → _____
(2) _____ → _____
(3) _____ → _____

07

형용사와 부사

01 형용사

① 형용사의 쓰임 1 - 한정적 용법

1 명사 앞에서 명사를 꾸며 준다.

Egypt is a **large** *country* in northern Africa.

I made a **simple** *sketch* on the T-shirt with a pencil.

2 -thing, -body, -one으로 끝나는 대명사는 형용사가 뒤에서 꾸며 준다.

Fred always tried to create *something* **new**.

Do you know *anybody* **generous** like Mr. Roberts?

⊕ PLUS 형용사의 위치
- 관사(a / an / the) + 형용사 + 명사 ex. a **beautiful** flower, the **cute** girl
- 지시형용사 / 소유격 대명사 + 형용사 + 명사 ex. this **small** box, her **new** shoes

② 형용사의 쓰임 2 - 서술적 용법

1 주격 보어: 동사 뒤에서 주어를 설명해 준다.

The sky in fall is **clear** and **blue**.

My school uniform looks **good** on me.

2 목적격 보어: 목적어 뒤에서 목적어를 설명해 준다.

Teresa found *her daughter* **sick**.

⊕ PLUS 보어로만 쓰이는 형용사
alive(살아 있는), afraid(두려워하는), alike(비슷한), awake(깨어 있는), asleep(잠든), alone(혼자인)
ex. The tiger is **alive**. (O) It is an **alive** tiger. (×)

③ 수량을 나타내는 형용사

많은	조금 있는, 약간의	거의 없는	수식하는 말
many	a few	few	셀 수 있는 명사의 복수형
much	a little	little	셀 수 없는 명사
a lot of / lots of	some / any		셀 수 있는 명사의 복수형 / 셀 수 없는 명사

He made **many** *mistakes* on the last exam.

We can get **much** *information* from the Internet.

Sandra wrote **a few** beautiful *poems*.

Few *people* bought the black dress.

A little *knowledge* is a dangerous thing.

I spent all my money, so I have **little** *money* now.

A 다음 괄호 안에서 알맞은 것을 고르시오.

1 This bread smells (fresh / freshly) and delicious.

2 I want to tell her (nice something / something nice).

3 I'm going to take pictures of (strange / strangely) plants.

4 He often visited his grandma's while she was (live / alive).

B 다음 괄호 안에서 알맞지 <u>않은</u> 것을 고르시오.

1 Do you need (a little / lots of / many) help?

2 I put a little (milk / blueberries / honey) on my cereal.

3 (Many / Much / A few) classmates made fun of him.

4 (Little / Few / Many) people came to the party.

C 다음 우리말과 의미가 같도록 빈칸에 들어갈 알맞은 말을 [보기]에서 골라 쓰시오.

┌ 보기 ┐
| many | much | few | a few | little | a little |

1 연못에 물이 거의 없고 개구리도 거의 없다.

→ There is _____ water and _____ frogs in the pond.

2 아프리카의 많은 아이들이 굶어 죽어가고 있다.

→ _____ children in Africa are dying of hunger.

3 Stella는 내일 그녀의 사무실에서 할 일이 많다.

→ Stella has _____ work to do at her office tomorrow.

4 우리는 그 가게에서 잡지 몇 권과 물건들을 샀다.

→ We bought _____ magazines and things from the shop.

D 다음 문장의 밑줄 친 부분을 어법상 알맞은 형태로 고쳐 쓰시오.

1 The T-shirt has <u>a little</u> tiny holes.

2 She drinks too <u>many</u> coffee.

3 Put <u>fresh these</u> vegetables in the basket.

4 There are many <u>places wonderful</u> in Turkey.

5 Have you noticed <u>strange anything</u> about the Han River lately?

02 부사

1 부사의 쓰임

1 동사, 형용사, 부사를 꾸며 준다.

We **sincerely** *appreciate* your assistance. (동사 수식)

Her smartphone is **quite** *different* from mine. (형용사 수식)

Time passed **very** *quickly*. (부사 수식)

2 문장 전체를 꾸며 줄 수 있다.

Unfortunately, *I won't be able to attend the meeting*. (문장 전체 수식)

2 부사의 형태

1 형용사 → 부사 만들기

대부분의 형용사	+ -ly	kind → kindly	nice → nicely	loud → loudly
「자음 + y」로 끝나는 형용사	-y → -ily	easy → easily	angry → angrily	happy → happily

I will focus on every class and take notes **carefully**.

I have been **happily** married for over 20 years.

2 주의해야 할 부사의 형태

형용사와 형태가 같은 부사	hard(단단한, 열심히 하는, 어려운 – 열심히), high(높은 – 높이), late(늦은 – 늦게) near(가까운 – 가까이), fast(빠른 – 빨리), early(이른 – 일찍)
「부사 + ly」가 다른 뜻을 가지는 부사	hard → hardly(거의 ~ 않는), high → highly(매우) late → lately(최근에), near → nearly(거의)

She doesn't want to sit on the **hard** chair. (형용사)

I will study **hard** to get good grades. (부사)

That report is **hardly** surprising. (부사)

⊕ **PLUS** 「명사 + ly」 vs. 「형용사 + ly」
- 「명사 + ly」→ 형용사 ex. friendly, lovely, costly 등
- 「형용사 + ly」→ 부사 ex. slowly, politely, carefully 등

3 빈도부사

어떤 일이 얼마나 자주 일어나는지를 나타내는 부사를 빈도부사라고 하며, be동사나 조동사 뒤, 일반동사 앞에 위치한다.

always	usually	often	sometimes	seldom	never
항상	대개, 보통	종종	가끔	거의 ~ 않는	결코 ~ 않는
100%	>	>	>	>	0%

Wild horses *are* **always** ready to run away quickly. (be동사 뒤)

You *should* **always** wear sunscreen in the sun! (조동사 뒤)

Diane **sometimes** *thinks* about her future. (일반동사 앞)

A 다음 괄호 안에서 알맞은 것을 고르시오.

1 (Fortunately / Fortunate), he did make it.

2 The elderly lady was crossing the street (careful / carefully).

3 Kevin jumps and catches the ball very (good / well).

4 The museum opens (late / lately) and closes early in winter.

B 다음 우리말과 의미가 같도록 빈칸에 알맞은 말을 [보기]에서 골라 쓰시오.

> ┤ 보기 ├
> high / highly   hard / hardly   near / nearly

1 그는 그 반지를 정가의 거의 10배 가격으로 팔았다.

→ He sold the ring for _____ 10 times the regular price.

2 비가 거세게 올 때면, 엄마는 보통 음악을 들으신다.

→ When it rains _____, my mom usually listens to music.

3 그녀의 목소리가 너무 낮아서, 우리는 그녀의 말을 거의 들을 수 없었다.

→ Because her voice was so low, we could _____ hear her.

C 다음 괄호 안의 단어를 알맞은 곳에 넣어 문장을 다시 쓰시오.

1 There is a dense fog along the coast. (often)

→ _____

2 He misses any opportunities in business. (never)

→ _____

3 You will be my best friend. (always)

→ _____

4 Children's books and toys have bright colors. (usually)

→ _____

D 다음 문장의 밑줄 친 부분을 어법상 알맞은 형태로 고쳐 쓰시오.

1 The boy can write a lot of words <u>correct</u>.

2 Henry's arguments were <u>high</u> critical to the issue.

3 The schoolyard <u>always is</u> crowded during lunchtime.

4 The woman was <u>deep</u> moved by the movie.

03 원급, 비교급, 최상급

1 원급 비교

원급 비교는 둘을 비교하여 정도가 같을 때 쓰며 형용사나 부사의 원급을 사용한다.

as + 원급 + as	~만큼 …핸[하게]

Your laptop computer is **as old as** mine.
Mike plays sports **as well as** Alex.

> ⊕ **PLUS** 비교 대상은 문법적으로 동일해야 한다.
> Your shoes are bigger than mine.(○)
> Your shoes are bigger than me.(×)

2 비교급 비교, 최상급 비교

1 비교급 비교: 둘 중 하나가 '더 ~하다'라고 말할 때 쓰며 형용사나 부사의 비교급을 사용한다.

비교급 + than	~보다 더 …핸[하게]

Silver is much **cheaper than** gold.
Old shoes are **more comfortable than** new shoes.

2 최상급 비교: 셋 이상을 비교하여 '가장 ~하다'라고 말할 때 쓰며 형용사나 부사의 최상급을 사용한다.

the + 최상급(+ 명사) + in[of] ~	~에서[~ 중에서] 가장 …핸[하게]

He wants to climb **the tallest** mountain **of** the seven continents.
This bag is **the most expensive in** this store.

> ⊕ **PLUS** in vs. of
> • the + 최상급(+명사) + in + 단수명사 / 장소 / 집단 ex. in the class, in the city, in Korea 등
> • the + 최상급(+명사) + of + 복수명사 / 숫자 / 기간 ex. of them, of his friends, of the three, of the year 등

3 비교급과 최상급 만들기

	방법		원급 – 비교급 – 최상급
규칙	대부분의 형용사 / 부사	+ -er / -est	long – longer – longest
	-e로 끝나는 형용사 / 부사	+ -r / -st	large – larger – largest
	「단모음 + 단자음」으로 끝나는 형용사 / 부사	자음 반복 + -er / -est	big – bigger – biggest
	「자음 + y」로 끝나는 형용사 / 부사	-y → -ier / -iest	busy – busier – busiest
	2음절 이상의 형용사 / 부사	more / most + 원급	careful – more careful – most careful
불규칙	good / well – better – best, bad / ill – worse – worst, many / much – more – most, little – less – least		

The weather of Britain is **worse** than that of Korea.
Antarctica is **the least** populated place in the world.

> ⊕ **PLUS** 규칙 변화의 예외
> 「형용사 + ly」형태의 부사는 앞에 more, most를 붙여서 비교급, 최상급을 만든다.
> ex. slowly – more slowly – most slowly

A   다음 괄호 안에서 알맞은 것을 고르시오.

1   He is not so bad (as / so / than) I first thought.

2   What is the most precious thing to you (in / of) your bag?

3   The red car is (more / most) expensive than the blue car.

4   Rural life is usually (peacefuler / more peaceful) than city life.

B   다음 괄호 안에 주어진 단어를 빈칸에 알맞은 형태로 바꿔 쓰시오. (단, 바꿀 필요가 <u>없는</u> 경우 그대로 쓸 것)

1   Berlin is _____ city of the four. (big)

2   Riding a bicycle uses _____ calories than walking. (many)

3   Friendship is _____ thing in my life. (important)

4   Jenny's clothes aren't as _____ as Mary's clothes. (fashionable)

C   다음 우리말과 의미가 같도록 괄호 안에 주어진 단어를 이용하여 문장을 완성하시오.

1   호랑이가 늑대보다 더 위험하다. (dangerous)

→ The tiger is _____ the wolf.

2   이 재킷은 전시된 모든 옷 중에 가장 저렴하다. (cheap)

→ This jacket is _____ all the clothes on display.

3   Roy는 그의 아버지만큼 조심스럽게 운전했다. (carefully)

→ Roy drove _____ his father.

4   소희가 그녀의 반에서 가장 많은 사진들을 찍었다. (many, picture)

→ Sohee took _____ her class.

D   다음 [보기]와 같이 두 문장을 한 문장으로 쓸 때 빈칸에 알맞은 말을 쓰시오.

┌ 보기 ├
Sally gets up at 7:30. Tom gets up at 7:50. (early)
→ Sally gets up <u>earlier than</u> Tom.

1   This movie was not dramatic. Its original was dramatic. (dramatic)

→ This movie was _____ its original.

2   Seoul is about 120 km from here. Busan is about 230 km from here. (near)

→ Seoul is _____ Busan from here.

3   The hamburger is 8 dollars. The ice cream is 5 dollars. The milk is 4 dollars. (expensive)

→ The hamburger is _____ the three.

A 다음 우리말과 의미가 같도록 괄호 안의 말을 이용하여 문장을 완성하시오.

1 아무도 위험한 물건을 가지고 다니지 못하게 되어 있다. (dangerous, anything)

→ Nobody is allowed to carry _____ .

2 아이들이 안전하게 길을 건너고 있다. (safe)

→ The children are crossing the street _____ .

3 어항에 물고기가 거의 없다. (fish, few)

→ There are _____ in the fish tank.

4 KTX가 지하철보다 더 빨리 달린다. (fast)

→ The KTX runs _____ the subway.

5 남극 대륙은 세계에서 가장 추운 곳이다. (cold)

→ Antarctica is _____ place in the world.

B 다음 우리말과 의미가 같도록 괄호 안의 말을 바르게 배열하시오.

1 너는 따뜻한 것을 먹는 게 좋겠다. (have, warm, should, something, you)

→ _____

2 그녀는 그녀의 어머니만큼 많이 먹었다. (much, as, she, ate, as, her, did, mother)

→ _____

3 사람들은 보통 하루에 세끼를 먹는다. (eat, usually, people, three meals)

→ _____ a day.

4 제동이는 그의 반에서 가장 용감한 소년이다. (in, the, boy, class, bravest, his)

→ Jedong is _____ .

5 세계의 많은 사람들이 코로나 바이러스에 대해 걱정했다.
(corona virus, people, a lot of, worried about)

→ _____ in the world.

○────────○ 🗐 Answers p.14

C 다음 문장에서 어법상 <u>어색한</u> 부분을 고쳐 문장을 다시 쓰시오.

1 Deserts are dry land with few plants and water.

→ _____

2 Ella purchases never her clothes online.

→ _____

3 She looks very happily at school nowadays.

→ _____

4 Many men dream of driving safely and fastly.

→ _____

5 Pinocchio's nose is not as long as an elephant.

→ _____

6 While inventors are looking for one thing, they discover different something.

→ _____

D 다음 우리말과 의미가 같도록 괄호 안에 주어진 말을 이용하여 문장을 완성하시오. (단, 필요한 것만 이용할 것)

1 그 나라의 남쪽은 북쪽보다 더 따뜻하다. (warm, as, than)

→ The south of the country _____.

2 이 침대는 저 침대만큼 편안하지 않다. (comfortable, as, than)

→ This bed is _____.

3 불고기가 그 식당에서 가장 인기 있는 음식이다. (popular, food, in, of)

→ *Bulgogi* _____.

4 그녀는 그녀의 여동생보다 더 많은 용돈을 받는다. (receive, allowance, as, than)

→ She _____.

5 김 선생님은 모든 선생님들 중에서 가장 명확한 설명을 한다.
(clear, explanations, in, of, all the teachers)

→ Ms. Kim gives _____.

01 짝지어진 단어의 관계가 나머지와 <u>다른</u> 것은?

① sad - sadly
② real - really
③ happy - happily
④ friend - friendly
⑤ careful - carefully

[02-05] 다음 빈칸에 들어갈 말로 알맞은 것을 고르시오.

02

I watched a very _____ movie yesterday.

① sadly
② scary
③ badly
④ funnily
⑤ interestingly

03

I woke up _____, so I missed the school bus.

① bad
② late
③ quiet
④ loud
⑤ lately

04

Jane is so hungry now, but she has _____ money.

① little
② few
③ many
④ much
⑤ a lot of

05

This restaurant is _____ than that one.

① kind
② worst
③ cleaner
④ delicious
⑤ the most expensive

[06-07] 다음 빈칸에 들어갈 말로 알맞지 <u>않은</u> 것을 고르시오.

06

There is _____ air in the yellow balloon.

① few
② some
③ little
④ lots of
⑤ a little

07

Molly is as _____ as her older sister.

① tall
② shy
③ pretty
④ wiser
⑤ diligent

08 다음 중 빈칸에 many[Many]가 들어갈 수 <u>없는</u> 것은?

① Don't eat too _____ sweets.
② There are _____ festivals in Korea.
③ I don't have _____ time for leisure.
④ Don't buy too _____ things on sale.
⑤ _____ kinds of flowers bloom in spring.

[09-11] 주어진 문장을 한 문장으로 바꿔 쓸 때 빈칸에 들어갈 말로 알맞은 것을 고르시오.

09

> Andy and Kate are twins. Andy is 13 years old. Kate is 13 years old, too.
> → Andy is _____ Kate.

① as old so
② as old as
③ older than
④ not as old as
⑤ oldest as

10

> Hana goes to school at 8 o'clock. Miso goes to school at 8 : 20.
> → Hana goes to school _____ Miso.

① as early as
② earlier than
③ later than
④ more early than
⑤ more late than

11

> Max, Minky, and Hugo are my pet dogs. Max runs faster than Hugo. Minky runs faster than Max.
> → Minky is _____ of the three.

① as fast as
② faster than
③ fastest
④ more fast
⑤ the fastest

[12-14] 다음 빈칸에 들어갈 말로 알맞게 짝지어진 것을 고르시오.

12

> · Linda always works _____.
> · I was very tired. So I could _____ walk.

① hard – hard
② hardly – hard
③ hard – hardly
④ hardly – hardly
⑤ hardly – hardest

13

> · There is no such thing as a _____ crime.
> · The music _____ matches the last scene of the movie.

① perfect - perfect
② perfectly - perfect
③ more perfect - perfect
④ perfect - perfectly
⑤ perfectly - more perfect

14

> · This melon is as _____ as honey.
> · They are _____ than us because of their simple diet.

① sweet – healthy
② sweet – healthier
③ sweeter – healthy
④ sweetest – healthier
⑤ sweeter – healthiest

15 빈칸에 공통으로 들어갈 말로 알맞은 것은?

> · Jordan is as _____ as Chris.
> · The bus turned the corner too _____.

① fast
② tall
③ strong
④ slowly
⑤ quickly

16 다음 중 그림의 내용과 일치하지 <u>않는</u> 것은?

Dave   Jim   Paul

① Dave is weaker than Paul.
② Paul is as strong as Jim.
③ Jim is stronger than Dave.
④ Dave is the weakest of the three.
⑤ Paul is the strongest of the three.

내신 빈출
17 다음 중 어법상 <u>틀린</u> 것은?

① Hurry up, it's nearly time for breakfast.
② There are few working couples in this city.
③ He runs very fast, and nobody can catch him.
④ The musical was more interesting than the movie.
⑤ The kids at the camp learned important something.

18 다음 우리말을 어법에 알맞게 영작할 때 빈칸 ⓐ에 들어갈 말로 알맞은 것은?

> 그는 걷기의 이점에 대해 사람들에게 자주 말한다.
> → He _____ ⓐ _____
> _____ _____ the benefits of walking.

① talks   ② to
③ often   ④ on
⑤ people

19 다음 문장과 의미가 같은 것은?

> Sue can't dance as well as Sam.

① Sam can dance as well as Sue.
② Sue can dance better than Sam.
③ Sam can dance better than Sue.
④ Sue can dance as badly as Sam.
⑤ Sam cannot dance as well as Sue.

[20-21] 다음 중 어법상 옳은 문장의 개수를 고르시오.

고난도
20

> ⓐ My girlfriend is an only daughter.
> ⓑ Amy cut the paper carefully with scissors.
> ⓒ It's 2 o'clock and my baby is still wake.
> ⓓ Much children know him.

① 없음   ② 1개   ③ 2개
④ 3개   ⑤ 4개

고난도
21

> ⓐ Mary's hair isn't as darker as my.
> ⓑ Chinese is most difficult than English.
> ⓒ The Sahara is the larger desert in Africa.
> ⓓ The architect designed the most beautiful building in the world.

① 없음   ② 1개   ③ 2개
④ 3개   ⑤ 4개

[22-23] 다음 중 어법상 틀린 것을 모두 고르시오.

22 ① My younger brother is always cute.

② The vet touched my puppy sick gently.

③ She bought a colorful skirt at the store.

④ Strange, there were no people in the park.

⑤ I saw something interesting in the back yard.

23 ① This is the smallest city in the world.

② Minsu's grades are highest than mine.

③ This medicine is the most bitter of all.

④ The backpack is as heavier as the box.

⑤ Spiders are more dangerous than snakes.

[24-25] 다음 우리말을 영어로 바르게 옮긴 것을 고르시오.

24
> 그들은 파티에서 노래를 거의 부르지 않았다.

① They sang few songs at the party.

② They sang little songs at the party.

③ They sang some songs at the party.

④ They sang a few songs at the party.

⑤ They sang a little songs at the party.

25
> 이 인형이 우리 가게에서 가장 인기 있다.

① This doll is the popularest in our shop.

② This doll is the popularest of our shop.

③ This doll is the most popular of our shop.

④ This doll is the most popular in our shop.

⑤ This doll is most popular than in our shop.

[26-28] 다음 괄호 안의 말을 알맞은 곳에 넣어 문장을 다시 쓰시오.

26
> You must throw trash on the street. (never)

→ _____

27
> She looks after her grandchildren. (often)

→ _____

28
> The Natural History Museum is popular with children. (always)

→ _____

[29-31] 다음 우리말과 의미가 같도록 괄호 안의 말을 바르게 배열하시오.

29
> 이 치즈는 저 치즈만큼 좋은 냄새가 난다.
> (smells, as, that cheese, as, this cheese, good)

→ _____

30
> 그는 그의 형보다 더 많은 돈을 쓴다.
> (than, more, he, his brother, spends, money)

→ _____

🔲 Answers p.14

31 타조는 세계에서 가장 큰 새이다.

(the world, in, the ostrich, bird, the, is, biggest)

→ _____

32 다음 글의 밑줄 친 ⓐ~ⓔ 중 어법상 틀린 것을 2개 찾아 기호를 쓰고 바르게 고쳐 쓰시오.

Minho and Bomi are siblings. Minho is ⓐunderline{older than} Bomi. Minho ⓑunderline{eats usually} breakfast, but Bomi never eats breakfast. Minho and Bomi always go to school together. They are ⓒunderline{hard late} for school. They seldom fight with each other. They ⓓunderline{often ride} a bike after school. Bomi can ride a bike ⓔunderline{as well as} Minho.

(1) _____ → _____

(2) _____ → _____

33 다음 그림을 보고, 냉장고 안을 묘사하는 문장을 완성하시오.

(1) There are a few _____ _____ _____ in the refrigerator.

(2) There _____ _____ _____ milk and jam in the refrigerator.

(3) There are _____ cucumbers and onions in the refrigerator.

34 다음 표를 보고, 네 사람을 비교하는 글을 완성하시오.

	Miju	Suji	Dana	Eden
Height	163cm	172cm	163cm	170cm
Weight	55kg	55kg	57kg	60kg
Study Time / Day	2 hours	1 hour	2 hours	3 hours

Miju is _____ tall _____ Dana. Eden is _____ _____ tall _____ Suji. Eden is _____ _____ of the four. Suji studies _____ than Dana. Eden studies the _____.

35 다음은 스마트폰을 홍보하는 광고문이다. 주어진 [조건] 에 맞게 글을 완성하시오.

┌ 조건 ┐
• 괄호 안의 말을 이용할 것
• 비교 표현을 이용할 것

Think Big and Do Easy!

Are you looking for a special smartphone? Here is your dream phone, MX 3.

It is _____ _____ (smart) phone in the world. It is _____ _____ (thin) a wallet. It is _____ _____ _____ (light) paper. Why not try it right now?

Chapter

08

동사의 종류

01. 보어가 필요한 동사

1 주어 + 동사 + 주격 보어(명사 / 형용사)

be동사, keep, become, grow, get, turn 등은 주어를 보충 설명하는 주격 보어가 필요한 동사로 주격 보어 자리에 명사 또는 형용사가 온다.

My grandfather **is** *a veteran of Vietnam*.
　　　　　　　동사　　　주격 보어(명사)

Many students **become** *sick, or depressed* because of the pressure.
　　　　　　　동사　　　주격 보어(형용사)

2 주어 + 감각동사 + 주격 보어(형용사)

감각동사는 사람의 감각(시각, 청각, 촉각, 후각, 미각)을 나타내는 동사로 뒤에 형용사가 온다.

look + 형용사	~하게 보이다	smell + 형용사	~한 냄새가 나다
sound + 형용사	~하게 들리다	taste + 형용사	~한 맛이 나다
feel + 형용사	~하게 느끼다		

Your phone **looks** different from mine.
　　　　　　感각동사　주격 보어(형용사)

The story may **sound** *strange*, but it is true.

I **feel** *sick* with a bad headache.

It is sticky and **smells** *good*.

The boiled eggs **taste** *bad*.

⊕ PLUS　감각동사 + like + 명사: ~처럼 …하다
감각동사 뒤에 명사가 올 경우 명사 앞에 전치사 like를 써 준다.
ex. My baby **looks like** *an angel*.

3 주어 + 동사 + 목적어 + 목적격 보어

목적어를 보충 설명해 주는 목적격 보어가 필요한 동사들이 있으며, 목적격 보어로는 명사나 형용사가 쓰인다.

주어	make(~을 …로 만들다) call(~을 …라고 부르다) name(~을 …라고 이름 짓다)	목적어	목적격 보어(명사)
	make(~을 …하게 만들다) find(~이 …한 것을 알게 되다) keep(~을 …하게 유지하다)		목적격 보어(형용사)

I **call** my dog *Max*.
동사　목적어　목적격 보어(명사)

The song **made** Minho *a world star*.

Unfortunately, I **found** my purse *empty*.
　　　　　　　동사　　목적어　목적격 보어(형용사)

Amber always **keeps** her room *clean*.

Grammar Check Up

A 다음 괄호 안에서 알맞은 것을 고르시오.

1 This soup really tastes (good / well).

2 The thought of him made her (happy / happily).

3 The pencil case really looks like (cool / a horse).

4 He became (healthy / healthily) after regular exercise.

B 다음 [보기]의 (A), (B)에서 알맞은 것을 하나씩 골라 문장을 완성하시오. (단, 한 번씩만 쓸 것)

보기				
(A)	sounded	look like	made	found
(B)	a cook	helpful	angry	bad

1 Do I _____ _____ ?

2 Mom's voice _____ _____ then.

3 The hot weather _____ the milk _____ .

4 Jordan _____ the information _____ .

C 다음 우리말과 의미가 같도록 괄호 안의 말을 바르게 배열하시오.

1 그녀의 머리카락은 장미 냄새가 난다. (like, her hair, a rose, smells)

→ _____

2 그 신발은 편하고 멋져 보인다. (and, look, lovely, the shoes, comfortable)

→ _____

3 매일 아침 식사를 하는 것은 사람들을 활기차게 만든다.
   (people, eating, every day, makes, breakfast, energetic)

→ _____

4 나는 그 책이 상당히 유용하다는 것을 알았다. (I, found, helpful, the book, very)

→ _____

D 다음 문장의 밑줄 친 부분을 어법상 알맞은 형태로 고쳐 쓰시오.

1 This scarf feels softly.

2 His attitude made the teacher angrily.

3 It didn't look my school, but it was great.

4 Junho's voice sounded sadly on the phone.

02 목적어가 필요한 동사

1 주어 + 동사 + 목적어

want, love, have, eat 등은 목적어를 취하는 동사로 목적어와 함께 '~을 …하다'라고 해석한다.

They **had** *a bad harvest* this year.
　　　동사　　목적어

The police **found** *important evidence* at the scene.

Judy **enjoys** *playing* the clarinet and *painting* pictures.

2 수여동사 + 간접목적어 + 직접목적어

수여동사는 '~에게 …을 해 주다'라는 의미를 갖는 동사로 두 개의 목적어, 즉 간접목적어(~에게)와 직접목적어
(…을)를 갖는다.

주어	수여동사 (give, lend, show, make, send, bring, write, tell, teach, hand, buy, cook, ask 등)	간접목적어(~에게)	직접목적어(…을)

She **gave** the dog *some water and food*.
　　수여동사 간접목적어　　직접목적어

Tom **bought** them *toy helicopters*.

Can you **show** me *your registration card*?

3 수여동사 + 직접목적어 + 전치사 + 간접목적어

「수여동사 + 간접목적어 + 직접목적어」는 두 목적어의 순서를 바꿔「수여동사 + 직접목적어 + 전치사(to / for / of)
+ 간접목적어」의 순서로 쓸 수 있다.

give, bring, lend, send, tell, pass, show, teach 등		to	
make, buy, cook, find, get, order 등	직접목적어	for	간접목적어
ask, beg, demand 등		of	

Ron **gave** the king *eight gold coins*.
　　　간접목적어　　　직접목적어

→ Ron **gave** *eight gold coins* **to** the king.
　　　　직접목적어　　　간접목적어

My mom **bought** me *this game player*.

→ My mom **bought** *this game player* **for** me.

The reporters **asked** the actor *many questions*.

→ The reporters **asked** *many questions* **of** the actor.

⊕ **PLUS**　**make**의 다양한 쓰임
　• make + 목적어: ~을 만들다 *ex.* He **made** *a swing.*
　• make + 간접목적어 + 직접목적어: ~에게 …을 만들어 주다 *ex.* He **made** me *a swing.*
　• make + 목적어 + 목적격 보어: ~을 …하게[로] 만들다 *ex.* He **made** me *happy.*

A 다음 괄호 안에서 알맞은 것을 고르시오.

1 His wife told (him her ideas / her ideas him).

2 Chris bought Russian dolls (to / for) his sister.

3 The teacher handed the paper (to / for) me.

4 He sent (me / I) a book in return for my present.

B 다음 우리말과 의미가 같도록 괄호 안의 말을 바르게 배열하시오.

1 수호는 나에게 그의 수학 숙제를 빌려주었다. (me, his math homework, to, lent)

→ Suho _____ .

2 나의 삼촌은 나에게 편의점에 가는 법을 알려 주었다.

(to, me, the way, showed, the convenience store)

→ My uncle _____ .

3 Amanda는 그녀의 오빠에게 스웨터를 만들어 주었다. (her brother, a sweater, made, for)

→ Amanda _____ .

4 선생님은 그의 학생들에게 수업 중에 무서운 이야기를 해 주었다. (his students, to, a scary story, told)

→ The teacher _____ in class.

C 다음 문장을 [보기]와 같이 전치사가 포함된 문장으로 바꿔 쓰시오.

> ┤ 보기 ├
> The farmer sent us some potatoes.
> → The farmer <u>sent some potatoes to us</u>.

1 Adam found his niece the toy truck.

→ Adam _____ .

2 The teacher taught his students the law of gravity.

→ The teacher _____ .

3 The doctor showed us a documentary about nature.

→ The doctor _____ .

D 다음 문장의 밑줄 친 부분을 어법상 알맞은 형태로 고쳐 쓰시오.

1 They found <u>for him</u> his lost child.

2 Don't forget to send a postcard <u>for me</u>.

3 The chef always cooks special dishes <u>to customers</u>.

4 My colleagues gave a wedding present <u>me</u>.

A 다음 우리말과 의미가 같도록 괄호 안의 말을 이용하여 문장을 완성하시오.

1 이 커피 콩은 달콤한 초콜릿 냄새가 난다. (smell, sweet chocolate)

→ The coffee beans _____.

2 그 가수는 무대에서 긴장해 보이지 않는다. (look, nervous)

→ The singer _____ on the stage.

3 그 요리사의 파스타는 훌륭한 맛이 난다. (taste, wonderful)

→ The chef's pasta _____.

4 Jordan은 그의 책들을 파란색 상자 안에 넣었다. (put, his books)

→ Jordan _____ in the blue box.

5 우리는 하이킹하는 동안 매우 목이 말랐다. (feel, very, thirsty)

→ We _____ during the hike.

B 다음 문장을 [보기]와 같이 전치사가 포함된 문장으로 바꿔 쓰시오.

┌─ 보기 ┐
My aunt bought me a doll.
→ My aunt bought a doll for me.
└─────┘

1 Could you find this lady a seat?

→ Could you _____?

2 My dad made me a round table.

→ My dad _____.

3 She asked a man the way to the bank.

→ She _____.

4 My e-pal, Cindy wrote me an e-mail.

→ My e-pal, Cindy _____.

5 His brother passed him the remote control.

→ His brother _____.

C 다음 문장에서 어법상 <u>어색한</u> 부분을 고쳐 문장을 다시 쓰시오.

1 His English sounds German.

→ _____

2 She sent to me an essay of her journey.

→ _____

3 Our students became health and strong.

→ _____

4 She asked their names for the new students.

→ _____

5 She will give him to useful information about South America.

→ _____

D 다음 우리말과 의미가 같도록 괄호 안에 주어진 말을 이용하여 영작하시오.

1 Laura는 보통 창문들과 문들을 닫아 둔다. (keep, closed)

→ _____

2 너희 이모가 너에게 헝겊 인형을 만들어 주셨니? (a cloth doll)

→ _____

3 그 간호사는 그 환자에게 알약을 몇 개 주었다. (some pills)

→ _____

4 뉴욕은 너에게 진정한 도시의 삶을 보여 줄 것이다. (the real city life)

→ _____

5 오렌지는 달고 신 맛이 모두 난다. (oranges, sweet, sour, both)

→ _____

6 그 사건 이후에, 언론이 그를 훌륭한 남자로 만들었다. (the press, a good man)

→ After the incident, _____ .

[01-03] 다음 빈칸에 들어갈 말로 알맞은 것을 고르시오.

01

Her cake doesn't always taste _____.

① good
② badly
③ sweetly
④ honey
⑤ an orange

02

The medicine may make you _____.

① sadly
② tiredly
③ sleepy
④ happily
⑤ freshly

내신 빈출
03

The news made me _____.

① happily
② a star
③ angrily
④ shocking
⑤ to do it

[04-07] 다음 빈칸에 들어갈 말로 알맞지 <u>않은</u> 것을 고르시오.

04

The runner felt _____.

① tired
② cold
③ thirsty
④ nervously
⑤ like a winner

05

Kevin _____ Yujin a catalogue.

① brings
② gives
③ sends
④ passes
⑤ turns

06

Cindy _____ a model plane to her cousin.

① gave
② sent
③ made
④ showed
⑤ brought

07

They became _____ thanks to oil.

① rich
② happy
③ strongly
④ powerful
⑤ wealthy countries

08 다음 중 어법상 <u>틀린</u> 것은?

① Your family newspaper looks great.
② Kevin always keeps his desk messily.
③ My friends call me "K-pop Queen."
④ Mina's dad gave her some allowance.
⑤ The concert for poor children made us happy.

09 다음 빈칸에 들어갈 전치사로 알맞은 것은?

> Sumin asked Minsu's phone number _____ me.

① in   ② for
③ to   ④ of
⑤ about

10 다음 우리말과 의미가 같도록 괄호 안의 말을 바르게 배열할 때 네 번째로 오는 단어는?

> 나는 내 강아지에게 푹신한 쿠션을 만들어 주었다.
> (soft, my, made, a, cushion, I, dog)

① a   ② my
③ dog   ④ soft
⑤ cushion

[11-12] 다음 빈칸에 들어갈 말로 알맞게 짝지어진 것을 고르시오.

11
> · The movie made Susan _____.
> · The vet found the dog _____.

① a star – sickly   ② famous – sick
③ famous – sickly   ④ a star – sickness
⑤ famously – sick

12
> · His mom made _____ a milkshake.
> · The waiter brought a new knife _____.

① him – me   ② to him – me
③ him – to me   ④ him – of me
⑤ to him – to me

[13-14] 다음 우리말을 영어로 바르게 옮긴 것을 고르시오.

13
> 그는 차고가 비어 있다는 것을 알았다.

① He found empty the garage.
② He found the garage empty.
③ He found emptily the garage.
④ He found the garage emptily.
⑤ He found the garage to be emptily.

14
> Tony는 Ellen에게 그의 주소를 말해 주었다.

① Tony told to his address Ellen.
② Tony told to Ellen his address.
③ Tony told Ellen to his address.
④ Tony told his address to Ellen.
⑤ Tony told Ellen his address to.

고난도
15 빈칸에 공통으로 들어갈 말로 알맞은 것은?

> · No one _____ the movie boring.
> · They _____ him his car at the beach.
> · Between the rocks, Kevin _____ a snake.

① sent   ② found
③ showed   ④ thought
⑤ brought

16 빈칸에 들어갈 말이 나머지와 다른 것은?

① Don't give chocolate _____ dogs.

② He teaches *taekwondo* _____ us.

③ My aunt bought a watch _____ me.

④ I lent my old camera _____ my friend.

⑤ She brought a piece of cake _____ Sean.

17 다음 우리말을 어법에 알맞게 영작한 것은?

> Mike는 그의 선생님에게 진실을 말하지 않았다.

① Mike didn't tell his teacher the truth.

② Mike didn't tell the truth of his teacher.

③ Mike didn't tell his teacher to the truth

④ Mike didn't tell to his teacher the truth.

⑤ Mike didn't tell the truth for his teacher.

18 다음 밑줄 친 ① ~ ⑤ 중 어법상 틀린 것은?

> Jenny ① sent ② a few ③ songs ④ for ⑤ a producer last week.

19 밑줄 친 부분 중 문장에서의 역할이 나머지와 다른 것은?

① The kids became quiet.

② The man is an animal doctor.

③ I can't stay awake any longer.

④ Mike walked bravely in the forest.

⑤ Her cousin looks friendly and cute.

20 밑줄 친 부분 중 쓰임이 나머지와 다른 것은?

① His song made us bored.

② This scarf makes me warm.

③ She made people yellow ribbons.

④ A lot of homework made me tired.

⑤ Her mom made her a great swimmer.

21 다음 중 [보기]와 문장의 형태가 같은 것은?

> 보기
>
> The sky looks clear today.

① This glass breaks easily.

② He got an A on the math test.

③ His parents called him a "prince."

④ The teacher's voice sounds angry.

⑤ Brad gave his wife a birthday present.

22 다음 중 어법상 틀린 것은?

① The pudding tasted great.

② Bill became a good doctor.

③ Sun-dried laundry smells fresh.

④ Mina looked a baby at that time.

⑤ The weather gets warm in spring.

내신 빈출

23 다음 중 어법상 틀린 것을 모두 고르면?

① Dad cooked us fried chicken.

② He told us to his adventures.

③ John bought a baseball bat his son.

④ The police officer asked me my age.

⑤ My mom teaches sign language to the students.

[24-25] 다음 중 어법상 옳은 문장의 개수를 고르시오.

고난도

24

ⓐ Adam found her honest.
ⓑ His friends call "Jordan" him.
ⓒ Can you explain the problems to me?
ⓓ I bought for him a hamburger and a cola.

① 없음   ② 1개   ③ 2개
④ 3개   ⑤ 4개

고난도

25

ⓐ His socks smell terribly.
ⓑ Can you find my bracelet to me?
ⓒ The coach made the players great.
ⓓ How do I keep them alive?

① 없음   ② 1개   ③ 2개
④ 3개   ⑤ 4개

[26-28] 다음 두 문장의 의미가 같도록 빈칸에 알맞은 말을 쓰시오. (단, 전치사를 포함할 것)

26

My husband made me a cup of tea and a sandwich for breakfast.

= My husband made _____ _____

_____ _____ _____

_____ _____ _____ for breakfast.

27

You should show them your driver's licence.

= You should show _____ _____

_____ _____ _____ .

28

Steve asked me Susan's address.

= Steve asked _____ _____ _____

_____ .

[29-31] 다음 우리말과 의미가 같도록 괄호 안의 말을 바르게 배열하시오.

29

그녀는 그녀의 딸에게 웨딩드레스를 만들어 주었다.
(for, made, her daughter, a wedding dress)

→ She _____ .

30

나는 내 친구에게 과자를 좀 가져다주었다.
(my friend, brought, some cookies, I)

→ _____

31
> Clara의 부모님은 그녀를 훌륭한 골프 선수로 만들었다.
> (a good golfer, her, made)

→ Clara's parents _____.

32 다음 대화의 밑줄 친 ⓐ~ⓔ 중 어법상 틀린 것을 2개 찾아 기호를 쓰고 바르게 고쳐 쓰시오.

> A: I found the dog sleeping ⓐ soundly at the front door. Is he yours?
> B: Yes, he is. My dad got him from a pet shop. We ⓑ call him "Chorong."
> A: He feels ⓒ soft and he smells ⓓ well.
> B: I gave him a bath with shampoo this morning.
> A: You look happy.
> B: That's right. He makes me ⓔ happily.

(1) _____ → _____

(2) _____ → _____

33 다음 그림을 보고, 각 빈칸에 알맞은 말을 [보기]에서 골라 쓰시오.

┤ 보기 ├
dolls   stars   unique   have   save   strangely

(1) Starfish normally _____ five arms.

(2) Starfish feel _____.

(3) Starfish look like _____ in the sky.

34 다음 괄호 안의 말과 전치사를 이용하여 Tom이 생일날 받은 것을 문장으로 쓰시오. (단, 과거형으로 쓸 것)

(1) (a birthday cake, make)

→ Tom's mom _____.

(2) (a new bike, buy)

→ Tom's dad _____.

(3) (a smart watch, send)

→ Tom's uncle _____.

(4) (a T-shirt, bring)

→ Tom's friend, Joe _____.

35 다음은 Elise의 일기이다. 밑줄 친 우리말을 주어진 [조건]에 맞게 영어로 쓰시오.

┤ 조건 ├
• 괄호 안의 말을 이용할 것
• 필요하면 단어를 추가하거나 어형을 바꿀 것

> A few days ago, a family moved to our neighborhood. They had a son. (1) 그들은 그 소년을 Jack이라고 불렀다. (the boy, Jack, call) (2) 나는 그가 친절하다는 것을 알았다. (find, him, kind) (3) 그들은 우리에게 떡을 주었다 (us, give, a rice cake) to celebrate moving in.

(1) _____

(2) _____

(3) _____

09

접속사

01 and, but, or, so

① and : 그리고

서로 비슷하거나 연속되는 내용의 단어와 단어, 구와 구, 절과 절을 연결해 준다.

What *color* **and** *size* for a jacket do you want?

Elise *smiled sweetly* **and** *asked him for a favor*.

My son won the first prize, **and** *I was really happy*.

> **PLUS** 셋 이상을 연결하는 and / or
> and와 or로 셋 이상을 연결할 때, 앞에는 콤마를 쓰고 마지막에만 and 또는 or를 쓴다.
> ex. smart, handsome, **and** rich / grapes, watermelons, **or** strawberries

② but : 그러나

서로 반대되거나 대조되는 내용의 단어와 단어, 구와 구, 절과 절을 연결해 준다.

The problem is *simple* **but** *difficult*.

I want *to meet him* **but** *not to stay with him for a long time*.

I have a big family, **but** *my house is so small.*

③ or : 또는

1 둘 이상에서 선택하는 내용을 연결해 주는 접속사로, 단어와 단어, 구와 구, 절과 절을 연결해 준다.

Dark chocolate **or** *soda* can be a great stress reliever.

He *plays mobile games* **or** *flies his drone* on weekends.

2 선택의문문에서 or를 사용한다.

How do you go to the library, *by bus* **or** *on foot*?

> **PLUS** and로 연결된 주어 vs. or로 연결된 주어
> • and로 연결된 주어는 복수 취급한다.
>   ex. My brother **and** I *are* going to be golfers.
> • or로 연결된 주어는 or 뒤의 단어에 동사의 수를 맞춘다.
>   ex. My brother **or** I *am* going to be a golfer.

④ so : 그래서

원인과 결과에 해당하는 절과 절을 연결해 준다. so 앞에는 원인이, 뒤에는 결과가 나온다.

My birthday party will begin soon, **so** I'm very busy.
　　　　　원인　　　　　　　　　　결과

I was sick last night, **so** I couldn't sleep well.

A 다음 괄호 안에서 알맞은 것을 고르시오.

1 The parents will name their baby Jordan (and / or) Tyler.

2 He slept during the day, (but / so) he can't sleep now.

3 He feels like a new person (and / but) feels happy.

4 Your team or my team (is / are) going to win the prize.

5 The interviewers asked me questions (but / or) I couldn't answer any of them.

B 다음 문장이 자연스러운 의미가 되도록 [보기]에서 알맞은 말을 골라 그 기호를 쓰시오.

┌ 보기 ├
ⓐ or climb the emergency stairs   ⓑ but I missed the train
ⓒ so move back behind the yellow line   ⓓ and get on a rescue boat quickly

1 The train is arriving, _____.

2 I intended returning home by six _____.

3 You have to put on a life jacket, _____.

4 We can take the elevator, _____.

C 다음 빈칸에 들어갈 알맞은 접속사를 [보기]에서 골라 쓰시오. (단, 한 번씩만 쓸 것)

┌ 보기 ├
and   but   or   so

1 That soup tasted salty, _____ I added some water.

2 Which do you want, iced tea _____ iced coffee?

3 Hamburgers are more delicious than fruit _____ not healthy.

4 I am afraid of worms _____ Kelly is afraid of snakes.

D 다음 문장의 밑줄 친 부분을 어법상 알맞은 형태로 고쳐 쓰시오.

1 His movies are always interesting and <u>excite</u>.

2 He is strict to his children <u>or</u> friendly to other people.

3 We have little time, <u>but</u> we must go the shortest way.

4 A lot of goats and sheep <u>is</u> on the farm.

02 when, before, after

1 when: ~할 때

1 '~할 때'라는 뜻으로 시간[때]을 나타내는 부사절을 이끈다.

He looked so excited **when** he came back home.

She told her secrets to me **when** there was no one around.

2 부사절은 주절 앞이나 뒤에 모두 올 수 있는데, 앞에 올 경우 부사절의 끝에 콤마(,)를 찍는다.

When Jane was in middle school, she acted in a school play.

= Jane acted in a school play **when** she was in middle school.

⊕ PLUS 접속사 when vs. 의문사 when
- 접속사 when: ~할 때 ex. **When** I went into the house, the dogs began to bark.
- 의문사 when: 언제 ex. **When** did you plant these flowers? – I planted them yesterday.

2 before: ~하기 전에

'~하기 전에'라는 뜻의 시간을 나타내는 접속사로, 시간상 앞서 이루어지는 일을 나타내는 부사절을 이끈다.

Let's warm up **before** we get into the pool.

Before he had a boxing match, he trained hard every day.

Let's buy sleeping bags **before** we go camping.

3 after: ~한 후에

'~한 후에'라는 뜻의 시간을 나타내는 접속사로, 시간상 뒤에 이루어지는 일을 나타내는 부사절을 이끈다.

You should wash your hands **after** you come home.

After she visits a nice restaurant, she always writes about it on her blog.

He could drive to work **after** he found his car key.

⊕ PLUS 시간의 부사절에서의 미래 표현
시간의 부사절에서는 미래를 현재시제로 나타낸다.
ex. **After** I *walk* my dog, I will wash it. (O)
    After I *will walk* my dog, I will wash it. (×)
    When I *meet* her tomorrow, I'll give her the message. (O)
    When I *will meet* her tomorrow, I'll give her the message. (×)

Grammar Check Up

A 다음 괄호 안에서 알맞은 것을 고르시오.

1 (When / Before) she was younger, she was a shy kid.

2 We replied (before / after) we received an invitation from her.

3 When you (arrive / will arrive) there, he will be waiting for you.

4 I fell in love with Mary at first sight (after / when) I met her.

5 Check the pockets (after / before) you send your clothes to the laundry.

B 다음 문장이 자연스러운 의미가 되도록 [보기]에서 알맞은 말을 골라 그 기호를 쓰시오.

┌ 보기 ┐
ⓐ when we went to college   ⓑ after I walked in the rain for hours
ⓒ before he visited Gyeongju   ⓓ when it snows

1 I got a severe cold _____.

2 We had different dreams _____.

3 He studied the history of Silla _____.

4 You'd better not drive _____.

C 다음 문장에서 어법상 <u>어색한</u> 부분을 찾아 바르게 고쳐 쓰시오.

1 When they read the map, they began to go east.   _____ → _____

2 Can you spare some time after it's convenient?   _____ → _____

3 Get back home before it will get dark.   _____ → _____

4 Before he turned on the computer, he checked his e-mail.   _____ → _____

D 다음 두 문장을 한 문장으로 바꿔 쓸 때, 빈칸에 알맞은 말을 쓰시오.

1 He stayed in the hospital for a month. He was in a car accident.

→ After _____.

2 Alice jogs for half an hour. She takes a shower.

→ Before _____.

3 Use "please." You ask a favor of other people.

→ When _____

03 because, if, that

1 because : ~ 때문에

1 '~ 때문에'라는 뜻으로 이유나 원인을 나타내는 부사절을 이끈다.

Let's give the girl a hand **because** she can't lift the box.

Because it keeps her awake at night, she doesn't drink coffee.

2 because of(~ 때문에)는 전치사구이므로 뒤에 절이 아닌 명사(구)가 이어진다.

The train was delayed **because of** *bad weather*.

> **⊕ PLUS** **because + 이유[원인] vs. so + 결과**
>
> **Because** the school is far, Dad drives me to school every morning.
> 이유[원인]   결과
>
> = The school is far, **so** Dad drives me to school every morning.
>   이유[원인]   결과

2 if : 만약 ~한다면

1 '만약 ~한다면'이라는 뜻으로 조건을 나타내는 부사절을 이끈다.

You'd get there in time **if** you run all the way.

If I have a 3D printer, I'll make a house for my family.

2 if ~ not은 접속사 unless로 바꿔 쓸 수 있다.

Don't come **if** I **don't** tell you to.

= Don't come **unless** I tell you to.

> **⊕ PLUS** **조건의 부사절에서의 미래 표현**
>
> 조건의 부사절에서도 시간의 부사절과 마찬가지로 미래를 현재시제로 나타낸다.
> ex. **If** it *rains* tomorrow, we will stay at the hotel. (O)
>   **If** it *will rain* tomorrow, we will stay at the hotel. (×)

3 that : ~하는 것

접속사 that은 명사절을 이끌며, that이 이끄는 절은 문장에서 주어, 목적어, 보어 역할을 한다.

1 주어 역할: '~하는 것은[것이]'으로 해석하며 단수 취급한다.

That I am a hard worker is my greatest advantage.
        주어

2 목적어 역할: '~하는 것을'로 해석하며 이때 that은 생략할 수 있다.

They think **(that)** there is water on Mars.
                    목적어

3 보어 역할: '~하는 것(이다)'으로 해석한다.

The trouble is **that** they don't have enough time.
                        보어

> **⊕ PLUS** **가주어와 진주어**
>
> 주어로 쓰인 that절은 가주어 it을 사용한 문장으로 바꿔 쓰는 것이 일반적이다.
> **That** you should listen to your teacher is important.
>   주어
> → **It** is important **that** you should listen to your teacher.
>   가주어   진주어

Grammar Check Up

A 다음 괄호 안에서 알맞은 것을 고르시오.

1 The fact is (if / that) Korean food can be loved by anyone.

2 If you (get / will get) up early tomorrow, you will see the first snow.

3 I will forgive him (because / if) he told me the truth.

4 (If / Unless) you like to take pictures, you might become a photographer.

5 The baseball game was canceled (because / because of) the rain.

B 다음 문장이 자연스러운 의미가 되도록 [보기]에서 알맞은 말을 골라 그 기호를 쓰시오.

보기
ⓐ that some people hit their pets
ⓑ because of thick fog
ⓒ if the gym is near my house
ⓓ if you go to a library

1 I will go and work out every day _____.

2 It is shocking _____.

3 You should not talk too loudly _____.

4 All planes can't take off _____.

C 다음 문장에서 어법상 <u>어색한</u> 부분을 찾아 바르게 고쳐 쓰시오.

1 That is true that Mr. Brown was taken to the hospital last night. _____ → _____

2 The twin babies often fight because their toys. _____ → _____

3 If you will join the website, you may find your old friends. _____ → _____

4 The dog will bite you because you throw a stone at it. _____ → _____

D 다음 두 문장의 의미가 같도록 빈칸에 알맞은 말을 쓰시오.

1 That there are treasures on the island is false.

→ It is false _____.

2 Someone stole my passport, so I couldn't get on the plane.

→ I couldn't get on the plane _____.

3 The dress is very expensive because a world-famous designer made it.

→ A world-famous designer made the dress, _____.

4 If you don't eat vegetables, you will be unhealthy.

→ _____, you will be unhealthy.

A 다음 우리말과 의미가 같도록 빈칸에 알맞은 접속사를 쓰시오.

1 만약 그들이 불법적으로 동물을 사냥한다면, 나는 경찰에 신고할 것이다.

→ _____ they hunt animals illegally, I will report to the police.

2 나는 오늘 오후에 낮잠을 자거나 TV를 볼 것이다.

→ I will take a nap _____ watch TV this afternoon.

3 Susie는 흰색 블라우스와 파란색 치마를 입었다.

→ Susie wore a white blouse _____ a blue skirt.

4 그녀는 방을 청소하기 전에 창문을 연다.

→ She opens the windows _____ she cleans the room.

5 교통 신호등이 빨간색이 되었을 때 차들이 멈추었다.

→ The cars stopped _____ the traffic light went red.

B 다음 두 문장을 한 문장으로 바꿔 쓸 때, [보기]에서 알맞은 접속사를 골라 문장을 완성하시오. (단, 한 번씩만 쓸 것)

> 보기
>
> after   but   that   so   because

1 He was quiet. His dad was sleeping.

→ He was quiet _____.

2 He is very rich. He can buy whatever he wants.

→ He is very rich, _____.

3 People know. The elephant can draw a picture.

→ People know _____.

4 She peeled an apple. She cut it into four pieces.

→ _____, she cut it into four pieces.

5 It's true that this necklace looks expensive. It only costs 50 dollars.

→ It's true that this necklace looks expensive, _____.

C 다음 [보기]의 (A), (B)에서 알맞은 말을 하나씩 골라 문장을 완성하시오. (단, 한 번씩만 쓸 것)

보기					
(A)	but	or	before	after	because

(B)	a tablet PC at home	I found it on the street
	she isn't still good at it	it closed
	she gained weight lately	

1 To send a package, I hurried to the post office _____.

2 She began to exercise hard _____.

3 She takes piano lessons every Friday, _____.

4 Do you have a notebook computer _____?

5 I took the wallet to the police _____.

D 다음 우리말과 의미가 같도록 괄호 안에 주어진 말과 알맞은 접속사를 이용하여 문장을 완성하시오. (단, 필요하면 형태를 바꿀 것)

1 어떤 사람들은 고양이가 행운을 가져온다고 믿었다. (bring, good luck)

→ Some people believed _____.

2 나는 충분한 돈이 없어서 식료품을 살 수 없다. (buy, groceries)

→ I don't have enough money, _____.

3 그 편지가 늦게 왔기 때문에 그는 기회를 놓쳤다. (come, late)

→ He missed the chance _____.

4 그녀는 그녀의 가족과 떨어져 살 때 외로웠다. (live away, from)

→ She was lonely _____.

5 내가 대도시로 이사를 간다면, 나는 일주일에 한 번 영화를 볼 것이다. (move to, a big city)

→ _____, I'll watch a movie once a week.

[01-03] 다음 빈칸에 들어갈 말로 알맞은 것을 고르시오.

01

> I thought he was tough _____ it was not true.

① or
② so
③ but
④ that
⑤ because

02

> He eats a lot of sweets, _____ he has bad teeth.

① if
② so
③ that
④ before
⑤ because

03

> Did you lose your purse _____ leave it at home?

① or
② and
③ but
④ when
⑤ because

[04-06] 다음 빈칸에 공통으로 들어갈 말로 알맞은 것을 고르시오.

04

> · I heard _____ Mike is a police officer.
> · Her dream is _____ she will become the best stylist.

① and
② but
③ when
④ that
⑤ because

05

> · _____ does the next train leave for Busan?
> · _____ you see her, say hello to her for me.

① If
② And
③ After
④ Before
⑤ When

06

> · The bread went bad _____ the hot weather.
> · She's happy _____ her pets.

① or
② and
③ after
④ because
⑤ because of

07 다음 중 밑줄 친 부분의 쓰임이 나머지와 다른 것은?

① When I left home, it started to rain.
② When she was younger, she was a shy kid.
③ When I was young, I liked to play baseball.
④ When are you going to do your homework?
⑤ What were you doing when your mom got home?

[08-09] 다음 두 문장을 한 문장으로 바꿔 쓸 때 빈칸에 들어갈 말로 알맞은 것을 고르시오.

08

> My father and I had lunch. Then we took a walk in the park.
> → _____ my father and I had lunch, we took a walk in the park.

① If
② Before
③ Because
④ When
⑤ After

09

My sister will win the first prize at the contest. I believe that.
→ I believe _____ my sister will win the first prize at the contest.

① as   ② if
③ that   ④ so
⑤ then

[10-12] 다음 빈칸에 들어갈 말로 알맞게 짝지어진 것을 고르시오.

10

· Gilbert _____ Anna are working in the field.
· It was cold this morning, _____ it is warm now.

① or – so   ② but – if
③ and – but   ④ but – and
⑤ and – because

11

· The ground was white _____ the snow fell.
· Let's have lunch _____ the movie starts.

① if – before   ② that – after
③ after – before   ④ because – if
⑤ before – when

내신 빈출
12

· He thinks _____ the comic book is boring.
· Drink a glass of water _____ you are thirsty.

① if – but   ② that – if
③ after – that   ④ when – before
⑤ that – and

[13-14] 다음 우리말을 영어로 바르게 옮긴 것을 고르시오.

13

우리가 가는 길에 카페를 지나가면, 나는 커피를 살 거야.

① If we pass a cafe on the way, I'll buy coffee.
② We pass a cafe on the way if I'll buy coffee.
③ If we'll pass a cafe on the way, I'll buy coffee.
④ We pass a cafe on the way and I'll buy coffee.
⑤ We pass a cafe on the way, so I'll buy coffee.

14

그는 대학에 다닐 때 의학을 공부했다.

① He studied medicine before he went to college.
② He studied medicine after he went to college.
③ He studied medicine when he went to college.
④ He went to college when he studied medicine.
⑤ Before he studied medicine, he went to college.

15 다음 두 문장을 한 문장으로 바꿀 때 알맞은 것을 <u>모두</u> 고르면?

I played online games. Then I went to bed.

① I went to bed after I played online games.
② I went to bed when I played online games.
③ After I went to bed, I played online games.
④ I went to bed before I played online games.
⑤ Before I went to bed, I played online games.

16 빈칸에 들어갈 접속사가 나머지와 <u>다른</u> 것은?

① Rocks _____ stones feel hard.
② Clara is very kind _____ pretty.
③ Go straight one block _____ turn right.
④ She grew up, _____ she became a model.
⑤ He was hungry, _____ he couldn't eat anything.

17 밑줄 친 부분 중 생략할 수 있는 것은?

① I took care of my sister <u>and</u> my cousin.

② Do you think <u>that</u> she is the best singer?

③ You get green <u>if</u> you mix blue and yellow.

④ He ran away <u>when</u> the police officer shouted.

⑤ My baby brother cried <u>because</u> he wanted something.

18 다음 중 어법상 틀린 것은?

① Is she at the library or at the post office?

② The students say cheese when they take pictures.

③ If I will go back to my hometown, I will farm there.

④ His cell phone doesn't work, so he needs a new one.

⑤ Sally thinks that she is the most beautiful in the class.

19 다음 중 빈칸에 because[Because]가 들어갈 수 없는 것은?

① Don't touch it _____ it is very hot.

② Jane is old _____ she can climb the stairs quickly.

③ I was so happy _____ Jake gave me a present.

④ _____ he was sick, he couldn't come to my party.

⑤ We don't have to go to school _____ today is a holiday.

20 [보기]의 밑줄 친 부분과 쓰임이 다른 것은?

보기
They say <u>that</u> there will be lots of snow tomorrow in the city.

① They know <u>that</u> she was badly injured.

② Do you think <u>that</u> he is a great actor?

③ My parents hope <u>that</u> I will be a teacher.

④ How can we know <u>that</u> without any information?

⑤ I believe <u>that</u> we spend too much money on clothes.

21 다음 중 의미하는 바가 나머지와 다른 것은?

① I missed my flight because of a traffic jam.

② I missed my flight so there was a traffic jam.

③ There was a traffic jam, so I missed my flight.

④ I missed my flight because there was a traffic jam.

⑤ Because there was a traffic jam, I missed my flight.

[22-23] 다음 중 어법상 틀린 것을 모두 고르시오.

22 ① She had toast and a glass of milk.

② Which can you play, the violin and the cello?

③ He will buy a doll or a ring for his sister.

④ Semi was sick, but she didn't go to school.

⑤ I drank too much coffee, so I couldn't sleep.

고난도
23 ① Unless I have enough money, I'll buy a laptop.
② When Nancy is free, she usually reads a book.
③ We stopped talking when he came into the room.
④ After you buy clothes, you should check the price.
⑤ Before I get on the plane, I'll go to the Duty Free shop.

고난도
24 다음 중 어법상 옳은 문장의 개수는?

ⓐ Take out the garbage when you go out.
ⓑ You should go home before it's too dark.
ⓒ I know if she is going to move tomorrow.
ⓓ If you won't walk quietly, the dog will bark at you.

① 없음　　　② 1개　　　③ 2개
④ 3개　　　⑤ 4개

고난도
25 다음 중 어법상 옳은 것으로 알맞게 짝지어진 것은?

ⓐ If you don't water the plants, they will die.
ⓑ Sora doesn't like history because of it's boring.
ⓒ When he has a sore throat, he eats ice cream.
ⓓ That the moon is smaller than the earth is true.
ⓔ Put the book back on my desk before you read it.

① ⓐ, ⓓ　　　　② ⓐ, ⓑ, ⓓ
③ ⓐ, ⓒ, ⓓ　　　④ ⓑ, ⓒ, ⓓ
⑤ ⓑ, ⓒ, ⓓ, ⓔ

[26-29] 다음 두 문장의 의미가 같도록 접속사를 이용하여 빈칸에 알맞은 말을 쓰시오.

26
Pizza was expensive, so Nick ordered pasta.

= Nick ordered pasta _____ _____.

27
That nuclear power is carbon-free is false.

= It is false _____.

28
After he drank some water, he began to eat dinner.

= _____, he drank some water.

29
If you don't follow traffic rules, you will have to pay a fine.

= _____, you will have to pay a fine.

[30-32] 다음 우리말과 의미가 같도록 괄호 안의 말을 바르게 배열하시오.

30
네가 주의 깊게 듣는 것이 중요하다.
(listen, that, it, carefully, is, you, important)

→ _____

31

> 나는 마트에 가기 전에 항상 쇼핑 목록을 만든다.
> (go to, before, the mart, I)

→ I always make a shopping list

_____ .

32

> 그 놀이공원이 이곳에서 멀지 않으면, 우리는 그곳에 걸어갈 것이다.
> (isn't, here, if, far from, the amusement park)

→ _____ ,
we will walk there.

33 다음 [보기]의 (A)와 (B)에서 알맞은 문장을 하나씩 골라 접속사를 사용하여 한 문장으로 연결하시오. (단, 한 번씩만 쓸 것)

┌ 보기 ┐
(A)   He looked sad.
      You should be careful.
      You turn right at the corner.

(B)   You will see the building.
      He missed the school bus.
      You ride your bike on the street.
└─────┘

(1) _____

(2) _____

(3) _____

34 다음 표를 보고, 두 사람의 일과를 비교하는 글을 완성하시오.

	Tom	Sejin
get home	3:30	4:30
eat a snack	3:30-4:00	4:30-5:00
do his homework	5:00-6:30	8:30-11:00
go to sleep	10:30	11:30

> Sejin gets home _____ Tom gets home. Both Tom _____ Sejin eat a snack as soon as they get home. Sejin does his homework _____ Tom does his homework. Tom goes to sleep _____ Sejin goes to sleep.

35 다음 '에너지를 절약하는 방법'에 관한 문장을 [조건]에 맞게 완성하시오.

┌ 조건 ┐
• 괄호 안의 말을 포함하여 쓸 것
• 접속사 before, when, or 중 하나를 포함하여 쓸 것
• 10단어 이내로 쓸 것
└─────┘

Ways to Save Energy

(1) We should _____
_____ .
   (unplug, computer, not, in use)

(2) We should _____ .
   (ride, bike, walk, school)

(3) We should _____ .
   (turn off, light, go out)

Chapter

10

전치사

01 시간을 나타내는 전치사

1 at, on, in

'~에'라는 뜻으로 시간을 나타내는 말 앞에 쓰며, 뒤에 오는 말에 따라 구분하여 사용한다.

at	+ 시각, 특정 시점	at 3 o'clock, at noon, at night
on	+ 날짜, 요일, 특정한 날	on March 4, on Sunday, on Christmas Day
in	+ 월, 계절, 연도, 세기, 오전 / 오후 / 저녁	in May, in (the) spring, in 2017, in the morning

The flight to Paris will leave **at** 7 p.m.

I heard a strange voice **at** night.

I'll take part in the marathon race **on** August 15.

Mary often eats brunch **on** Sundays.

I often travel to Zürich, Switzerland **in** summer.

In the evening, we tried different street foods.

⊕ **PLUS** 하루의 때를 나타내는 말
- 하루의 때를 나타내는 말과 전치사
  ex. **in** the morning, **at** noon, **in** the afternoon, **in** the evening, **at** night, **at** midnight
- 때를 나타내는 말 앞에 this, last, next, every 등이 올 경우 전치사를 쓰지 않는다.
  ex. I'm leaving for London **next Friday**. (O)
      I'm leaving for London **on next Friday**. (×)

2 그 밖의 시간을 나타내는 전치사(구)

before	~ 전에	after	~ 후에
for	~ 동안	during	~ 동안
by	~까지	until[till]	~까지
from A to B	A부터 B까지	between A and B	A와 B 사이에

Please hand in your essay **before** January 15.

After the nap, you may focus better.

The typhoon hit the island **for** a short time.

During *Chuseok*, Koreans spend time with their family.

He ordered the soldiers, "Get there **by** eight o'clock."

They delayed the decision **until** next month.

My boss will go on a trip to Sydney **from** Monday **to** Wednesday.

Breakfast is served **between** 7 a.m. **and** 10 a.m.

⊕ **PLUS** for vs. during
- for + 숫자로 된 구체적인 기간
  ex. **for** a week, **for** 20 minutes, **for** three hours
- during + 특정 기간을 나타내는 명사(구)
  ex. **during** the meal, **during** the game, **during** the winter

Grammar Check Up

A 다음 괄호 안에서 알맞은 것을 고르시오.

1 You must not walk alone (at / on / in) night in this city.

2 Why is it hotter (at / on / in) summer than (at / on / in) winter?

3 (At / On / In) Sundays, we had cold noodles.

4 Shadows become longer (at / on / in) the evening.

5 Children dress up as ghosts and monsters (at / on / in) Halloween.

B 다음 빈칸에 for 또는 during 중 알맞은 것을 쓰시오.

1 I hiked on the mountain _____ a few days.

2 Where were you _____ your working hours?

3 The computers were down _____ three hours.

4 You will feel great _____ the class if you eat a good breakfast.

5 She was an important figure _____ the Cold War.

C 다음 문장에서 어법상 <u>어색한</u> 부분을 찾아 바르게 고쳐 쓰시오.

1 Office workers usually work after nine to six.   _____ → _____

2 I will be in this country during a month on business.   _____ → _____

3 Football started in England on the 19th century.   _____ → _____

4 The market opens between December until April every year.   _____ → _____

5 He didn't say a word for the meal.   _____ → _____

D 다음 우리말과 의미가 같도록 괄호 안의 말을 이용하여 문장을 완성하시오.

1 우리는 모두 저녁 식사 후에 배가 아팠다. (dinner)

 → We all had stomachaches _____.

2 입장료가 화요일에는 무료이다. (Tuesdays)

 → Admission is free _____.

3 나의 엄마는 밤 늦게까지 나를 기다리신다. (night)

 → My mom waits for me _____.

4 저녁 8시에서 9시 사이에 분수 쇼가 있다. (eight, nine)

 → There is a fountain show _____ p.m.

02 장소를 나타내는 전치사

1 at, on, in

at	+ 비교적 좁은 장소나 지점	~에	at home, at the airport, at the bus stop
on	+ 접촉해 있는 장소, 표면	~에, ~ 위에	on the wall, on the table, on the street
in	+ 비교적 넓은 장소, 공간의 내부 + 하늘, 바다, 우주 등	~에, ~ 안에	in Seoul, in Korea, in the room in the sky, in the sea, in space

There is a stranger **at** the door.
She waited **at** the bus stop for thirty minutes.

There is a large map of Seoul **on** the wall.
Take a book from the bookshelf and place it **on** the table.

A great artist, Pablo Picasso was born **in** Spain.
They will stay **in** space for about 10 months.

2 그 밖의 장소를 나타내는 전치사(구)

over	(떨어져서) ~ 위에	under	(떨어져서) ~ 아래에
in front of	~ 앞에	behind	~ 뒤에
next to / beside / by	~ 옆에	near	~ 근처에
from A to B	A부터 B까지	across from	~ 맞은편에
between A and B	A와 B 사이에	among	(셋 이상) ~ 사이에

We crossed the long bridge **over** the river.
The kids found gifts **under** the Christmas tree.

There is a bus stop **in front of** the Plaza Shopping Mall.
We have a flower garden **behind** our house.

The man **next to** me on the plane was very talkative.
The fans gathered **near** the movie star.

What's the earliest flight time **from** Seoul **to** Paris?
The convenience store is just **across from** the theater.

⊕ **PLUS** **between vs. among**
둘 다 '~ 사이에'라는 뜻이지만 between은 둘 사이일 때, among은 셋 이상 사이일 때 사용한다.
ex. Minsu is sitting **between** the twin brothers.
She is standing **among** many dogs.

Grammar Check Up

A 다음 괄호 안에서 알맞은 것을 고르시오.

1 Sit up straight (at / on / in) the horse.

2 Did you enjoy yourself (at / on / in) the party?

3 How do you spend your time (at / on / in) work?

4 Write your name (at / on / in) the name tag.

5 We can see a lot of windmills (at / on / in) the Netherlands.

B 다음 그림의 상황에 맞도록 빈칸에 알맞은 전치사(구)를 쓰시오.

1 There are some books _____ the sofa.

2 _____ _____ _____ the sofa, there is a yellow table.

3 There is a big box _____ the table.

4 Some toys and dolls are _____ the box.

5 The cute puppies are sleeping _____ the table.

6 _____ _____ the table, their mother is eating food.

C 다음 우리말과 의미가 같도록 괄호 안의 말을 이용하여 문장을 완성하시오.

1 한복 대여점은 고궁 건너편에 있다. (the palace)

  → The *hanbok* rental shop is _____.

2 그 개구리는 돌아가신 엄마를 개울 근처에 묻었다. (the stream)

  → The frog buried its dead mother _____.

3 우리는 시청역 앞에서 만날 예정이다. (City Hall Station)

  → We're going to meet _____.

4 헬리콥터가 불타고 있는 나무들 위에서 날고 있다. (the burning trees)

  → A helicopter is flying _____.

A 다음 빈칸에 공통으로 들어갈 알맞은 말을 [보기]에서 골라 쓰시오.

| 보기 |
| at   on   in   between   from |

1 My uncle is going to join the army _____ March.

   We stayed _____ Los Angeles at that time.

2 Some flowers bloom only _____ night.

   She was talking to her friend _____ the front door.

3 Avoid the sun _____ 10 a.m. and 4 p.m.

   My store is _____ a flower shop and a bookstore.

4 She didn't stay at home _____ New Year's Day.

   Did you see my purse _____ the table?

5 He was U.S. President _____ 2009 to 2016.

   We traveled _____ Paris to Nice by train.

B 다음 우리말과 의미가 같도록 괄호 안의 말을 이용하여 문장을 완성하시오.

1 때때로 그는 다리 아래에서 잠을 잤다. (the bridge)

   → Sometimes, he slept _____.

2 외제 차 한 대가 내 차 앞에서 달리고 있었다. (my car)

   → A foreign car was running _____.

3 모빌이 아기 침대 위에 걸려 있다. (the baby bed)

   → A mobile is hanging _____.

4 우리는 파티가 끝난 후에 집에 늦게 도착했다. (the party)

   → We arrived home late _____.

5 Jessica는 인터뷰하는 동안 매우 긴장했다. (the interview)

   → Jessica felt very nervous _____.

6 나는 재활용 상자 뒤에서 가방 하나를 발견했다. (the recycling box)

   → I found a bag _____.

C 다음 우리말과 의미가 같도록 괄호 안의 말을 바르게 배열하시오. (단, 전치사를 추가할 것)

1 그 영화는 처음부터 끝까지 환상적이었다. (start, fantastic, was, finish)

→ The film _____ .

2 카페 옆에 커피 자판기가 있다니 재미있다. (the cafe, is, a coffee machine, there)

→ It is funny that _____ .

3 그 당시, 사람들은 겨울 동안에 신선한 음식을 구할 수 없었다. (get, the winter, fresh food)

→ At that time, people could not _____ .

4 내일까지 그것에 대한 정보를 수집하자. (tomorrow, information, collect, that, about)

→ Let's _____ .

5 대부분의 아이들이 초등학교 전에 유치원에 다닌다. (kindergarten, go to, elementary school)

→ Most children _____ .

D 괄호 안의 우리말과 표현을 이용하여 질문에 알맞은 대답을 완성하시오.

1 A: When did you leave China?

B: We _____ .
(우리는 2019년에 그 나라를 떠났어. / leave, the country)

2 A: Where did he hide when his father was angry at him?

B: He _____ . (그는 그의 엄마 뒤에 숨었어. / hide)

3 A: Was the girl putting on her dress?

B: No. She _____ .
(그녀는 거울 앞에서 화장하고 있었어. / put on makeup, the mirror)

4 A: How long can the seal dive in the sea?

B: One type of seal can _____ !
(물개 중의 한 종류는 두 시간 동안 잠수할 수 있어! / dive)

5 A: What is the dog doing?

B: It _____ .
(그것은 정육점 건너편에 앉아 있어. / sit, the meat shop)

[01-04] 다음 빈칸에 들어갈 말로 알맞은 것을 고르시오.

01

| _____ a rainy day, I wear a raincoat. |

① At
② On
③ In
④ Until
⑤ During

02

| Frank jogs _____ 7:00 to 8:00 in the morning. |

① at
② for
③ until
④ from
⑤ between

03

| She bumped into a boy and fell _____ the ice. |

① at
② on
③ in
④ over
⑤ under

04

| My aunt lives _____ Melbourne, Australia. |

① in
② on
③ at
④ over
⑤ among

[05-07] 다음 빈칸에 공통으로 들어갈 말로 알맞은 것을 고르시오.

05 내신 빈출

| • Camels usually live _____ the desert.
• Did you take a nap _____ the afternoon? |

① at
② on
③ in
④ for
⑤ next to

06

| • We often do our shopping _____ midnight on hot summer days.
• There were no empty seats _____ the concert. |

① at
② on
③ in
④ to
⑤ by

07

| • He worked in a restaurant _____ two years.
• My dog sleeps _____ three hours in the afternoon. |

① at
② for
③ until
④ while
⑤ during

08 다음 빈칸에 들어갈 말로 알맞지 않은 것은?

| Kevin and Cindy visited us in _____. |

① summer
② October
③ Saturday
④ 2021
⑤ the afternoon

📖 Answers p.19

[09-10] 다음 우리말과 의미가 같도록 빈칸에 들어갈 전치사로 알맞은 것을 고르시오.

09

나는 수업 시간 동안 잠이 들었다.
→ I fell asleep _____ class.

① for
② at
③ from
④ on
⑤ during

10

그 정원은 여름에 아름답다.
→ The garden is lovely _____ summer.

① for
② at
③ in
④ on
⑤ to

11 다음 중 빈칸에 들어가지 <u>않는</u> 것은?

· The letter _____ the desk is mine.
· There are classes _____ Monday to Friday.
· Let's meet _____ the bus stop _____ Monday.
· He won the 'Superstar K' audition _____ 2015.

① at
② in
③ from
④ on
⑤ for

[12-13] 다음 대화의 빈칸에 들어갈 말로 알맞게 짝지어진 것을 고르시오.

12

A: What did you get _____ Children's Day from your mom and dad?
B: I received a gift box from them. Some cookies were _____ it.

① on - in
② on - at
③ at - in
④ during - at
⑤ for - in

13

A: Why did you run from the school _____ the subway station?
B: I had to arrive there _____ 5 o'clock.

① to - by
② to - until
③ at - by
④ for - until
⑤ in - by

[14-15] 다음 그림을 보고, 빈칸에 들어갈 말로 알맞은 것을 고르시오.

14

The fire station is _____ the department store.

① among
② in front of
③ across from
④ between
⑤ next to

15

The museum is _____ the hospital.

① behind
② over
③ between
④ next to
⑤ under

16 다음 우리말을 어법에 맞게 영작할 때 빈칸 ⓐ에 들어갈 말로 알맞은 것은?

빵집은 은행과 꽃집 사이에 있다.
→ The bakery _____ ⓐ _____
_____ _____ the flower shop.

① bank
② is
③ and
④ the
⑤ between

[17-18] 다음 빈칸에 들어갈 말이 나머지와 **다른** 것을 고르시오.

고난도

17 ① The birds live _____ the cage.

② The sun rose high _____ the sky.

③ There is an old clock _____ the wall.

④ My grandma put some eggs _____ the basket.

⑤ Mt. Everest is the highest mountain _____ the world.

18 ① Don't call me _____ the evening.

② My sister was born _____ March of 2011.

③ He usually takes a shower _____ the morning.

④ I have an appointment with the doctor _____ 4.

⑤ Fresh vegetables are more expensive _____ winter.

[19-20] 다음 영화 상영표를 보고, 빈칸에 들어갈 말로 알맞게 짝지어진 것을 고르시오.

Movie Schedule	
Minions	2 p.m. ~ 3 p.m.
Mission Impossible	4 p.m. ~ 6 p.m.
Veteran	7 p.m. ~ 9 p.m.

19

Minions starts _____ two o'clock and shows _____ an hour.

① at - for ② in - for

③ at - in ④ by - during

⑤ in - during

20

Mission Impossible shows _____ *Minions* and shows _____ 4 to 6 p.m.

① behind - during ② after - from

③ before - between ④ behind - from

⑤ after - between

21 다음 우리말을 영어로 바르게 옮긴 것은?

그들은 두바이와 서울 사이에 직항편 운항을 시작할 것이다.

① They will begin non-stop flights from Dubai and Seoul.

② They will begin non-stop flights from Dubai among Seoul.

③ They will begin non-stop flights among Dubai and Seoul.

④ They will begin non-stop flights between Dubai to Seoul.

⑤ They will begin non-stop flights between Dubai and Seoul.

[22-23] 다음 중 어법상 **틀린** 것을 **모두** 고르시오.

고난도

22 ① Tie the rope on the tree.

② Come and sit down next to me.

③ You shouldn't stand behind the car.

④ The baby is sleeping over the bed.

⑤ There is a truck in front of the gate.

23 ① Owls usually hunt at night.

② You may use my car on Saturday.

③ Living conditions were bad for the war.

④ I sit quietly and read a book in the evening.

⑤ They are beginning to spend money in this winter.

[24-25] 다음 중 어법상 옳은 문장의 개수를 고르시오.

고난도
24
ⓐ Will you stay here by tomorrow?
ⓑ We don't go to school in Buddha's Birthday.
ⓒ The airplane leaves at 10 in the morning.
ⓓ In Korea, it snows a lot during the winter.

① 없음　　② 1개　　③ 2개
④ 3개　　⑤ 4개

25
ⓐ Kevin sat next to the driver.
ⓑ Put a cushion behind your back.
ⓒ There is a big park near our school.
ⓓ The train runs between Seoul to Busan.

① 없음　　② 1개　　③ 2개
④ 3개　　⑤ 4개

[26-28] 다음 두 문장의 의미가 같도록 빈칸에 알맞은 전치사를 쓰시오.

26
Mr. White has lunch at the cafeteria, and then he takes a walk.

= Mr. White takes a walk _____ lunch.

27
The teacher is walking in front of the students.

= The students are walking _____ the teacher.

28
My mom started knitting at 3 o'clock and stopped it at 6 o'clock.

= My mom knitted _____ 3 hours.

[29-31] 다음 우리말과 의미가 같도록 괄호 안의 말을 바르게 배열하시오.

29
갑자기 그의 뒤에 머리가 긴 귀신이 나타났다.
(appeared, him, behind, a ghost with long hair)

→ Suddenly _____

_____.

30
세종대왕은 1418년부터 1450년까지 통치했다.
(1418, 1450, to, from, ruled)

→ King Sejong _____.

31
나는 극장 앞에서 자선 공연을 했다.
(of, front, a benefit performance, the theater, in)

→ I gave _____

_____.

32 다음 대화의 밑줄 친 ⓐ~ⓕ 중 어법상 **틀린** 것을 3개 찾아 기호를 쓰고 바르게 고쳐 쓰시오.

> A: What time do you get up ⓐ <u>in the morning</u>?
> B: I usually get up ⓑ <u>on 7 o'clock</u>.
> A: Do you go to school ⓒ <u>after the breakfast</u>?
> B: No. I skip breakfast. I must leave my house ⓓ <u>before 8 o'clock</u>.
> A: You must be hungry. Aren't you hungry ⓔ <u>at the school</u>?
> B: Yes, a little bit.
> A: Then, do you eat lunch ⓕ <u>at noon</u>?
> B: Yes, I do.

(1) _____ → _____

(2) _____ → _____

(3) _____ → _____

33 다음 그림을 보고, 빈칸에 알맞은 말을 [보기]에서 골라 쓰시오.

┌─ 보기 ─────────────────────────┐
  in   in front of   next to   on
└────────────────────────────────┘

(1) A white mouse is _____ a plate.

(2) A gray mouse is _____ a bowl.

(3) Two mice are _____ some cheese.

(4) There is a girl _____ the door.

34 다음 그림을 보고, 각각의 장소를 묘사하는 글을 완성하시오.

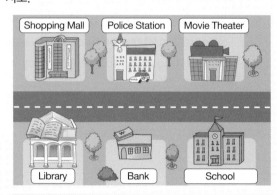

> The movie theater is _____ the police station. The shopping mall is _____ the library. The school is _____ the movie theater. The library is _____ the bank. The police station is _____ the movie theater _____ the shopping mall.

35 다음은 Jack의 하루 일과표이다. 표를 보고 일기를 완성하시오. (단, 숫자는 영어로 쓰시오.)

7 : 00 a.m.	get up
7 : 30 a.m.	have breakfast
8 : 00 a.m.	leave for school
9 : 00 a.m. ~ 12 : 00 p.m.	take classes
1 : 00 p.m. ~ 4 : 00 p.m.	take classes
5 : 00 p.m.	come back home
7 : 00 p.m. ~ 10 : 00 p.m.	do my homework
10 : 00 p.m. ~ 12 : 00 p.m.	break (TV, online games ...)
12 : 30 a.m.	go to bed

> I get up _____ a.m. I have breakfast at seven thirty a.m. I leave for school _____ a.m. I take classes _____ six hours. I come back home _____ p.m. I finish my homework by _____ p.m. I watch TV or play online games for _____. I go to bed _____ one a.m.

Chapter

11

to부정사와 동명사

01 to부정사

1 to부정사의 형태와 의미

to부정사는 「to + 동사원형」의 형태로 동사가 아닌 명사, 부사, 형용사처럼 쓰이는 말이다.

To exercise the brain is not easy. (명사)
We should wear seatbelts **to be** safe. (부사)
A merchant had many shoes **to sell**. (형용사)

2 명사로 쓰이는 to부정사

to부정사가 명사처럼 문장에서 주어, 보어, 목적어 역할을 하며 '~하는 것'으로 해석한다.

1 주어 역할: '~하는 것은'으로 해석하며, 이 경우 보통 가주어 it을 사용하여 「It ~ to부정사」 형태로 쓴다.
　　　　　주어로 쓰인 to부정사는 단수 취급한다.

To watch movies through online streaming *is* interesting.
→ **It** is interesting **to watch** movies through online streaming.

2 보어 역할: ~하는 것(이다)

Our wish is **to keep** peace between the nations.

3 목적어 역할: ~하는 것을

My dad decided **to have** some downtime every weekend.

3 부사로 쓰이는 to부정사

to부정사가 부사처럼 동사, 형용사 등을 수식하여 어떤 일의 목적, 감정의 원인, 결과 등을 나타낸다.

1 목적: ~하기 위해서, ~하러

He turned off the light **to save** electricity.

2 감정의 원인: ~해서

I was surprised **to hear** a cat crying over the rain.

3 결과: (…해서 그 결과) ~하다

The boy grew up **to be** a respected president.

4 형용사로 쓰이는 to부정사

to부정사가 형용사처럼 명사나 대명사를 뒤에서 꾸며 주며 '~할, ~하는'으로 해석한다.

The policeman is helping *the elderly woman* **to collect** the recyclables.
There are *many places* **to see** in Busan.

⊕ PLUS **-thing + 형용사 + to부정사**
-thing으로 끝나는 대명사를 형용사와 함께 수식할 경우 「-thing + 형용사 + to부정사」의 순서로 쓴다.
ex. I want to buy **something warm to wear**.

A 다음 괄호 안에서 알맞은 것을 고르시오.

1 (It / That) is not easy to find a steady job these days.

2 To help other people in need (is / are) rewarding.

3 The man hopes (go / to go) to the North Pole someday.

4 She is knitting a scarf (give / to give) to him.

5 I was pleased to (meet / meeting) my old friend by chance.

B 다음 밑줄 친 to부정사의 쓰임을 [보기]에서 골라 기호를 쓰시오.

┌ 보기 ┐
ⓐ 명사적 용법   ⓑ 형용사적 용법   ⓒ 부사적 용법

1 He decided to change his job this year.

2 Koreans need spoons and chopsticks to eat with.

3 She woke up to find herself alone in the house.

4 My plan for this vacation is to volunteer at an animal shelter.

5 We should all do our best to live in a peaceful world.

C 다음 우리말과 의미가 같도록 괄호 안의 말을 이용하여 문장을 완성하시오.

1 나의 언니의 직업은 인테리어 디자인을 하는 것이다. (do, interior design)

→ My sister's job is _____ .

2 나 혼자 그 일을 끝마치는 것은 힘들었다. (finish, by oneself)

→ It was hard _____ .

3 나는 시험에서 많은 실수를 해서 슬펐다. (make, a lot of mistakes)

→ I was sad _____ on the test.

D 다음 문장의 밑줄 친 부분의 뜻을 우리말로 쓰시오.

1 The prince grew up to become a cruel king.

2 He cooked some food to give to his sick dog.

3 They turned on the TV to watch the baseball match.

4 It was interesting to prepare for the surprise party.

5 They are happy to make new friends in the club.

02 동명사

1 동명사의 형태와 의미

1 동명사는 「동사원형 + -ing」의 형태로 동사가 아닌 명사처럼 쓰이는 말이며, 문장에서 주어, 보어, 목적어 역할을 한다.

Living without smartphones is difficult for us these days. (주어)

His wish is **becoming** a famous webtoon artist. (보어)

She began **wearing** her school uniform every day. (목적어)

2 동명사는 명사로 쓰이는 to부정사와 같은 역할을 한다.

Watching the weather report is useful.

= **To watch** the weather report is useful.

> **⊕ PLUS** 동명사 vs. 현재분사
> 둘 다 「동사원형 + -ing」로 형태는 같지만 역할이 다르다.
> · 동명사: 명사로 쓰이며 주어, 보어, 목적어 역할을 함
>   ex. **Sleeping** in the car is dangerous.
> · 현재분사: 형용사로 쓰이며 진행형에 쓰임
>   ex. Who is the **crying** child over there?

2 동명사의 쓰임

1 주어: '~하는 것은'으로 해석하며 단수 취급한다.

Telling sad news to them is hard for me.

Traveling in Paris was a great experience.

2 보어: ~하는 것(이다)

My last job was **selling** books on TV home shopping.

The best way to get there is **taking** the subway.

3 동사의 목적어: ~하는 것을

When can you finish **writing** a book review?

I like **staying** home and **taking** a rest on weekends.

4 전치사의 목적어: 동명사는 명사처럼 전치사의 목적어로도 쓸 수 있다. *cf.* to부정사는 전치사의 목적어로 쓸 수 없다.

I'm doing my group project about **designing** classroom walls.
_{to design (×)}

> **⊕ PLUS** 동명사 vs. to부정사
> 둘 다 목적어로 쓰이지만 문장의 동사에 따라 취할 수 있는 목적어가 다르다.
> · 동명사만 목적어로 취하는 동사: enjoy, finish, mind, avoid, stop, keep, practice, give up 등
> · to부정사만 목적어로 취하는 동사: want, hope, wish, would like, decide, plan, learn, promise 등
> · 둘 다 목적어로 취하는 동사: like, love, hate, begin, start, continue 등

目 Answers p.21

A 다음 괄호 안에서 알맞은 것을 <u>모두</u> 고르시오.

1 The fat cat loves (lying / to lie) on the floor all day.

2 The new worker decided (to get / getting) a driver's license.

3 I'm looking forward to (see / seeing) you in person.

4 We're trying to avoid (to start / starting) a war.

5 (Overeating / To overeat) is not good for your health.

B 다음 문장의 밑줄 친 부분을 어법상 알맞은 형태로 고쳐 쓰시오.

1 How about <u>meet</u> an hour early at the station?

2 The company's new business is <u>make</u> electric cars.

3 Would you mind <u>to mail</u> this letter on your way to the gym?

4 <u>Walk</u> up the stairs is impossible for my grandma.

5 He was the first person to finish <u>solve</u> the puzzle.

C 다음 빈칸에 들어갈 알맞은 말을 [보기]에서 골라 알맞은 형태로 바꿔 쓰시오. (단, 한 번씩만 쓸 것)

보기

| look | have | tell | play | hurt |

1 _____ around the old castle was interesting.

2 Don't be afraid of _____ people to stop smoking.

3 I really hate _____ other people's feelings.

4 My little sister enjoys _____ with her dolls.

5 His wish is _____ some true friends.

D 다음 우리말과 의미가 같도록 괄호 안의 말을 이용하여 문장을 완성하시오.

1 제 아들의 돌잔치에 와 주셔서 감사합니다. (come, first birthday party)

→ Thank you for _____.

2 그 사원 안에서는 반바지를 입는 것을 피해야 한다. (wear, shorts)

→ We should avoid _____ in the temple.

3 아름다운 돌을 수집하는 것은 내 취미 중 하나이다. (collect, beautiful stones)

→ _____ is one of my hobbies.

A 다음 우리말과 의미가 같도록 괄호 안의 말을 이용하여 문장을 완성하시오.

1 나의 삼촌은 나무로 물건 만드는 것을 잘하신다. (make, things)

  → My uncle is good at _____ out of wood.

2 그러한 야생 구역에서 혼자 머무는 것은 위험하다. (stay alone, a wild area)

  → It is dangerous _____ .

3 그의 임무는 모든 회원들에게 문자 메시지를 보내는 것이다. (send, text messages)

  → His mission is _____ to all members.

4 그들은 그 소파를 일주일 이내에 배달하기로 약속했다. (deliver, the sofa)

  → They promised _____ within a week.

5 나의 부모님은 나의 옛날 사진 보는 것을 즐기신다. (look at, my old photos)

  → My parents enjoy _____ .

B 다음 우리말과 의미가 같도록 괄호 안의 말을 바르게 배열하시오.

1 새로운 것을 발견하는 것은 항상 흥미롭다. (exciting, to, always, discover, something, new)

  → It is _____ .

2 Linda의 직업은 건물을 디자인하는 것이다. (buildings, design, to)

  → Linda's job is _____ .

3 그는 먹을 약간의 과일을 사러 슈퍼마켓에 갔다. (some fruit, eat, to, buy, to)

  → He went to the supermarket _____ .

4 우리 할아버지는 100살까지 사셨다. (100 years old, lived, to be)

  → My grandfather _____ .

5 나는 공원에서 몇몇 가수들을 보고 깜짝 놀랐다. (see, a few, surprised, singers, to)

  → I was _____ at the park.

○─────○ 📖 Answers p.21

C 다음 두 문장을 한 문장으로 나타낼 때 빈칸에 알맞은 말을 쓰시오.

1 I will improve my English. That's my first goal this year.

→ My first goal this year is _____.

2 Harry was very angry. He saw a lot of trash on the mountain.

→ Harry was very angry _____.

3 He practiced hard to break the world record. He didn't give up.

→ He didn't give up _____.

4 I wanted to write down my daily life in a notebook. So I bought one.

→ I bought a notebook _____.

5 We will do volunteer work at a nursing home. How about doing it together?

→ How about _____ _____ together?

D 다음 우리말과 의미가 같도록 괄호 안에 주어진 말을 이용하여 영작하시오.

1 너의 꿈을 포기하지 않는 것은 정말 중요하다. (it, really important, give up)

→ _____

2 나는 그날 한 마디도 하고 싶지 않았다. (want, say a word)

→ _____

3 우리는 앉아서 쉴 장소를 찾고 있었다. (look for, a place, sit and take a rest)

→ _____

4 그는 자정까지 계속해서 일했다. (continue, work, until midnight)

→ _____

5 한밤중에 시끄럽게 해서 죄송합니다. (be sorry for, make noise, in the middle of the night)

→ _____

[01-04] 다음 빈칸에 들어갈 말로 알맞은 것을 고르시오.

01

> I'm so excited _____ the actor in the hit drama.

① see   ② saw
③ sees   ④ to see
⑤ to seeing

02

> _____ the chef's recipe is easy for us.

① Follow   ② Follows
③ Following   ④ To followed
⑤ To Following

03

> She is knitting woolen hats _____ to the African babies.

① send   ② sends
③ sending   ④ to send
⑤ to sending

04

> Don't drink too much water before _____ to bed.

① go   ② to go
③ goes   ④ to going
⑤ going

[05-07] 다음 빈칸에 공통으로 들어갈 말로 알맞은 것을 고르시오.

05

> · He grew up _____ respect from many people.
> · I want _____ a friend like her.

① have   ② having
③ to have   ④ had
⑤ to having

06

> · He is _____ around the world on his bike without any money.
> · He is old and tired of _____ long distances.

① travel   ② traveled
③ traveling   ④ to travel
⑤ to travels

07

> · He _____ to prepare meals for his family.
> · The monkey _____ taking a bath in the hot spring.

① likes   ② minds
③ plans   ④ wishes
⑤ keeps

08 다음 우리말을 어법에 맞게 영작할 때 빈칸 ⓐ에 들어갈 말로 알맞은 것은?

> 가족과 함께 할 몇 가지 재미있는 것들을 생각해 보아라.
> → Think of _____ _____ _____
> _____ ⓐ _____ with your family.

① to   ② do
③ things   ④ some
⑤ interesting

09 다음 중 밑줄 친 to의 쓰임이 나머지와 <u>다른</u> 것은?

① Are you ready <u>to</u> order?

② I like <u>to</u> cook Italian food.

③ I want <u>to</u> have many friends.

④ He hopes <u>to</u> be an astronaut.

⑤ Sometimes I talk <u>to</u> her about you.

[10-12] 다음 빈칸에 들어갈 말로 알맞지 <u>않은</u> 것을 고르시오.

10

> The dog _____ to sleep under the shade of the trees.

① likes ② loves

③ continues ④ enjoys

⑤ starts

11

> My cousin _____ riding a bike along the river.

① loved ② planned

③ started ④ enjoyed

⑤ practiced

고난도
12

> Mandy hates _____.

① drinking black coffee

② to go out when it rains

③ tie her hair with a band

④ to take selfies

⑤ watching historical dramas

[13-14] 다음 우리말을 영어로 바르게 옮긴 것을 고르시오.

13

> 나는 입을 예쁜 것이 필요하다.

① I need something pretty wearing.

② I need pretty something to wear.

③ I need something to wear pretty.

④ I need pretty something wearing.

⑤ I need something pretty to wear.

14

> 야생 버섯을 먹는 것은 위험하다.

① Eat wild mushrooms is dangerous.

② It is dangerous eat wild mushrooms.

③ It is dangerous to eat wild mushrooms.

④ This is dangerous to eat wild mushrooms.

⑤ That is dangerous to eat wild mushrooms.

[15-16] 다음 빈칸에 들어갈 말로 알맞게 짝지어진 것을 고르시오.

내신 빈출
15

> · We finished _____ the swing.
> · I decided _____ kind to others.

① paint – to be ② painting – to be

③ painting – being ④ to paint – to be

⑤ to paint – being

16

> · My sister's hobby is _____ origami.
> · Semi went to the cafeteria _____ lunch.

① make – to eat ② makes – eat

③ making – eating ④ making – to eat

⑤ to make – eating

고난도
17 다음 중 어법상 틀린 것은?

① Tony wanted to get something drinking.

② Amy went to the library to return a book.

③ Jack is interested in watching horror movies.

④ Sam decided to make some cookies for her.

⑤ I'm good at memorizing the phone numbers.

20 다음 중 어법상 틀린 것을 <u>모두</u> 고르면?

① Mom decided buying a new car.

② Henry turned off the TV to study.

③ The horses stopped to run suddenly.

④ We have nothing special to offer you.

⑤ Mom uses the Internet to buy some cat food.

[18-19] 다음 [보기]의 밑줄 친 부분과 쓰임이 같은 것을 고르시오.

내신 빈출
18

| 보기 |
She wants <u>to know</u> his phone number.

① Allen took a bus <u>to go</u> to the museum.

② I have something important <u>to tell</u> you.

③ I was pleased <u>to see</u> my favorite writer.

④ <u>To sleep</u> regularly is good for your health.

⑤ He went to the post office <u>to send</u> a letter.

[21-22] 다음 중 어법상 옳은 문장의 개수를 고르시오.

고난도
21

ⓐ Please give me to drink something cold.

ⓑ He's afraid of looking foolish in front of his friends.

ⓒ Matthew will learn controlling a drone.

ⓓ Mike was surprised to hear her quiet voice.

① 없음　　　　② 1개　　　　③ 2개

④ 3개　　　　⑤ 4개

19

| 보기 |
Tom ran <u>to kick</u> the ball.

① Daniel wants <u>to learn</u> Korean.

② She was happy <u>to pass</u> the test.

③ There are many places <u>to visit</u> in China.

④ Mina's goal is <u>to lose</u> weight this summer.

⑤ I loved <u>to make</u> snowmen when I was a child.

22

ⓐ Mozart lived being 35 years old.

ⓑ Cheating on exams are very bad.

ⓒ It isn't easy to live out of the city.

ⓓ I enjoy napping in the afternoon.

① 없음　　　　② 1개　　　　③ 2개

④ 3개　　　　⑤ 4개

[23-24] 다음 중 밑줄 친 부분의 쓰임이 나머지와 다른 것을 고르시오.

23
① My job is to take care of patients.
② To do your best is very important.
③ I want to get some rest right now.
④ The team's goal is to win the game.
⑤ I have a lot of homework to do today.

내신 빈출
24
① Fishing on a boat is fun.
② My sister is making paper dolls.
③ Don't be afraid of making mistakes.
④ Her dream is becoming a cartoonist.
⑤ How about going shopping this Friday?

25 다음 우리말을 영어로 바르게 옮긴 것은?

> 헬멧 없이 자전거를 타는 것은 위험하다.

① Ride a bike without a helmet is dangerous.
② Riding a bike without a helmet is dangerous.
③ To ride a bike without a helmet are dangerous.
④ To riding a bike without a helmet is dangerous.
⑤ Rides a bike with without a helmet are dangerous.

[26-27] 다음 우리말과 의미가 같도록 괄호 안의 말을 이용하여 문장을 완성하시오.

26
> 내 우산을 찾아 줘서 고마워. (find, my umbrella)

→ Thank you for _____ .

27
> 저에게 보여 줄 것이 있나요? (show, me)

→ Do you have anything _____ ?

[28-29] 다음 두 문장을 to부정사를 이용하여 한 문장으로 바꿀 때 빈칸에 알맞은 말을 쓰시오.

28
> The workers were pleased.
> They received a bonus.

→ The workers were _____ .

29
> Some doctors visited the island.
> They wanted to look after the patients.

→ Some doctors visited the island _____
_____ .

[30-32] 다음 우리말과 의미가 같도록 괄호 안의 말을 바르게 배열하시오. (단, 필요하면 형태를 바꿀 것)

30
> Nancy는 빵을 좀 사기 위해 빵집에 갔다.
> (buy, some bread, the bakery)

→ Nancy went to _____ .

31

계단을 이용하는 것은 지구에 좋다.
(the stairs, good, is, use)

→ _____ for the earth.

32

우리 가구를 옮길 트럭이 밖에서 기다리고 있다.
(move, our furniture, a truck)

→ _____ is
waiting outside.

33 다음은 이사 간 친구 Jack이 Billy에게 보낸 편지이다. 밑줄 친 ⓐ~ⓔ 중 어법상 **틀린** 것을 3개 찾아 기호를 쓰고 바르게 고쳐 쓰시오.

Hi, Billy. How are you? I'm well now. Thank you ⓐ for send me a letter. I was very glad ⓑ to receive your letter. Thank you for the present and the book, too. I enjoyed ⓒ to read the book a lot. It was very interesting. I was happy ⓓ to hear that you are coming here. I look forward ⓔ to see you soon. I miss you and the other friends a lot. Let's keep in touch.

Love, Jack

(1) _____ → _____
(2) _____ → _____
(3) _____ → _____

34 다음 (A), (B)의 어구를 하나씩 사용하여 [보기]처럼 to부정사를 포함한 완전한 문장으로 쓰시오.

(A)	I saved money
	She turned on the light
	Sarah went to the hairshop
	A lot of people go to Egypt
(B)	have a haircut
	look for her bag
	see the Pyramids
	buy his birthday present

┌ 보기 ┐
A lot of people go to Egypt to see the Pyramids.

(1) _____
(2) _____
(3) _____

35 다음은 James의 주말여행 계획표이다. 표를 보고 글을 완성하시오.

PLAN ✈	Take a trip to Bear's Resort
To Do ☺	ski 1 : 00 p.m. ~ 3 : 30 p.m.
	swim 8 : 00 p.m. ~ 9 : 30 p.m.
Not To Do ☹	play computer games, read a book

I am planning _____ Bear's Resort. I want _____ in the day and _____ at night. I don't want _____ _____ and _____ there. I can't wait my trip.

Chapter

12

문장의 종류

01 의문사가 있는 의문문

1 who, what, which

1 who (누구, 누가): 사람에 대해 물을 때 쓰며, 목적격은 whom(누구를)이지만 who를 더 자주 사용한다.
Who bought these donuts for you? – My brother bought them for me.
Who(m) did your mom cook this food for? – For the guests.

2 what (무엇): 사물에 대해 묻거나 사람의 직업 등을 물을 때 쓰며, 의문형용사(무슨 ~)로도 쓰인다.
What did he study at university? – He studied Politics.
What *kind* of webtoons are you interested in? – I'm interested in Korean webtoons.

3 which (어느 것): 주로 정해진 대상에서 선택을 물을 때 쓰며, 의문형용사(어느 ~)로도 쓰인다.
Which is cheaper, an e-book or an audio book? – An audio book is cheaper than an e-book by 1,000 won.
Which *dessert* do you want, ice cream or cake? – I want both of them.

⊕ PLUS **whose** (누구의, 누구의 것)
who의 소유격, 소유대명사로 소유를 물을 때 쓴다.
ex. **Whose** is this pencil case? / **Whose** pencil case is this? – It's Dave's.

2 when, where, why, how

when	언제 〈시간〉	why	왜 〈이유〉
where	어디서, 어디에 〈장소〉	how	어떻게, 어떤 〈방법, 상태〉

When will there be COVID-19 vaccines for children? – We don't know for sure.
Where is this place on the map? – It's right here.
Why does Johnny look so happy? – Because he got a gift from his grandparents.
How can I get to City Hall? – You can get there by subway.

3 how + 형용사 / 부사

1 하나의 의문사처럼 쓰여 나이, 키, 빈도, 기간, 거리, 무게, 높이, 개수, 양 등을 물을 때 사용한다.

how old	how tall	how often	how long	how far
몇 살의	얼마나 큰[높은]	얼마나 자주	얼마나 오래[긴]	얼마나 먼

How often do you meet your old friend? – We usually meet about once a month.
How long does it take to interview two people? – It usually takes 3 hours.

2 how many + 셀 수 있는 명사의 복수형 (개수) / how much + 셀 수 없는 명사 (양)
How many *hours* a day do you watch YouTube videos? – I watch them about 3 hours.
How much *time* do you need to do that? – I need one hour.

A 다음 괄호 안에서 알맞은 것을 고르시오.

1 (Which / Whose) umbrella did he borrow?

2 (Who / Where) do you have lunch with at lunchtime?

3 (Where / When) do they get back from their trip?

4 (How / Why) does this spaghetti taste so strange?

5 (Which / What) hotel will you stay at, the Park View Hotel or the Hamilton Hotel?

B 다음 대화의 빈칸에 알맞은 의문사를 쓰시오.

1 A: _____ does Laura want as her math teacher? B: She wants Ms. White.

2 A: _____ would you like your eggs? B: Make the eggs sunny-side up, please.

3 A: _____ color will you use to paint it? B: I'll use white and pink.

4 A: _____ did you live before you moved here? B: I lived in a small town.

5 A: _____ does your mom go to work? B: She goes by subway.

C 다음 문장에서 어법상 어색한 부분을 찾아 바르게 고쳐 쓰시오.

1 A: What movies do you like better, horrors or comedies? _____ → _____
    B: I like comedies.

2 A: How long is it to the nearest hospital? _____ → _____
    B: It's 10 km from here.

3 A: How many pocket money do you use in a month? _____ → _____
    B: I use about 50,000 won.

D 다음 우리말과 의미가 같도록 알맞은 의문사를 써서 문장을 완성하시오.

1 너는 가족들에게 '사랑해'라고 얼마나 자주 말하니?

    → _____ "I love you" to your family?

2 너는 하루에 몇 잔의 커피를 마시니?

    → _____ in a day?

3 너는 운전을 배웠을 때 몇 살이었니?

    → _____ when you learned to drive?

02 명령문, 청유문

1 명령문

상대방에게 '~해라', '~하지 마라'라고 명령하거나 요청, 부탁할 때 사용하는 문장이다.

1 긍정 명령문: 동사원형 ~. (~해라.)

Be quiet, please.

Remember the safety rule!

Check out the book from the library.

2 부정 명령문: Don't[Never] + 동사원형 ~. (~하지 마라.)

Don't be shy about giving your opinion.

Don't look back, and **don't stop** until you've reached safety.

Never give up when faced with a challenge.

> ⊕ **PLUS**
> - 명령문의 앞이나 뒤에 please를 붙이면 공손한 표현이 된다. please가 문장 뒤에 오면 please 앞에 콤마(,)를 쓴다.
>   ex. **Please** open the door. / Open the door**, please**.
> - 명령문 + and / or
>
> | 명령문 + and | ~해라, 그러면 …할 것이다 | **Press** the blue button, **and** the door will open. |
> |---|---|---|
> | 명령문 + or | ~해라, 그렇지 않으면 …할 것이다 | **Press** the blue button, **or** the door will close. |

2 청유문

상대방에게 자신과 함께 '~하자'라고 청유 또는 제안할 때 사용하는 문장으로, Let's로 시작한다. Let's는 Let us의 줄임말이다.

1 긍정 청유문: Let's + 동사원형 ~. (~하자.)

Let's be proud of our country, Korea.

Let's have a race to the end of the beach.

Let's watch the director's new film.

2 부정 청유문: Let's not + 동사원형 ~. (~하지 말자.)

Let's not be too serious!

Let's not quarrel about such unimportant matters.

Let's not buy anything in that store.

> ⊕ **PLUS** 제안하는 다양한 표현
> **Let's enjoy** ourselves at the festival.
> = **Shall we enjoy** ourselves at the festival?
> = **How[What] about enjoying** ourselves at the festival?
> = **Why don't we enjoy** ourselves at the festival?

Grammar Check Up

A 다음 괄호 안에서 알맞은 것을 고르시오.

1 (Are / Be) quick about it.

2 (Not / Don't) talk a lot on the phone.

3 Let's (build / builds) a sandcastle on the beach.

4 (Never fly / Fly never) the drones in this area.

5 (Don't let's / Let's not) travel by ship in the future.

B 다음 문장을 괄호 안의 지시대로 바꿔 쓰시오.

1 You should open the package carefully. (긍정 명령문으로)

    → _____

2 Why don't we wait until the prices are lower? (Let's를 사용한 청유문으로)

    → _____

3 You shouldn't do business with a friend. (부정 명령문으로)

    → _____

C 다음 문장에서 어법상 <u>어색한</u> 부분을 찾아 바르게 고쳐 쓰시오.

1 Let's to be true friends.   _____ → _____

2 Don't are afraid of wild animals in the forest.   _____ → _____

3 Chooses the freshest watermelon among them.   _____ → _____

4 Let's don't cross that old wooden bridge.   _____ → _____

5 Never clicks links from unknown sources.   _____ → _____

D 다음 우리말과 의미가 같도록 괄호 안의 말을 이용하여 문장을 완성하시오.

1 쇼핑 센터 대신에 전통 시장에서 쇼핑을 하자. (shop, at the traditional market)

    → _____ instead of the shopping center.

2 우리가 통화할 때 절대 우리 대화를 녹음하지 마시오. (record, our conversation)

    → _____ when we talk on the phone.

3 지난 실수는 잊어버려라. 지난 얘기는 꺼내지 말자. (forget, bring)

    → _____ about the past mistakes. _____ the past.

03 부가의문문, 감탄문

1 부가의문문

상대방에게 어떤 사실을 확인하거나 동의를 구할 때 평서문 뒤에 덧붙이는 의문문으로, '그렇지?', '그렇지 않니?'로 해석한다.

1 부가의문문 만들기: 긍정문 뒤에는 부정의 부가의문문, 부정문 뒤에는 긍정의 부가의문문을 쓴다.

평서문	부가의문문	규칙
긍정문,	동사 + not + 주어?	1. 동사: be동사 → be동사, 조동사 → 조동사, 일반동사 → do동사
부정문,	동사 + 주어?	2. 주어: 항상 대명사 사용 3. 부정문: 축약형 사용

You *are* thinking about buying the tablet PC, **aren't you**?
The movie *was* really boring, **wasn't it**?

Nick *will* be our class president, **won't he**?
James *can't* speak Japanese well, **can he**?

She *had* a graduation concert yesterday, **didn't she**?
You *don't* like others who are different, **do you**?

2 부가의문문에 대한 대답: 대답하는 내용이 긍정이면 Yes, 부정이면 No로 답한다.

They will go to Spain, **won't they**?
- **Yes**, they **will**. / **No**, they **won't**.

Mary is talking nonsense, **isn't she**?
- **Yes**, she **is**. / **No**, she **isn't**.

⊕ **PLUS** 명령문과 청유문의 부가의문문

명령문, will you?	~해라, 알았지?	Do your homework, **will you**?
Let's ~, shall we?	~하자, 그럴 거지?	Let's watch TV, **shall we**?

2 감탄문

'정말[매우] ~하구나!'의 의미로 기쁨, 슬픔, 놀람 등의 감정을 표현하는 문장이다. 감탄문은 의문사 what 또는 how로 시작한다.

what으로 시작하는 감탄문	What + a(n) + 형용사 + 단수명사(+ 주어 + 동사)!
how로 시작하는 감탄문	How + 형용사 / 부사(+ 주어 + 동사)!

What a wonderful day it is!
How fresh the salad is!

⊕ **PLUS** what + 형용사 + 복수명사 / 셀 수 없는 명사(+ 주어 + 동사)!
what 감탄문에서 명사가 복수명사이거나 셀 수 없는 명사일 경우 부정관사 a 또는 an을 쓰지 않는다.
ex. **What terrible traffic jams** they are!
What tasty chocolate it is!

A 다음 괄호 안에서 알맞은 것을 고르시오.

1 The girl can stand on her head, (doesn't / can't) she?

2 Emma wants to move to a new apartment, (isn't / doesn't) she?

3 To eat too much isn't good for the health, (is / did) it?

4 (What / How) a beautiful night it is!

5 (What / How) peaceful this place is!

B 다음 빈칸에 알맞은 부가의문문을 써서 문장을 완성하시오.

1 That old tree looks so ugly, _____?

2 Let's spend more time with our family, _____?

3 Bob is bored with his job in the big city, _____?

4 The mountain climbers didn't start a fire, _____?

5 Pick me up at the railway station tomorrow, _____?

C 다음 문장을 감탄문으로 바꿔 쓸 때 빈칸에 알맞은 말을 쓰시오.

1 They are very dangerous stairs. → _____ they are!

2 The turtle is very slow. → _____ the turtle is!

3 The politician is very honest. → _____ the politician is!

4 The 3-D technology is very interesting. → _____ the 3-D technology is!

5 They are really beautiful flowers. → _____ they are!

D 다음 우리말과 의미가 같도록 괄호 안의 말을 이용하여 문장을 완성하시오.

1 그 이야기는 한국에서부터 전해졌어, 그렇지 않니? (from Korea)

→ The story is _____, _____?

2 당신들의 눈은 정말로 중요해요! (important)

→ _____ your eyes are!

3 그들은 정말 무례한 파파라치구나! (rude, paparazzi)

→ _____ they are!

A 다음 우리말과 의미가 같도록 괄호 안의 말을 이용하여 문장을 완성하시오.

1 너는 그 인형을 어디에서 샀니? (buy)

→ _____ the doll?

2 왜 명왕성은 행성이 아니니? (Pluto)

→ _____ a planet?

3 코미디 프로그램과 다큐멘터리 중 어떤 프로그램을 보고 싶니? (program, see)

→ _____, comedy program or documentary?

4 더러운 손으로 입을 만지지 마라. (touch, your mouth)

→ _____ with your dirty hands.

5 Kevin과 Ann은 깜짝 파티를 할 거지, 그렇지 않니? (will, have)

→ Kevin and Ann _____ a surprise party, _____?

B 다음 우리말과 의미가 같도록 괄호 안의 말을 바르게 배열하시오.

1 그것은 정말 작은 새구나! (it, a, what, is, bird, small, !)

→ _____

2 그녀는 이탈리아에서 얼마나 오래 살았니? (how, did, long, she, live, in, Italy, ?)

→ _____

3 지금은 그녀에게 화내지 말자. (let's, not, be, with, her, angry, right now)

→ _____

4 Susan은 어떻게 그녀의 반지를 찾았니? (find, Susan, her ring, how, did, ?)

→ _____

5 너는 제과점에서 누구를 만날 거니? (at the bakery, will, meet, who, you, ?)

→ _____

C 다음 괄호 안의 지시대로 주어진 상황 속의 인물에게 할 말을 완성하시오.

1 I want to make a time capsule with Lucy together. (Let's 제안문으로)

to Lucy: _____ with me.

2 I think that Tina should improve her scores on the next exams. (명령문으로)

to Tina: _____

3 I am surprised at Henry's chair. It is really comfortable. (형용사를 강조하는 감탄문으로)

to Henry: _____

4 I'm surprised at the web application Andy made. It is very useful. (명사를 강조하는 감탄문으로)

to Andy: _____

5 I think Kate had a bad dream last night. (부가의문문으로)

to Kate: _____

D 다음 우리말과 의미가 같도록 괄호 안에 주어진 말을 이용하여 영작하시오.

1 밤에 잘 자고 싶으면, 낮잠을 자지 마라. (take a nap)

→ _____ if you want to sleep well at night.

2 실종된 사람은 키가 얼마나 되나요? (the missing person)

→ _____

3 우리와 함께 얼마나 오래 머무르실 계획입니까? (be planning to, stay)

→ _____

4 그 예술가는 우리보다 더 창의적이야, 그렇지 않니? (the artist, more creative)

→ _____

5 새들이 정말 빨리 날고 있구나! (fast, fly)

→ _____

[01-04] 다음 빈칸에 들어갈 말로 알맞은 것을 고르시오.

01

> A: _____ was Brian late for school?
> B: Because he missed the school bus.

① How   ② Why
③ When   ④ Where
⑤ Which

02

> _____ in line.

① No cut   ② Not cut
③ Don't cut   ④ Aren't use
⑤ Don't cutting

03

> The cat can't climb down the tree,
> _____?

① is it   ② does it
③ can it   ④ doesn't it
⑤ can't it

04

> _____ bitter the medicine tastes!

① How   ② What
③ Be   ④ Very
⑤ Really

내신 빈출

05 다음 대화의 빈칸에 공통으로 들어갈 말로 알맞은 것은?

> A: May I help you?
> B: Yes, please. I'm looking for a shirt for my dad.
> A: _____ does your father do?
> B: He is a farmer.
> A: _____ color do you want?
> B: Green, please.

① How   ② What
③ Which   ④ Where
⑤ Who

[06-07] 다음 대화의 빈칸에 알맞은 의문사를 쓰시오.

06

> A: _____ did you take this picture?
> B: I took it last week.

07

> A: _____ will you choose, buying a new phone or fixing your phone?
> B: I will buy a new one.

[08-10] 다음 빈칸에 알맞은 부가의문문을 쓰시오.

08

> Your sister likes potato pizza,
> _____?

09

> That electric car on TV is perfect,
> _____?

10

You will have dinner with Jason,
_____?

📖 Answers p.23

[14-15] 다음 문장 중 의미가 나머지와 다른 것을 고르시오.

14 ① Let's make the fruitcake for mom.
② Please make the fruitcake for mom.
③ Shall we make the fruitcake for mom?
④ How about making the fruitcake for mom?
⑤ Why don't we make the fruitcake for mom?

[11-12] 다음 빈칸에 들어갈 말로 알맞게 짝지어진 것을 고르시오.

내신 빈출
11

· _____ tall players they are!
· _____ nice the bike is!

① How – How
② What – How
③ How – What
④ What – What
⑤ What – Which

15 ① Don't take photos in the art museum.
② Never take photos in the art museum.
③ Let's not take photos in the art museum.
④ You mustn't take photos in the art museum.
⑤ You shouldn't take photos in the art museum.

12

· _____ is his nickname?
· _____ will you go tomorrow?

① Who – Where
② Who – When
③ Which – What
④ What – Who
⑤ What – Where

고난도
16 다음 중 밑줄 친 When[when]의 쓰임이 나머지와 다른 것은?

① When did you come back?
② Do you know when the class starts?
③ When are you going to buy this book?
④ I don't talk to mom when she is angry.
⑤ Can you remember when Peter's birthday is?

13 다음 중 빈칸에 들어갈 말이 나머지와 다른 것은?

① _____ a nice day it is!
② _____ kind your sister is!
③ _____ tall trees those are!
④ _____ useful information it is!
⑤ _____ a big dress the girl wears!

내신 빈출

17 다음 빈칸 (A), (B), (C)에 들어갈 말로 알맞게 짝지어진 것은?

> · She will teach math, ___(A)___ ?
>
> · Let's have a look at it, ___(B)___ ?
>
> · You don't need it, ___(C)___ ?

	(A)		(B)		(C)
①	will she	–	shall we	–	don't it
②	won't she	–	let we	–	do you
③	will she	–	shall we	–	do you
④	won't she	–	shall we	–	do you
⑤	will she	–	let we	–	does it

[18-19] 다음 우리말을 영어로 바르게 옮긴 것을 고르시오.

18

> 너는 문을 잠그지 않았지, 그렇지?

① You locked the door, did you?

② You locked the door, didn't you?

③ You didn't lock the door, did you?

④ You didn't lock the door, were you?

⑤ You didn't lock the door, didn't you?

19

> 정말 환상적인 석양이구나!

① How fantastic sunset is!

② What fantastic sunset is!

③ How a fantastic sunset it is!

④ What fantastic a sunset it is!

⑤ What a fantastic sunset it is!

[20-21] 다음 짝지어진 대화 중 어색한 것을 고르시오.

20 ① A: Whose backpack is that?

  B: It is Minsu's.

② A: How does he go to work?

  B: He goes to work by car.

③ A: Where is the bookstore?

  B: It is near the subway station.

④ A: Which do you want, coffee or tea?

  B: Yes, I want a cup of coffee.

⑤ A: Who is the woman in the photo?

  B: She is my aunt.

21 ① A: How old is your dog?

  B: It is only 3 months old.

② A: How far is the hospital?

  B: I go there by bus.

③ A: How long did you live in Jeju?

  B: For five years.

④ A: How often does he take a shower?

  B: Every day.

⑤ A: How much are these sneakers?

  B: They are 22 dollars.

[22-23] 다음 중 어법상 틀린 것을 모두 고르시오.

22 ① It isn't a sad story, is it?

② Don't make a noise, do you?

③ Sam didn't use my laptop, did he?

④ James lost his camera, doesn't he?

⑤ Plastic is bad for the environment, isn't it?

23 ① What cute the robot is!

② How nice gloves he has!

③ What a good friend James is!

④ What a beautiful night it was!

⑤ How exciting the golf game is!

[24-25] 다음 중 어법상 옳은 것으로 알맞게 짝지어진 것을 고르시오.

24
> ⓐ How high is that hill?
> ⓑ Why did Fabien move to Seoul?
> ⓒ What is her eraser, this or that?
> ⓓ When did you watch the musical?
> ⓔ How much lemons are there in the basket?

① ⓑ, ⓒ   ② ⓒ, ⓔ

③ ⓐ, ⓑ, ⓓ   ④ ⓒ, ⓓ, ⓔ

⑤ ⓐ, ⓒ, ⓓ, ⓔ

고난도
25
> ⓐ Please helps your brother.
> ⓑ Not be angry at me, please.
> ⓒ Don't worry about the exam.
> ⓓ Let's going to the Italian restaurant.
> ⓔ Put the trash in the trash can.

① ⓑ, ⓒ   ② ⓒ, ⓔ

③ ⓐ, ⓒ, ⓔ   ④ ⓒ, ⓓ, ⓔ

⑤ ⓐ, ⓑ, ⓓ, ⓔ

[26-27] 다음 주어진 문장을 명령문으로 바꿔 쓰시오.

26
> You should wait in line to order food.

→ _____

27
> You shouldn't go down to the basement.

→ _____

[28-29] 다음 주어진 문장을 감탄문으로 바꿔 쓰시오.

28
> The traditional Korean story is very touching.

→ How _____ !

29
> The love story has a very happy ending.

→ What _____ !

[30-31] 다음 우리말과 의미가 같도록 괄호 안의 말을 바르게 배열하시오.

30
> 음식을 낭비하지 말자.
> (food, not, waste, let's)

→ _____

31
> 엄마를 귀찮게 하지 마, 그럴 거지?
> (bother, you, don't, will, mom, ?)

→ _____

32 다음 대화를 읽고, 주어진 [조건]에 맞게 빈칸 ⓐ, ⓑ에 알맞은 말을 쓰시오.

> A: Hi, James. Can you go shopping with me after school?
> B: You went shopping with your sister yesterday, _____ⓐ_____?
> A: Yes. But I forgot to buy a mask.
> B: Umm. I'm sorry, but I have to exercise with my friend today.
> A: Exercise? _____ⓑ_____, do you?
> B: No, I don't. I want to be healthy, so I decided to exercise every day from now on.

┤ 조건 ├
• ⓐ는 사실 여부를 확인하는 2단어로 쓸 것
• ⓑ는 다음의 말을 모두 이용할 것: like, exercise

ⓐ _____

ⓑ _____

33 다음 그림을 보고, 대화를 완성하시오.

(1) A: _____ _____ books does Suji want to borrow?

  B: She wants to borrow three books.

(2) A: _____ _____ Mr. Lee _____ for a living?

  B: He is a librarian.

(3) A: _____ _____ does the library close?

  B: It closes at 6 p.m.

34 다음 그림을 묘사하는 문장을 주어진 [조건]에 맞게 영어로 쓰시오.

┤ 조건 ├
• 다음의 말을 모두 이용할 것: be, expensive, how
• 필요시 단어를 추가하거나 변형할 것

_____ _____ _____ _____ _____!

35 다음 대화의 밑줄 친 ⓐ~ⓔ 중 어법상 틀린 것을 3개 찾아 기호를 쓰고 바르게 고쳐 쓰시오.

> A: You're good at *taekwondo*, ⓐ don't you?
> B: Yes, ⓑ I am.
> A: What ⓒ exciting sport it is!
> B: Yes, ⓓ it is. I practice it every day.
> A: ⓔ How much hours a day do you practice *taekwondo*?
> B: About 2 hours.

(1) _____ → _____

(2) _____ → _____

(3) _____ → _____

MEMO

MEMO

중학 국어의 문을 두드려라!

똑똑한 독해
중학 국어

똑똑

중학 국어 비문학 독해+어휘

똑똑한 독해

똑독

중학 국어
비문학
독해+어휘

실전편
3

1 비문학 독해의 기본이 되는 독해력과 어휘력을 동시에 습득
2 중학교 국어·도덕·사회·과학·음악·미술 교과서 연계 배경지식 강화
3 수능형 서술형 논술형 등 다양한 유형의 문제로 단계별 실력 향상

이투스북

똑똑한 독해
똑독
중학 국어
문법
기본편

똑독 중학 국어 **문법**

똑똑한 독해
똑독
중학 국어
어휘
1

똑독 중학 국어 **어휘**

GRAMMAR MASTER

MASTER

Level 1

WORKBOOK

ETOOS book

GRAMMAR MASTER

WORKBOOK

Level 1

Practice **01** 인칭대명사

01-1 다음 괄호 안에서 알맞은 것을 고르시오.

1 Miso is (he / his) sister.
2 (It / Its) is for your birthday.
3 The children like (their / them).
4 The book on the table is (her / hers).
5 Martha invites (I / me) to her party.
6 (We / Our) are middle school students.
7 The pen is not Cathy's. It's (my / mine).
8 The babies always need (us / our).
9 The artist is proud of (his / him) painting.
10 Mr. Smith is (our / ours) good neighbor.

01-2 다음 문장의 밑줄 친 부분을 인칭대명사로 바꿔 쓰시오.

1 Mike lives in New York City. _____
2 Henry and I are at the library. _____
3 She always carries the smartphone. _____
4 Jenny and you are my best friends. _____
5 My schoolbag's color is red. _____
6 It was my brother's birthday last Monday. _____
7 Andy and I find a sign on the street. _____
8 These presents are for my niece and nephew. _____

01-3 다음 빈칸에 괄호 안의 단어를 알맞은 형태로 쓰시오.

1 The backpack is _____. (I)
2 Mike and I often visit _____. (he)
3 _____ go to school together. (they)
4 _____ hair is brown and long. (you)
5 He is my nephew. _____ name is Eric. (he)
6 Emily is their daughter. They love _____. (she)
7 Sue does _____ homework after dinner. (she)
8 The cake in the refrigerator is _____. (you)
9 _____ English teacher is kind to all students. (we)

01-4 다음 문장의 밑줄 친 부분을 어법상 알맞은 형태로 고쳐 쓰시오.

1 Tony cleans him room. _____
2 My brother helps mine. _____

3 Your are a baseball player.   _____
4 This isn't her umbrella. Her is blue.   _____
5 Tom and Jerry play soccer. I know their.   _____
6 The presents on the table are our.   _____
7 My shoes are black but he are white.   _____
8 She is a new nurse in the hospital. Hers name is Sue.   _____
9 Gina loves her new computer. She uses them every day.   _____

01 -5 다음 빈칸에 들어갈 말을 [보기]에서 골라 알맞은 형태로 쓰시오. (단, 중복 가능)

┌─ 보기 ─────────────────────────────────────┐
│   he   she   it   they   │
└──┘

1 I eat a hamburger. _____ is delicious.
2 We have two dogs. We love _____.
3 I like my classmates. _____ are friendly.
4 Mr. Park is my math teacher. _____ is kind.
5 Sandy is 9 months old. _____ hands are small.
6 I know them. _____ job is teaching sports.
7 Paul lives on the other side. That's _____ house.
8 My little sister is seven years old. This doll is for _____.

01 -6 다음 우리말과 의미가 같도록 빈칸에 알맞은 말을 쓰시오.

1 나는 그의 여동생의 이름을 알지 못한다.
  → _____ don't know _____ sister's name.
2 Sam은 달걀을 좋아한다. 그는 매일 그것들을 먹는다.
  → Sam likes eggs. _____ eats _____ every day.
3 나의 형은 매우 바쁘다. 나는 그를 도와준다.
  → _____ brother is very busy. I help _____.
4 그의 개는 닥스훈트이다. 그것의 다리들은 짧다.
  → _____ dog is a Dachshund. _____ legs are short.
5 Jessica는 우리의 이웃이다. 그녀는 영국에서 왔다.
  → Jessica is _____ neighbor. _____ is from England.
6 Tina의 수학 점수는 완벽하다. 그녀는 그것을 매우 자랑스러워한다.
  → Tina's math grades are perfect. _____ is very proud of _____.
7 Mike의 삼촌은 대단한 농구선수이다. 나는 그를 많이 좋아한다.
  → _____ uncle is a great basketball player. I like _____ a lot.

02 -1 다음 빈칸에 알맞은 be동사의 현재형을 쓰시오.

1 It _____ a useful book.

2 I _____ very tired today.

3 We _____ in the same class.

4 Blair and Jimmy _____ from Australia.

5 Mr. Han _____ my homeroom teacher.

6 You _____ a brave police officer.

7 Lots of paintings _____ in this museum.

8 The post office _____ opposite to the bank.

9 My sister _____ at her desk in her room.

02 -2 다음 빈칸에 알맞은 be동사의 과거형을 쓰시오.

1 They _____ the new students.

2 It _____ rainy in Seoul yesterday.

3 The stories _____ very interesting.

4 Daniel _____ surprised at the news.

5 His aunt _____ a famous photographer.

6 Emily and Anne _____ great swimmers.

7 The pond in the garden _____ full of frogs.

8 Three books and a dictionary _____ on the desk.

02 -3 다음 괄호 안에서 알맞은 것을 고르시오.

1 Her favorite subject (is / are) music.

2 Mike and I (am / are) in the same club.

3 They (is / are) at the Moon Hotel in Seattle.

4 We (are / were) at the park yesterday.

5 The players (are / were) very excited then.

6 My father's office (is / are) on the third floor.

7 All the students in this class (is / are) so smart.

02-4 다음 빈칸에 There is 또는 There are 중 알맞은 것을 쓰시오.

1 _____ a bench in the yard.
2 _____ some meat in the refrigerator.
3 _____ two windows in his room.
4 _____ many students in the library.
5 _____ a squirrel in the tree.
6 _____ five pencils in my pencil case.
7 _____ a piano next to the sofa.
8 _____ three pictures on the wall.

02-5 다음 문장의 밑줄 친 부분을 어법상 알맞은 형태로 고쳐 쓰시오.

1 This box <u>are</u> big and heavy.   _____
2 I <u>is</u> thirteen years old.   _____
3 Jennifer <u>was</u> interested in fashion now.   _____
4 There <u>were</u> a concert at school last week.   _____
5 My dad <u>is</u> a history teacher before.   _____
6 There <u>are</u> some cheese in the kitchen.   _____
7 The singer's voice <u>are</u> deep and loud.   _____
8 Ted and Scott <u>was</u> ready for a bike ride then.   _____

02-6 다음 우리말과 의미가 같도록 괄호 안의 말을 이용하여 문장을 완성하시오.

1 나의 부모님은 연세가 같으시다. (my parents)
→ _____ the same age.
2 Henry와 Matt는 나의 좋은 이웃들이었다. (Henry and Matt)
→ _____ my good neighbors.
3 그의 스마트폰은 너의 것과 다르다. (his smartphone)
→ _____ different from yours.
4 10월에는 휴일이 많이 있다. (there)
→ _____ many holidays in October.
5 그녀의 침실에는 거울이 3개 있었다. (there)
→ _____ three mirrors in her bedroom.
6 내 지갑은 내 외투 주머니 안에 있었다. (my purse)
→ _____ in the pocket of my jacket.
7 Sue와 Judy는 작년에 나의 급우들이었다. (Sue and Judy)
→ _____ my classmates last year.

be동사의 부정문과 의문문

03-1 다음 괄호 안에서 알맞은 것을 고르시오.

1 (Was / Were) Steve rich then?
2 Bananas (isn't / aren't) expensive.
3 She (isn't / wasn't) on the phone now.
4 (Are / Were) you at the bank this morning?
5 There (isn't / aren't) many students in the library.
6 Lucy and Pam (isn't / aren't) from Spain.
7 (Is / Are) Kevin and Jimmy at the park?
8 The movie about the dog (wasn't / weren't) interesting.

03-2 다음 문장을 부정문으로 바꿔 쓰시오. (단, 줄임말로 쓸 것)

1 I'm afraid of snakes.
→ _____

2 He was a soldier last year.
→ _____

3 There is enough time for you.
→ _____

4 There are enough chairs for everyone.
→ _____

5 Judy and Julie were my neighbors last year.
→ _____

03-3 다음 괄호 안의 말을 이용하여 대화를 완성하시오.

1 A: _____ ready for the trip? (you)
B: Yes, _____ am.
2 A: _____ good at soccer? (your uncle)
B: Yes, _____ was.
3 A: _____ in Paris a week ago? (your brothers)
B: No, _____ weren't.
4 A: _____ a twin? (Amanda)
B: Yes, _____ is.
5 A: _____ in the north of the USA? (Canada)
B: Yes, _____ is.
6 A: _____ about computer programming? (these books)
B: No, _____ aren't.

⊟ Answers p.26

03 -4 다음 문장의 밑줄 친 부분을 어법상 알맞은 형태로 고쳐 쓰시오.

1   <u>Were</u> Steve Jobs diligent?   _____

2   <u>Is</u> they oranges and apples?   _____

3   You <u>isn't</u> kind to your friends.   _____

4   <u>Are</u> her nickname "Dancing Queen?"   _____

5   <u>Are</u> you at the concert yesterday?   _____

6   <u>Are</u> there an elephant in the picture?   _____

7   This <u>aren't</u> your pizza. It is Tony's pizza.   _____

8   I <u>was</u> a teacher, but I was an animal doctor.   _____

9   I <u>amn't</u> afraid of the barking dog.   _____

10 <u>Were</u> it so hot last night in Korea?   _____

11 I <u>am</u> afraid of the dark in my childhood.   _____

12 There <u>wasn't</u> many interesting programs on TV last night.   _____

03 -5 다음 질문에 대한 알맞은 대답을 완성하시오.

1   A: Is there a calendar on the wall?
    B: Yes, _____ _____.

2   A: Is there a toilet near here?
    B: No, _____ _____.

3   A: Are there many clouds in the sky?
    B: Yes, _____ _____.

4   A: Are there any candies in his pocket?
    B: No, _____ _____.

5   A: Is your slipper in the doghouse?
    B: No, _____ _____.

6   A: Were you at the hospital last week?
    B: Yes, _____ _____.

7   A: Was your photo album in the attic?
    B: Yes, _____ _____.

8   A: Is the girl in a red dress your sister?
    B: No, _____ _____.

9   A: Were you and your family in Canada last year?
    B: Yes, _____ _____.

10 A: Are there many roller coasters in the amusement park?
    B: No, _____ _____.

Chapter Test

01 다음 빈칸에 들어갈 말로 알맞은 것은?

> My father and I _____ in the stadium now.

① is ② am ③ are
④ was ⑤ were

02 다음 빈칸에 공통으로 들어갈 말로 적절한 것은?

> · The last lesson _____ about wild animals.
> · I _____ upset by Dave's behavior yesterday.

① is ② am ③ are
④ was ⑤ were

03 다음 빈칸에 들어갈 말로 알맞지 <u>않은</u> 것은?

> _____ is popular among the students.

① Mr. Homes
② Emma and Lisa
③ The band's song
④ The shopping mall
⑤ The restaurant's sandwich

04 다음 빈칸에 알맞은 말이 순서대로 짝지어진 것은?

> · The music festival _____ exciting last Friday.
> · Many buildings in New York _____ very tall.

① is – is ② is – are
③ was – is ④ was – are
⑤ were – are

05 다음 중 밑줄 친 부분을 인칭대명사로 <u>잘못</u> 바꾼 것은?

① <u>Mr. Simpson</u> wasn't a greedy person.
   → He
② That girl next to Anna is <u>Fred's</u> sister.
   → his
③ The dictionary on the table is <u>Sonya's</u>.
   → her
④ Lisa was interested in <u>Korean pop music</u>.
   → it
⑤ <u>Brian and I</u> are in the park with our dogs.
   → We

06 다음 질문에 대한 대답으로 알맞은 것은?

> Were you late for school yesterday?

① Yes, I am. ② Yes, I was.
③ Yes, you were. ④ No, I am not.
⑤ No, you weren't.

07 다음 중 빈칸에 들어갈 be동사가 나머지와 <u>다른</u> 것은?

① There _____ dancers on the stage.
② There _____ someone in my room.
③ There _____ many birds in the sky.
④ There _____ old stamps in this album.
⑤ There _____ colorful crayons in the box.

08 다음 중 빈칸에 들어갈 be동사의 형태가 같은 것끼리 짝지어진 것은?

> · The stamp in the box ⓐ _____ very old.
> · Steve ⓑ _____ a soldier in World War II.
> · A few skaters ⓒ _____ on the ice rink now.
> · There ⓓ _____ a supermarket around the corner ten years ago.

① ⓐ, ⓑ ② ⓐ, ⓒ ③ ⓑ, ⓓ
④ ⓐ, ⓑ, ⓒ ⑤ ⓑ, ⓒ, ⓓ

09 다음 중 어법상 틀린 것은?

① Are you ready to help others?
② Victoria and her mother aren't tall.
③ London is a capital city of England.
④ Was Claire and Kate close friends last year?
⑤ Some students in the classroom are so noisy.

10 다음 중 어법상 옳은 문장의 개수는?

· There isn't many people in the theater.
· The Eiffel Tower in Paris is very famous.
· Dave was so hungry after school yesterday.
· It was American Independence day yesterday.
· Are you in Rome with your family last summer?

① 1개　② 2개　③ 3개　④ 4개　⑤ 5개

11 다음 빈칸 ⓐ와 ⓑ에 들어갈 알맞은 인칭대명사를 쓰시오.

Tony is a great engineer. ⓐ _____ is interested in robots. This robot is ⓑ _____.

12 다음 문장을 괄호 안의 지시에 따라 바꿔 쓰시오.

The beach was full of people yesterday.

(부정문)
→ _____
(의문문)
→ _____

13 다음 대화의 빈칸 ⓐ~ⓒ에 들어갈 말을 알맞은 형태로 쓰시오.

A: ⓐ _____ you and James in the new restaurant last night?
B: Yes, ⓑ _____ _____. The food ⓒ _____ great.

14 다음 밑줄 친 ⓐ~ⓔ 중 어법상 틀린 것을 2개 찾아 그 기호를 쓰고, 바르게 고쳐 쓰시오.

Lucy and Laura ⓐ is sisters. They ⓑ are elementary school students. ⓒ Theirs hobbies are different. ⓓ Lucy's favorite subject is science. ⓔ Laura's favorite subject is math.

(1) _____ → _____
(2) _____ → _____

15 다음 우리말과 의미가 같도록 [조건]에 맞게 바르게 영작하시오.

지난번 영어 시험이 나에게는 어렵지 않았다.

┤조건├
1. the English exam, difficult for를 이용할 것
2. 필요시 단어를 추가할 것
3. 주어와 동사를 갖춘 완전한 문장으로 쓸 것
4. 대·소문자 및 구두점에 유의할 것

→ _____

Practice 01 **일반동사의 현재형**

01 -1 다음 괄호 안에서 알맞은 것을 고르시오.

1 She (need / needs) a new printer now.
2 You (know / knows) my cell phone number.
3 Brad and Nick (play / plays) tennis after school.
4 Andrew (wash / washes) his hands before meals.
5 My brother and I (miss / misses) our parents.
6 The P.E. class (finish / finishes) at 4.
7 The river (flow / flows) into the Atlantic Ocean.
8 My father and I (go / goes) camping on weekends.

01 -2 다음 괄호 안의 동사를 현재형으로 써서 문장을 완성하시오.

1 The puppy _____ milk and cheese. (like)
2 She _____ cookies for her children. (make)
3 Jessica _____ her homework in the evening. (do)
4 Mr. Park _____ history at a middle school. (teach)
5 My brother _____ about his school grades. (worry)
6 Ms. Smith _____ the eggs and milk in the bowl. (mix)
7 The boy _____ the drone in the field. (fly)
8 The band _____ for an hour every day. (practice)
9 The World Cup _____ place every four years. (take)

01 -3 다음 밑줄 친 부분을 괄호 안의 말로 바꿔 쓸 때, 빈칸에 알맞은 말을 쓰시오.

1 We enjoy taking pictures. (My brother)
   → _____ taking pictures.
2 They help their parents on weekends. (Tom)
   → _____ his parents on weekends.
3 I deliver newspapers in the morning. (The man)
   → _____ newspapers in the morning.
4 I carry a notebook computer in my hand. (An elderly man)
   → _____ a notebook computer in his hand.
5 I water the plants once a week. (My mother)
   → _____ the plants once a week.
6 Most students come to class on time every day. (Peter)
   → _____ to class on time every day.

01-4 다음 문장의 밑줄 친 부분을 어법상 알맞은 형태로 고쳐 쓰시오. (단, 현재형으로 쓸 것)

1 The cars <u>has</u> three doors.   _____

2 My sister <u>take</u> a shower every day.   _____

3 The old women <u>wears</u> glasses for reading.   _____

4 Miso <u>live</u> in London with her grandmother.   _____

5 These days, my grandpa <u>sleep</u> for an hour after lunch.   _____

6 The house <u>stand</u> on the top of the hill.   _____

7 The man <u>sit</u> in the same seat every day.   _____

01-5 다음 빈칸에 들어갈 알맞은 말을 [보기]에서 골라 현재형을 써서 문장을 완성하시오. (단, 한 번씩만 쓸 것)

┌─ 보기 ┐
│   do   buy   spend   remember   study   stop   hide   │
└──┘

1 I _____ her name and face well.

2 My father _____ the dishes after dinner.

3 You _____ lots of time with your pets.

4 Minsu _____ math without a calculator.

5 Ms. Kim _____ fish at the traditional market.

6 The bus _____ right in front of the post office.

7 My dog often _____ my slippers under the sofa.

01-6 다음 우리말과 의미가 같도록 괄호 안의 말을 이용하여 문장을 완성하시오.

1 나는 매일 아침 머리를 빗는다. (I, brush)
    → _____ my hair every morning.

2 그 비행기는 오후 3시에 도착한다. (the airplane, arrive)
    → _____ at three in the afternoon.

3 Owen은 신문에 영화에 관한 글을 쓴다. (Owen, write)
    → _____ about movies for a newspaper.

4 그녀는 건강을 위해서 우유를 많이 마신다. (she, drink)
    → _____ a lot of milk for her health.

5 Jane과 Judy는 수요일에 바이올린 강습이 있다. (Jane and Judy, have)
    → _____ a violin lesson on Wednesday.

6 내 친구들과 나는 매달 자원봉사를 한다. (my friends and I, do)
    → _____ volunteer work every month.

7 내 사촌은 다른 여러 나라의 동전들을 수집한다. (my cousin, collect)
    → _____ coins from many different countries.

02 -1 다음 괄호 안에서 알맞은 것을 고르시오.

1 My sister (learns / learned) Chinese in 2020.
2 She (drinks / drank) two cups of tea this morning.
3 John (read / readed) a magazine in the library.
4 They (take / took) plastic glasses for the picnic last Sunday.
5 The tourists (arrive / arrived) at the airport last night.
6 We (move / moved) into a new house last month.
7 I (drop / dropped) a cup on the floor a few minutes ago.

02 -2 다음 괄호 안의 동사를 과거형으로 써서 문장을 완성하시오.

1 Sally _____ the ring under the bed. (find)
2 His uncle _____ 12 sheep on his farm. (raise)
3 The woman _____ the piano last night. (play)
4 Paul _____ some questions three hours ago. (ask)
5 My mother _____ a green dress for the party. (wear)
6 James _____ his eyes tight under the blanket. (close)
7 The waiter _____ the main dishes on a tray. (bring)
8 The children on the bus _____ a cheerful song. (sing)

02 -3 다음 [보기]와 같이 과거형 문장으로 바꿔 쓸 때, 빈칸에 알맞은 말을 쓰시오.

┌ 보기 ┐
　　The train starts at 10 o'clock. → The train started at 10 o'clock yesterday.
└────┘

1 I send email to my friend.
→ _____ an hour ago.
2 Michael calls his grandmother.
→ _____ last night.
3 Her family visits an amusement park.
→ _____ last weekend.
4 Lisa takes a taxi to the airport.
→ _____ yesterday morning.
5 Troy learns to play the guitar in a band.
→ _____ last year.
6 My uncle studies math at university.
→ _____ four years ago.

02 -4 다음 문장의 밑줄 친 부분을 어법상 알맞은 형태로 고쳐 쓰시오.

1 I <u>get</u> up at six this morning.   _____

2 Jimmy <u>needed</u> our help now.   _____

3 It <u>rains</u> yesterday, but it is sunny today.   _____

4 My dad <u>comes</u> back home late last night.   _____

5 The boys <u>fly</u> model airplanes two days ago.   _____

6 Jessica <u>tries</u> hard to get good grades last semester. _____

7 We <u>see</u> the polar bears at the zoo last week.   _____

02 -5 다음 빈칸에 들어갈 알맞은 말을 [보기]에서 골라 과거형을 써서 문장을 완성하시오. (단, 한 번씩만 쓸 것)

┌─ 보기 ┐
| sleep | get | go | make | catch | open | build | walk |

1 You _____ swimming with your family.

2 Minho _____ for eleven hours last night.

3 The stationery store _____ at 10 yesterday.

4 I _____ many friends at my new school.

5 Jim and his father _____ fish in the river.

6 She _____ some presents last Christmas.

7 My school _____ a new swimming pool recently.

8 They _____ together slowly through the woods.

02 -6 다음 우리말과 의미가 같도록 괄호 안의 말을 이용하여 문장을 완성하시오.

1 우리는 지난주 금요일에 그 영화를 봤다. (we, watch)

→ _____ the movie last Friday.

2 그들은 어제 오후에 축구를 했다. (they, play)

→ _____ soccer yesterday afternoon.

3 Kate는 어제 머리 스타일을 바꾸었다. (Kate, change)

→ _____ her hairstyle yesterday.

4 Kevin과 Sam은 지난달에 유성우를 보았다. (Kevin and Sam, see)

→ _____ meteor showers last month.

5 그녀는 시장에서 채소를 좀 샀다. (she, buy)

→ _____ some vegetables at the market.

6 나는 그 책들을 선반에 다시 갖다 놓았다. (I, carry)

→ _____ the books back to the shelf.

7 내 남동생은 문을 열려고 아래층으로 뛰어 내려갔다. (my brother, run)

→ _____ downstairs to answer the door.

일반동사의 부정문과 의문문

03-1 다음 괄호 안에서 알맞은 것을 고르시오.

1 I (don't / am not) listen to pop music.

2 Hana (didn't / doesn't) help her mom last weekend.

3 (Are / Do) you jump rope in the morning?

4 (Do / Does) your mother need an alarm clock?

5 It (isn't / doesn't) snow in Hawaii in winter.

6 (Do / Did) you knock on the door a few minutes ago?

03-2 다음 문장을 부정문으로 바꿔 쓰시오. (단, 줄임말로 쓸 것)

1 David wears glasses in class.

→ _____

2 I wanted ice cream for dessert.

→ _____

3 Children like carrots.

→ _____

4 I take a bath every evening.

→ _____

5 My roommate comes from Australia.

→ _____

6 Bill wrote a report about blue whales.

→ _____

03-3 다음 문장을 의문문으로 바꿔 쓰시오.

1 The duck swam in the pond then.

→ _____

2 David washes his face before breakfast.

→ _____

3 The boys broke the classroom window.

→ _____

4 Many tourists visit the beautiful lake.

→ _____

5 The children made this great sandcastle.

→ _____

03-4 다음 문장의 밑줄 친 부분을 어법상 알맞은 형태로 고쳐 쓰시오.

1 We doesn't go to school on Sundays. _____
2 Jake didn't told a lie to his teacher then. _____
3 She don't drinks coffee. She drinks milk. _____
4 Do she take a walk in the evening? _____
5 Does John visit you yesterday, too? _____
6 Do you see the soccer game last night? _____
7 Evan didn't finished the computer course. _____

03-5 다음 괄호 안의 말을 이용하여 의문문을 완성하시오.

1 A: _____ to work by car? (your father, go)
  B: No, he doesn't. He goes to work by bus.
2 A: _____ water in the morning? (you, drink)
  B: Yes, I do. I drink a glass of water every morning.
3 A: _____ the stars in the sky? (they, look at)
  B: No, they didn't. It was cloudy.
4 A: _____ the elephant show in Thailand? (Alice, see)
  B: Yes, she did. She said it was good.
5 A: _____ in the white building? (Kate, work)
  B: No, she doesn't. She works in the pink building.
6 A: _____ early on weekends? (you, get up)
  B: No, I don't. I oversleep on weekends.
7 A: _____ his vacation in France? (your cousin, spend)
  B: Yes, he did. He had a great time there.

03-6 다음 우리말과 의미가 같도록 괄호 안의 말을 바르게 배열하시오.

1 내 여동생은 매운 음식을 먹지 않는다. (eat, doesn't, spicy food, my sister)
  → _____

2 Pablo는 한국 음식을 좋아하니? (Korean food, Pablo, like, does, ?)
  → _____

3 너는 그녀를 위해 사과 파이를 만들었니? (make, you, for her, an apple pie, did, ?)
  → _____

4 너는 제주도에서 호텔에 머무르니? (stay, in Jejudo, do, at a hotel, you, ?)
  → _____

5 그 기사는 신문에 나오지 않았다. (in, appear, the article, the newspaper, didn't)
  → _____

6 경찰관이 너에게 몇 가지 질문들을 물었니? (you, did, some questions, the police officer, of, ask, ?)
  → _____

Chapter Test

01 다음 빈칸에 들어갈 말로 알맞은 것은?

_____ tries to protect the environment.

① They
② My friends
③ Joshua and I
④ A lot of people
⑤ The organization

02 다음 빈칸에 공통으로 들어갈 말로 알맞은 것은?

· _____ you agree with John on the matter last time?
· The player _____ not score many goals in yesterday's game.

① Do[do]
② Did[did]
③ Was[was]
④ Does[does]
⑤ Were[were]

03 다음 빈칸에 들어갈 말로 알맞지 <u>않은</u> 것은?

Judy _____ last weekend.

① made a delicious cake
② went to the bookstore downtown
③ watches a basketball game on TV
④ bought many things at the flea market
⑤ visited an amusement park with her friends

04 다음 빈칸에 들어갈 말로 알맞게 짝지어진 것은?

· Does the word _____ with the letter "s"?
· The thief _____ the crown from the museum last night.

① begin – steals
② begin – stole
③ began – steals
④ begins – stole
⑤ begins – steals

05 다음 우리말을 어법에 알맞게 영작한 것은?

네가 또 내 영어 사전을 가져갔니?

① Do you take my English dictionary again?
② Do you took my English dictionary again?
③ Are you take my English dictionary again?
④ Did you take my English dictionary again?
⑤ Did you took my English dictionary again?

06 짝지어진 대화 중 어법상 <u>어색한</u> 것은?

① A: Do you feel good today?
   B: Yes, I do.
② A: Did your pen cost two dollars?
   B: No, it didn't.
③ A: Did your father make this chair?
   B: Yes, he did.
④ A: Do Mr. Evans teaches English at school?
   B: No, he doesn't.
⑤ A: Were you at the bus stop an hour ago?
   B: Yes, I was.

07 다음 중 빈칸에 들어갈 말이 나머지와 <u>다른</u> 것은?
(단, 대·소문자 무시할 것)

① I _____ not go hiking yesterday.
② _____ someone open the window last night?
③ _____ Martha in Seoul with her parents two years ago?
④ My mother _____ not take the dog for a walk last Friday.
⑤ The train to Paris _____ not stop at this station last month.

08 다음 중 밑줄 친 부분의 쓰임이 나머지와 다른 것은?

① I do not eat fast food so often.
② Steve does a lot of fun activities.
③ They did not stay long in London.
④ Did you finish your homework last night?
⑤ Do you want to go on a picnic tomorrow?

09 다음 중 어법상 틀린 것은?

① Did you sleep well last night?
② I translated the title of the book.
③ Does the shop sell chocolate ice cream?
④ The bus tour lasted for about three hours.
⑤ Carol didn't apologized to me for her mistake.

10 다음 중 어법상 옳은 문장의 개수는?

- Did the boy picked up the flowers?
- I opened the door for the old lady.
- Emma finded some money on the street.
- Does it rains a lot in April in the country?
- Peter didn't eat the cookies in the basket.

① 1개   ② 2개   ③ 3개   ④ 4개   ⑤ 5개

11 다음 우리말과 의미가 같도록 괄호 안의 말을 바르게 배열하시오.

나는 매일 일기를 쓰지 않는다.
(every day, keep, don't, I, a diary)

→ _____

12 다음 문장에서 어법상 틀린 부분을 찾아 바르게 고쳐 쓰시오.

Does Wendy wears blue jeans every day?

_____ → _____

13 다음 대화의 빈칸 ⓐ~ⓒ에 들어갈 do의 알맞은 형태를 각각 쓰시오.

A: ⓐ _____ the wind blow hard last night?
B: Yes, it ⓑ _____ . I ⓒ _____ sleep well last night because of the noise of the wind.

14 다음 글의 각 빈칸에 들어갈 말을 [보기]에서 골라 알맞은 형태로 쓰시오.

보기
take   go   have   hear   play

Last night I _____ to a K-pop concert. I _____ very good songs there. The K-pop bands _____ a lot of famous songs. I _____ many pictures of the bands. I _____ a great time at the concert.

15 다음 우리말과 의미가 같도록 [조건]에 맞게 문장을 완성하시오.

2002년 월드컵이 한국에서 열렸니?

조건
1. the 2002 World Cup, take place를 이용하여 총 7단어로 쓸 것 2. 필요시 단어를 추가할 것

→ _____
in Korea?

Practice 01 **현재시제, 과거시제**

01-1 다음 괄호 안에서 알맞은 것을 고르시오.

1 A friend in need (is / was) a friend indeed.
2 The puppies (are / were) born three days ago.
3 The moon (moves / moved) around the earth.
4 The train (arrives / arrived) 10 minutes late yesterday.
5 Greg (goes / went) shopping with his mom last week.
6 All work and no play (makes / made) Jack a dull boy.
7 Alexander Graham Bell (invents / invented) the telephone in 1876.

01-2 다음 문장을 과거시제로 바꿔 쓰시오.

1 Sam meets Mike at the gym.
→ _____

2 Jenny doesn't join a book club.
→ _____

3 I have lunch at the park with my friend.
→ _____

4 Mom peels potatoes for curry and rice.
→ _____

5 Lewis is a violinist in the orchestra.
→ _____

6 The cat doesn't enjoy running after a mouse.
→ _____

01-3 다음 괄호 안의 단어를 이용하여 문장을 완성하시오.

1 They _____ their house in 1995. (build)
2 Jimmy _____ camping every Saturday. (go)
3 She _____ Tolstoy's *War and Peace* last week. (read)
4 My sister and I _____ the musical two weeks ago. (watch)
5 The earth _____ from west to east. (rotate)
6 Admiral Yi Sun-shin _____ the Japanese Navy. (defeat)
7 I usually _____ my lunch to the office nowadays. (bring)
8 Twenty-eight minus seven _____ twenty-one. (equal)
9 I _____ enough time to finish my homework then. (have)

01-4 다음 문장의 밑줄 친 부분을 어법상 알맞은 형태로 고쳐 쓰시오.

1 Yesterday <u>is</u> my first day at school. _____

2 The Titanic <u>sinks</u> on April 15, 1912. _____

3 It <u>rained</u> a lot in summer in Korea. _____

4 My grandma <u>was</u> sick in the hospital now. _____

5 It <u>stops</u> snowing an hour ago. _____

6 A rolling stone <u>gathered</u> no moss. _____

7 Ricky <u>spends</u> his free time at the gym yesterday. _____

01-5 다음 우리말과 의미가 같도록 [보기]에서 알맞은 말을 골라 문장을 완성하시오. (단, 한 번씩만 쓸 것)

┌─ 보기 ───┐
│   watch   take   give   play   be   explain   │
└──┘

1 나는 부모님을 위해 피아노를 연주했다.

→ I _____ the piano for my parents.

2 아빠는 나에게 한 달에 한 번 용돈을 주신다.

→ Dad _____ pocket money to me once a month.

3 그는 방에서 망원경으로 별들을 보았다.

→ He _____ the stars through a telescope in his room.

4 한국인들은 보통 여름에 휴가를 간다.

→ Koreans usually _____ a vacation in summer.

5 작년 크리스마스에는, 그 광장에 큰 나무가 있었다.

→ Last Christmas, there _____ a big tree in the square.

6 Ford 선생님은 학생들에게 그 구절을 다시 설명해 주셨다.

→ Mr. Ford _____ that passage again to the students.

01-6 다음 우리말과 의미가 같도록 괄호 안의 말을 바르게 배열하시오. (단, 필요하면 동사의 형태를 바꿀 것)

1 그들은 지금 강 가까이에 산다. (near, live, the river, now)

→ They _____.

2 엄마는 지금 새 냉장고를 원하신다. (a new refrigerator, now, want)

→ Mom _____.

3 Andy는 어제 오후에 자전거를 탔다. (a bike, yesterday afternoon, ride)

→ Andy _____.

4 그 아기는 우리에게 미소를 지었다. (us, at, smile)

→ The baby _____.

5 Alfred는 항상 손톱을 물어뜯는다. (all the time, bite, his fingernails)

→ Alfred _____.

6 내 친구들과 나는 시내에 가기 위해 버스에 탔다. (the bus, get on, downtown, to go)

→ My friends and I _____.

02-1 다음 괄호 안에서 알맞은 것을 고르시오.

1 A boy is (runing / running) at the park.

2 (Are / Do) you listening to classical music now?

3 We (was taking / were taking) pictures at the beach.

4 My dad and my brother (painting / are painting) the door.

5 The goldfish were (dieing / dying) in the fishbowl.

6 Are the students (wait / waiting) to see the principal?

7 They are (take / taking) notes on their science experiment.

02-2 다음 문장을 진행시제로 바꿔 쓰시오.

1 Betty doesn't sleep in her room.

→ _____

2 The teacher writes something on the board.

→ _____

3 I didn't water the flowers then.

→ _____

4 They shopped at the new department store.

→ _____

5 Does the dog hide the bone in the ground?

→ _____

6 Some people travel around the world in their yacht.

→ _____

02-3 다음 괄호 안의 말을 이용하여 진행시제 의문문을 완성하시오.

1 A: _____ on the carpet? (Brian, lie)

B: Yes, he is. He is taking a rest.

2 A: _____ for a train? (they, wait)

B: Yes, they were. It arrived late.

3 A: _____ blue jeans? (your sister, wear)

B: No, she isn't. She is wearing a skirt.

4 A: _____ on the frozen lake? (you, skate)

B: No, we weren't. We were riding a sled.

5 A: _____ an exam now? (the students, take)

B: No, they aren't. The exam already finished an hour ago.

02 -4 다음 문장의 밑줄 친 부분을 어법상 알맞은 형태로 고쳐 쓰시오.

1 Are you <u>study</u> English now? _____

2 The birds <u>don't</u> singing on the roof. _____

3 Bill <u>was</u> cutting the paper with scissors now. _____

4 They <u>are</u> having a birthday party yesterday. _____

5 <u>Did</u> he doing the laundry then? _____

6 The audience was <u>shout</u> for the home team. _____

7 Are the firefighters <u>put</u> out a fire in the building? _____

02 -5 다음 괄호 안의 단어를 이용하여 진행시제 문장을 완성하시오. (단, 부정문은 줄임말로 쓸 것)

1 They _____ a roller coaster then. (ride)

2 We _____ hamburgers in the yard now. (eat)

3 My mom _____ a sweater in the armchair now. (knit)

4 _____ a strange man _____ on the door now? (knock)

5 Mr. Robert and his son _____ the elevator now. (not, take)

6 _____ Daniel _____ slowly to the bus stop then? (walk)

7 A lot of monkeys _____ around in the forest then. (run)

8 Emily _____ computer games last night. (not, play)

02 -6 다음 우리말과 의미가 같도록 괄호 안의 말을 이용하여 문장을 완성하시오.

1 그 트럭 운전사는 조심스럽게 운전하고 있다. (the truck driver, drive)
→ _____ carefully.

2 너는 이를 닦고 있지 않다. (you, brush)
→ _____ your teeth.

3 그녀는 설거지를 하고 있니? (she, wash)
→ _____ the dishes?

4 Kevin은 서점에서 책을 찾고 있었다. (Kevin, look for)
→ _____ a book at the bookstore.

5 한 소년이 거리에서 쓰레기를 줍고 있다. (a boy, pick up)
→ _____ garbage on the street.

6 우리는 그때 우리의 어린 시절에 관해 이야기하고 있었다. (we, talk)
→ _____ about our childhood at that time.

7 선생님이 교실에서 학생들 수를 세고 계신다. (the teacher, count)
→ _____ the students in the classroom.

03 -1 다음 괄호 안에서 알맞은 것을 고르시오.

1 It (wills / will) be sunny and warm tomorrow.

2 I (will not / not will) change my vacation plans.

3 They are going (go / to go) to the library by bus.

4 She (is / will) going to lose weight during the vacation.

5 The people (aren't / don't) going to make any noise.

6 The actor will (come / comes) to the ceremony in London.

7 We (will / are going) to build a shopping mall in this area.

03 -2 다음 문장을 will을 이용하여 미래시제로 바꿔 쓸 때, 빈칸에 알맞은 말을 쓰시오.

1 I win the cooking contest.

→ _____ the cooking contest.

2 He watches the movie with his friends.

→ _____ the movie with his friends.

3 Mike doesn't take a rest after lunch.

→ _____ a rest after lunch.

4 Does she see her earring under the bed?

→ _____ her earring under the bed?

5 Brian doesn't throw a party for his friend.

→ _____ a party for his friend.

6 The teacher gives a dictation test on Friday.

→ _____ a dictation test on Friday.

7 The company sends some samples to customers.

→ _____ some samples to customers.

03 -3 다음 문장을 be going to를 이용하여 미래시제로 바꿔 쓸 때, 빈칸에 알맞은 말을 쓰시오.

1 The children visit the toy factory.

→ _____ the toy factory.

2 My father doesn't drive to Busan.

→ _____ to Busan.

3 Do you learn Chinese?

→ _____ Chinese?

4 Martha wears a white T-shirt and jeans.

→ _____ a white T-shirt and jeans.

5 Do you eat lunch with Ann at the cafeteria?

→ _____ lunch with Ann at the cafeteria?

03-4 다음 문장의 밑줄 친 부분을 어법상 알맞은 형태로 고쳐 쓰시오.

1 Steve will <u>goes</u> to their wedding.　　　　　　　　＿＿＿＿＿＿＿＿＿＿

2 I'm going <u>call</u> you again tomorrow.　　　　　　　＿＿＿＿＿＿＿＿＿＿

3 We will <u>to go</u> to the beach this summer.　　　　＿＿＿＿＿＿＿＿＿＿

4 Will you <u>returning</u> the books next Friday?　　　＿＿＿＿＿＿＿＿＿＿

5 He <u>won't</u> going to leave tomorrow morning.　　　＿＿＿＿＿＿＿＿＿＿

6 <u>Do</u> you going to boil some water in the kettle?　＿＿＿＿＿＿＿＿＿＿

7 Ms. Johnson <u>wills</u> move to the new office next month.　＿＿＿＿＿＿＿＿＿＿

03-5 다음 [보기]에서 알맞은 말을 골라 괄호 안의 말을 이용하여 문장을 완성하시오. (단, 한 번씩만 쓸 것)

| 보기 |
| order　　be　　wear　　lecture　　travel　　live |

1 Janet ＿＿＿＿＿＿＿＿＿＿＿＿＿ fourteen years old next year. (will, not)

2 I ＿＿＿＿＿＿＿＿＿＿＿＿＿ a sandwich and a glass of milk. (be going to)

3 Bora ＿＿＿＿＿＿＿＿＿＿＿＿＿ a new dress tomorrow. (be going to, not)

4 Ms. Moon ＿＿＿＿＿＿＿＿＿＿＿＿＿ on Korean history next Thursday. (will)

5 ＿＿＿＿＿＿ you ＿＿＿＿＿＿＿＿＿ in the student's dormitory next year? (be going to)

6 We ＿＿＿＿＿＿＿＿＿＿＿＿＿ to Iceland to see the auroras this winter. (be going to)

03-6 다음 [보기]와 같이 괄호 안의 말을 이용하여 문장을 다시 쓰시오.

| 보기 |
| She fed the dog this morning. (will, tomorrow morning) |
| → She will feed the dog tomorrow morning. |

1 The exams started yesterday. (be going to, tomorrow)

　→ ＿＿＿＿＿＿＿＿＿＿＿＿＿＿＿＿＿＿＿＿＿＿＿＿＿

2 Karen wasn't busy this month. (be going to, next month)

　→ ＿＿＿＿＿＿＿＿＿＿＿＿＿＿＿＿＿＿＿＿＿＿＿＿＿

3 Dean bought hiking boots for hiking last week. (will, next week)

　→ ＿＿＿＿＿＿＿＿＿＿＿＿＿＿＿＿＿＿＿＿＿＿＿＿＿

4 We didn't invite Sandra to our home then. (will, this weekend)

　→ ＿＿＿＿＿＿＿＿＿＿＿＿＿＿＿＿＿＿＿＿＿＿＿＿＿

5 The island's volcano erupted last year. (will, sooner or later)

　→ ＿＿＿＿＿＿＿＿＿＿＿＿＿＿＿＿＿＿＿＿＿＿＿＿＿

6 I raised money for local charities last week. (be going to, next week)

　→ ＿＿＿＿＿＿＿＿＿＿＿＿＿＿＿＿＿＿＿＿＿＿＿＿＿

Chapter Test

01 다음 빈칸에 들어갈 말로 알맞은 것을 <u>모두</u> 고르면?

The construction _____ at the start of next year.

① begin
② began
③ will begin
④ was beginning
⑤ is going to begin

02 다음 빈칸에 들어갈 말로 알맞지 <u>않은</u> 것은?

Jake burned his finger on the hot water _____.

① then
② yesterday
③ last week
④ tomorrow
⑤ at that time

03 다음 중 어법상 옳은 것으로 알맞게 짝지어진 것은?

- James Naismith _____ basketball in 1891.
- The Earth _____ a day to spin on its axis.

① invents – takes
② invents – took
③ invented – takes
④ invented – took
⑤ will invent – is taking

04 다음 빈칸에 공통으로 들어갈 말로 알맞은 것은?

- My badminton rackets _____ in my room.
- We _____ going to set up the tent over there.
- The tourists _____ checking the map to the Grand Canyon now.

① is
② do
③ are
④ did
⑤ will

05 다음 우리말을 어법에 알맞게 영작한 것은?

경찰관들이 실종된 아이를 찾고 있니?

① Do the police officers look for the missing child?
② Will the police officers look for the missing child?
③ Are the police officers looking for the missing child?
④ Were the police officers looking for the missing child?
⑤ Did the police officers look for the missing child?

06 다음 중 부정문으로 <u>잘못</u> 바꾼 것은?

① Tim is playing a computer game.
   → Tim isn't playing a computer game.
② Carol and Ellen walk to school.
   → Carol and Ellen don't walk to school.
③ My new house will have two bathrooms.
   → My new house don't will have two bathrooms.
④ They are going to play basketball after school.
   → They aren't going to play basketball after school.
⑤ The actor is going to show up in the new movie.
   → The actor isn't going to show up in the new movie.

07 다음 중 밑줄 친 부분을 will로 바꿔 쓸 수 <u>없는</u> 것은?

① We <u>are going to</u> run to the theater.
② I <u>am going to</u> see the doctor this week.
③ The orchestra <u>is going to</u> perform a symphony.
④ Sally <u>is going to</u> the baker's to buy some bread.
⑤ Mr. Porter <u>is going to</u> make a speech at the meeting.

08 다음 중 밑줄 친 부분의 쓰임이 나머지와 <u>다른</u> 것은?

① Are you <u>going</u> to answer my questions?

② I'm <u>going</u> to take a math class at 9:00 today.

③ They are not <u>going</u> to sit in the waiting room.

④ The doctor is <u>going</u> to check my temperature.

⑤ We are <u>going</u> to an Italian restaurant downtown.

09 다음 중 어법상 <u>틀린</u> 것은?

① Raindrops splashed on the window.

② People will live longer in the future.

③ I was squeezing the oranges to make juice.

④ A journey of 1,000 miles began with a single step.

⑤ They are going to sell miniatures of the Eiffel Tower to visitors.

10 다음 중 어법상 옳은 문장의 개수는?

· A trip to the city wills take two hours.

· Will you come back early this evening?

· A monkey sometimes falls from the tree.

· I'm going to complaining about the noise outside.

· The announcer is speaking about the accident extremely fast.

① 1개 ② 2개 ③ 3개 ④ 4개 ⑤ 5개

11 다음 우리말과 의미가 같도록 괄호 안의 말을 바르게 배열하시오.

너는 절벽에서 번지 점프를 시도할 거니?
(you, at, bungee jumping, going, the cliff, to try, are, ?)

→ _____

12 다음 두 문장의 의미가 같도록 빈칸에 들어갈 알맞은 말을 쓰시오.

The exam won't start at 8:30 tomorrow.

= The exam _____ at 8:30 tomorrow.

13 다음 대화의 빈칸 ⓐ와 ⓑ에 들어갈 알맞은 말을 쓰시오.

A: ⓐ _____ the cat sleeping under the tree now?

B: No, it ⓑ _____. It went over the wall.

14 다음 우리말과 의미가 같도록 [조건]에 맞게 문장을 완성하시오.

그때 축구 선수들이 경기장에 들어오고 있었다.

┌ 조건 ┐
1. enter the stadium을 이용할 것
2. 필요시 단어를 추가하거나 어형을 바꿀 것

→ The soccer players _____ _____ then.

15 다음 Sue의 여행 일정표를 보고, 빈칸 ⓐ~ⓒ에 들어갈 알맞은 말을 쓰시오.

Yesterday	go to Namdaemun Market
Today	ride on a cable car
Tomorrow	visit Gyeongbokgung

Sue ⓐ _____ to Namdaemun Market to buy souvenirs yesterday. She ⓑ _____ on a cable car to N Seoul Tower now. She ⓒ _____ Gyeongbokgung in a traditional Korean costumes, *hanbok*, tomorrow.

Practice 01 can, may

01 -1 다음 괄호 안에서 알맞은 것을 고르시오.

1 Betty may (know / knows) Tom's secret.

2 It (not may / may not) rain this afternoon.

3 She doesn't have a key. She (can / can't) open the door.

4 Alex (may / mays) be a very talented singer.

5 I have a headache. (Can / May) you talk quietly?

01 -2 다음 문장을 be able to를 이용하여 바꿔 쓰시오.

1 I can get there in 10 minutes.

→ _____

2 She couldn't hear the telephone.

→ _____

3 The ostrich can't fly, but it can run fast.

→ _____

4 Can your dog walk on two feet?

→ _____

5 The bus can carry 80 passengers.

→ _____

6 We can stay healthy through sports.

→ _____

01 -3 다음 문장을 괄호 안의 지시대로 바꿔 쓰시오.

1 Maggie can do the work herself. (부정문)

→ _____

2 You can see lots of fish in the pond. (의문문)

→ _____

3 I may use this computer now. (의문문)

→ _____

4 They may be of the same age. (부정문)

→ _____

5 People can live on other planets. (의문문)

→ _____

6 The boy can stand on his hands. (부정문)

→ _____

01-4 다음 문장의 밑줄 친 부분을 어법상 알맞은 형태로 고쳐 쓰시오.

1 Harry may <u>is</u> absent from school. _____

2 I <u>don't can</u> find my smartphone. _____

3 <u>Do I may</u> borrow your umbrella? _____

4 We are able <u>protect</u> the earth by recycling. _____

5 <u>Can you able</u> to drive a 10-ton truck? _____

6 You <u>not can</u> master English in a few months. _____

7 It <u>mays</u> take 20 minutes to bake these cookies. _____

01-5 다음 우리말과 의미가 같도록 괄호 안의 말과 can 또는 may를 이용하여 문장을 완성하시오.

1 그 가방은 그녀의 것이 아닐지도 모른다. (be)

→ The bag _____.

2 너는 이 케이크를 먹어도 된다. (eat, this cake)

→ You _____.

3 그녀는 바이올린을 잘 연주할 수 있다. (play, the violin, well)

→ She _____.

4 우리는 이 돈으로 그 비싼 자동차를 살 수 없다. (buy, the expensive car)

→ We _____ with this money.

5 너는 밤에 늦게까지 깨어 있어도 된다. (stay up late)

→ You _____ at night.

6 고열은 독감의 징조일지도 모른다. (be, a sign of the flu)

→ A high temperature _____.

01-6 다음 우리말과 의미가 같도록 괄호 안의 말을 바르게 배열하시오.

1 Mike는 공원에 있을지도 모른다. (be, at the park, may, Mike)

→ _____

2 그 개는 높이 점프할 수 있다. (high, is, the dog, jump, to, able)

→ _____

3 너는 내일 일찍 일어날 수 있니? (get up, tomorrow, you, can, early, ?)

→ _____

4 그는 다섯 가지 언어를 말할 수 있니? (speak, able to, five languages, is, he, ?)

→ _____

5 우리는 물속에서 숨을 쉴 수 없다. (breathe, the water, able, we, under, not, are, to)

→ _____

6 관광객들은 이 타워에서 도시 전체를 볼 수 있다. (this tower, see, from, tourists, can, the whole city)

→ _____

02 -1 다음 괄호 안에서 알맞은 것을 고르시오.

1 She (have / has) to choose one.

2 You (must not / not must) fight each other.

3 She (has to / must) be Nancy's sister.

4 You (should / has to) take this medicine every day.

5 My father doesn't (must / have to) attend the meeting.

6 You (don't should / should not) press the red button.

7 You (must tell not / must not tell) the secret to Jane.

8 The actor's new movie (must / has) be interesting.

9 Children (don't must / must not) eat chocolate every day.

02 -2 다음 문장을 have to를 이용하여 바꿔 쓰시오.

1 The sailors must find the treasure.

→ _____

2 You must wash the blouse by hand.

→ _____

3 Kelly must have dinner before 6 today.

→ _____

4 Alex must change his Internet password.

→ _____

5 We must warm up before swimming.

→ _____

6 I must look up this word in the dictionary.

→ _____

02 -3 다음 문장의 밑줄 친 부분을 어법상 알맞은 형태로 고쳐 쓰시오.

1 Eric doesn't should skip the class.   _____

2 They must to speak in English in class.   _____

3 The tall man musts be a basketball player.   _____

4 You must to return this bike by tomorrow.   _____

5 The runners not must forget the game rules.   _____

6 Lucy don't have to make more sandwiches.   _____

7 You don't must sit too close to the monitor. _____

02-4 다음 괄호 안의 말과 mustn't 또는 don't[doesn't] have to를 이용하여 문장을 완성하시오.

1 Alex is very sleepy. He _____ a car. (drive)

2 This lake is very deep. We _____ here. (swim)

3 You may wear a cap. You _____ it off. (take)

4 The paint is still wet. You _____ the door. (touch)

5 Dad doesn't go to work today. He _____ up early. (get)

6 This is a library. You _____ loudly. (talk)

7 Nobody is hungry. I _____ anything. (cook)

02-5 다음 우리말과 의미가 같도록 괄호 안의 말을 이용하여 문장을 완성하시오.

1 그녀는 좋은 친구들이 많이 있음에 틀림없다. (have)

→ _____ a lot of good friends.

2 너는 내일 치과에 갈 필요가 없다. (go)

→ _____ to the dentist tomorrow.

3 너는 사람들을 외모로 판단해서는 안 된다. (should, judge)

→ _____ people by their appearance.

4 우리는 스마트폰에 시간을 낭비해서는 안 된다. (must, waste)

→ _____ time on smartphones.

5 사람들은 동물원의 동물들에게 먹이를 줘서는 안 된다. (must, feed)

→ _____ the animals in the zoo.

6 우리는 내일까지 이 일을 끝낼 필요가 없다. (have to, finish)

→ _____ this work by tomorrow.

02-6 다음 우리말과 의미가 같도록 괄호 안의 말을 바르게 배열하시오.

1 그는 취업 면접에서 정장을 입어야 한다. (a suit, has, he, to, wear)

→ _____ to the job interview.

2 그 교통사고는 심각한 게 틀림없다. (serious, the traffic accident, be, must)

→ _____

3 너는 이것에 대해 아무에게도 말하면 안 된다. (should, you, not, anyone, tell)

→ _____ about this.

4 그들은 그곳에 정시에 도착할 필요가 없다. (there, have to, they, arrive, don't)

→ _____ on time.

5 승객들은 기차를 타기 위해 티켓을 제시해야 한다. (passengers, present, must)

→ _____ their tickets to get on the train.

6 사람들은 공공장소에서 너무 시끄럽게 해서는 안 된다. (should, make, people, not)

→ _____ too much noise in public places.

Chapter Test

01 다음 빈칸에 공통으로 들어갈 말로 알맞은 것은?

> · _____ you guess the height of the tree?
> · _____ I borrow three books at a time from the library?

① Can   ② May   ③ Must
④ Should   ⑤ Have to

02 다음 빈칸에 들어갈 말로 알맞은 것은?

> Yesterday I _____ wait for 30 minutes to catch the school bus.

① may   ② must   ③ should
④ had to   ⑤ am able to

03 다음 빈칸에 들어갈 말로 알맞게 짝지어진 것은?

> · Judy got a bad cold. She _____ stay home.
> · He's a pilot. He _____ wear a uniform at work.

① could – can
② should – must
③ was able to – may not
④ must not – was able to
⑤ shouldn't – didn't have to

04 다음 중 의도하는 바가 나머지와 다른 것은?

① Don't make fires in the forest.
② You mustn't make fires in the forest.
③ You may not make fires in the forest.
④ You shouldn't make fires in the forest.
⑤ You don't have to make fires in the forest.

05 다음 중 짝지어진 두 문장의 의미가 같지 <u>않은</u> 것은?

① May I sit next to you?
   = Can I sit next to you?
② We must not walk on the grass.
   = We shouldn't walk on the grass.
③ My brother can juggle apples.
   = My brother is able to juggle apples.
④ I must buy all the books on the list.
   = I have to buy all the books on the list.
⑤ The old woman must be over a hundred.
   = The old woman has to be over a hundred.

06 다음 문장을 의문문으로 바르게 바꾼 것은?

> The doctor was able to treat the disease.

① Be able the doctor to treat the disease?
② Was the doctor able to treat the disease?
③ Do the doctor is able to treat the disease?
④ Did the doctor is able to treat the disease?
⑤ Does the doctor is able to treat the disease?

07 다음 우리말을 어법에 알맞게 영작한 것은?

> 내 계산에 실수가 있을지도 모른다.

① I can have a mistake in my calculations.
② I may have a mistake in my calculations.
③ I must have a mistake in my calculations.
④ I should have a mistake in my calculations.
⑤ I am able to have a mistake in my calculations.

08 다음 밑줄 친 부분의 의미가 나머지와 다른 것은?

① You <u>must</u> take an umbrella with you.

② You <u>must</u> wear a swimming cap in this pool.

③ I <u>must</u> return these books to the library today.

④ We <u>must</u> clean the windows. They are so dirty.

⑤ Someone is knocking on the door. It <u>must</u> be Kelly.

09 다음 중 어법상 틀린 것은?

① People should take care of nature.

② We may have some rain tomorrow.

③ Everyone will can join the club meeting.

④ You should not forget about the matter.

⑤ I have to write an essay about Asian cultures.

10 다음 중 어법상 옳은 문장의 개수는?

· Harry musted wear a funny hat.

· Do I may give some advice to you?

· You must not read a book in the car.

· We should not quarrel with our friends.

· I couldn't find a way to go to the train station.

① 1개   ② 2개   ③ 3개

④ 4개   ⑤ 5개

11 다음 대화의 빈칸 ⓐ와 ⓑ에 들어갈 알맞은 조동사를 쓰시오.

A: ⓐ _____ you move this box over there?

B: No, I ⓑ _____ . It is too heavy.

12 다음 문장을 부정문으로 바꿔 쓰시오.

You have to know the exact date of the event.

→ _____

13 다음 표지판을 보고, 괄호 안의 말을 이용하여 문장을 완성하시오.

You _____ your cell phone in the theater. (use)

14 다음 우리말과 의미가 같도록 [조건]에 맞게 문장을 완성하시오.

나는 스페인어로 숫자를 셀 수 있다.

┌ 조건 ┐
1. able, count numbers를 이용할 것
2. 필요시 단어를 추가할 것

→ I _____ in Spanish.

15 다음 빈칸 ⓐ~ⓒ에 들어갈 알맞은 말을 [A]와 [B]에서 각각 골라 글을 완성하시오.

[A]	can	must not	have to
[B]	touch	take	book

The wax museum is very popular. You ⓐ _____ a ticket in advance to get in there. You ⓑ _____ _____ photos with the wax figures of the famous people there. However, you ⓒ _____ them.

Practice 01 명사

01-1 다음 주어진 명사의 복수형을 쓰시오.

1	boy	_____	2	knife	_____
3	box	_____	4	dish	_____
5	foot	_____	6	potato	_____
7	man	_____	8	child	_____
9	ox	_____	10	sheep	_____
11	mouse	_____	12	candy	_____
13	photo	_____	14	baby	_____
15	carrot	_____	16	dress	_____
17	fish	_____	18	radio	_____
19	proof	_____	20	goose	_____
21	leaf	_____	22	hero	_____
23	tooth	_____	24	dictionary	_____

01-2 다음 괄호 안에서 알맞은 것을 고르시오.

1 My aunt is (doctor / a doctor).

2 (Water / A water) is very important to us.

3 Antonio was born in (Germany / a Germany).

4 There are a lot of fallen (leafs / leaves) in the yard.

5 Can you count the (sheep / sheeps) on the farm?

6 I usually brush my (tooths / teeth) three times a day.

7 I often wash the (dishs / dishes) on weekends.

8 We found several (boxs / boxes) in the attic.

9 For more (information / informations), visit our website.

01-3 다음 괄호 안의 말을 알맞은 형태로 바꿔 문장을 완성하시오.

1 Two _____ are crying in the room. (girl)

2 Three _____ stop at the bus stop. (bus)

3 Are there ten _____ in the park? (bench)

4 Five _____ were playing with a ball. (child)

5 You can find five _____ in this city. (library)

6 There is some _____ in the bathroom. (shampoo)

7 We took many _____ of the military parade. (photo)

8 I like to read detective _____ in my free time. (story)

01 -4 다음 문장의 밑줄 친 부분을 어법상 알맞은 형태로 고쳐 쓰시오.

1 A science is her favorite subject. _____
2 Alice has two tomatos every day. _____
3 There is a delicious cheese on the table. _____
4 He saved a lot of moneys for three years. _____
5 There were three woman in the taxi. _____
6 My English teacher comes from a Canada. _____
7 Two deers jumped across the road. _____
8 There is a Tom on the phone for you. _____
9 Kate is reading a book about butterflys. _____

01 -5 다음 [보기]에서 알맞은 말을 골라 괄호 안의 말을 이용하여 문장을 완성하시오. (단, 한 번씩만 쓸 것)

┌ 보기 ┐
| piece | sheet | glass | loaf | slice | cup |

1 The woman needs _____. (five, paper)
2 There are _____ in the basket. (five, bread)
3 They ordered _____ and cookies. (two, cake)
4 You should drink _____ a day for your health. (eight, water)
5 The waiter gave _____ to each person. (one, tea)
6 Put _____ and mustard on the bread. (three, ham)

01 -6 다음 우리말과 의미가 같도록 괄호 안의 말을 이용하여 문장을 완성하시오.

1 단지 안에 꿀이 조금 있다. (there, some, honey)
  → _____ in the jar.

2 강아지 세 마리가 소파 위에서 자고 있다. (puppy, sleep)
  → _____ on the sofa.

3 Lucy는 양말 두 켤레를 샀다. (buy, pair, sock)
  → Lucy _____.

4 Oliver는 가구 다섯 점을 팔았다. (sell, piece, furniture)
  → Oliver _____.

5 두 명의 아이들이 길을 따라 나란히 걷고 있다. (child, be, walk)
  → _____ side by side along the street.

6 나는 대개 목요일마다 많은 숙제를 해야 한다. (do, a lot of, homework)
  → I usually have to _____ on Thursdays.

02-1 다음 괄호 안에서 알맞은 것을 고르시오.

1 (A / An) egg is healthy food.

2 Tony is good at (math / a math).

3 Pablo needs (a / an) new uniform.

4 It's cold. Can I turn on (a / the) heater?

5 They will employ (a / an) honest person.

6 She often takes a walk in (a / the) morning.

7 Two girls are chatting. I know (a / the) girls.

8 Tom and Jerry speak (a Korean / Korean) well.

9 I watched (a / an) interesting documentary on TV last night.

10 There is a watch on the table. (A / The) watch is from switzerland.

11 There are many countries in (a / the) world.

12 The population is increasing at about 6% (a / the) year.

13 The man played (violin / the violin) with great expression.

14 I have (lunch / the lunch) from twelve o'clock to one o'clock.

02-2 다음 빈칸에 a, an, the 중 알맞은 것을 쓰시오. (단, 필요 <u>없는</u> 경우 ×표)

1 Betty eats _____ breakfast at eight.

2 His father is _____ famous painter.

3 The sun is larger than _____ earth.

4 I have _____ iguana. It is 5 years old.

5 The player runs 10 kilometers _____ day.

6 My brother always goes to _____ bed late.

7 Some boys play _____ soccer at the playground.

8 Dohyun arrived in _____ London by _____ airplane.

9 They have _____ car. They bought _____ car last month.

10 I have a ring. _____ ring is real gold.

11 _____ sky becomes dark early in winter.

12 Sherlock Holmes has much interest in _____ chemistry.

13 I have no time to go to _____ theater during the week.

02-3 다음 문장의 밑줄 친 부분을 어법상 알맞은 형태로 고쳐 쓰시오.

1 Do you like to swim in <u>a sea</u>?　　　　　_____

2 He goes to work by <u>the subway</u>.　　　　_____

3 You can buy anything on <u>Internet</u>.　　　_____

4 Sumi lives in <u>a apartment</u> in the city.　_____

5 We ate the dinner at a Chinese restaurant.   _____

6 I'm looking for an comfortable armchair.   _____

7 We bought a small and cozy cabin in an Alps.   _____

02-4 다음 우리말과 의미가 같도록 괄호 안의 말을 이용하여 문장을 완성하시오.

1 축구는 흥미진진한 스포츠이다. (exciting, sport)

→ Soccer is _____.

2 나는 우산 하나와 우비 하나를 살 것이다. (umbrella, raincoat)

→ I will buy _____ and _____.

3 Sam은 일주일에 한 번 영화를 보러 간다. (once, week)

→ Sam goes to the movies _____.

4 Kelly는 플루트를 연주할 수 있다. (play, flute)

→ Kelly is able to _____.

5 우리는 여름에 한밤중에 쇼핑을 한다. (midnight)

→ We do our shopping _____ in summer.

6 나는 햇빛을 피하기 위해 선글라스를 썼다. (avoid, sun)

→ I wore my sunglasses to _____.

7 그 공장은 영국 북부에 위치해 있다. (north, England)

→ The factory is located in _____.

02-5 다음 우리말과 의미가 같도록 괄호 안의 말을 바르게 배열하시오.

1 그 영화는 정오에 시작한다. (at, begins, the movie, noon)

→ _____

2 그녀는 학교에 가는 길에 라디오를 듣는다. (to, she, the radio, listens)

→ _____ on her way to school.

3 Jessica는 일주일에 두 번 교회에 간다. (a week, goes, church, to, twice)

→ Jessica _____.

4 나의 아침 식사는 우유 한 잔과 사과 한 개이다. (a glass of, an apple, milk, is, and)

→ My breakfast _____.

5 인터넷 속도는 우리에게 중요하다. (important, the Internet, us, is, to)

→ The speed of _____.

6 그 소년들은 빗속에서 야구를 계속했다. (baseball, continued, the boys, to play)

→ _____ in the rain.

7 어떤 사람들은 환경을 위해 자전거로 출근한다. (by, go, some people, to work, bike)

→ _____ for the environment.

01 다음 중 명사의 복수형이 <u>잘못</u> 짝지어진 것은?

① a leaf – many leaves

② a candy – six candies

③ a bench – ten benches

④ a woman – two women

⑤ a goose – three gooses

02 다음 빈칸에 들어갈 말로 알맞은 것은?

There is a _____ on the table.

① salt ② apple ③ paper

④ basket ⑤ shampoo

03 다음 빈칸에 들어갈 말로 알맞지 <u>않은</u> 것은?

I found a _____ on the bench in the park.

① cap ② pen ③ book

④ money ⑤ squirrel

04 다음 빈칸에 들어갈 말로 알맞게 짝지어진 것은?

• _____ unusual thing happened to me today.

• I bought a dictionary. _____ dictionary cost 20 dollars.

① A – A ② A – The

③ An – The ④ The – A

⑤ The – The

05 다음 우리말을 어법에 알맞게 영작한 것은?

우리는 저녁 식사 후에 함께 TV를 보았다.

① We watched TV together after dinner.

② We watched TV together after a dinner.

③ We watched a TV together after a dinner.

④ We watched a TV together after the dinner.

⑤ We watched the TV together after the dinner.

06 [보기]의 밑줄 친 부분과 의미가 같은 것은?

— 보기 —

I clean my room twice <u>a</u> week.

① I want <u>a</u> pair of sneakers.

② There is <u>a</u> big spider on the desk.

③ Alex was in the hospital for <u>a</u> week.

④ We are planning <u>a</u> trip to visit Oxford.

⑤ You have to take the medicine three times <u>a</u> day.

07 다음 중 빈칸에 들어갈 관사가 나머지와 <u>다른</u> 것은?

① Spain is _____ country of Europe.

② Picasso is _____ very famous artist.

③ Ms. Wise plays _____ cello in an orchestra.

④ I chose _____ black jacket for the meeting.

⑤ There is _____ special program on TV tonight.

08 다음 밑줄 친 부분 중 어법상 <u>틀린</u> 것은?

① The boy emptied <u>a bottle of water</u>.

② They saw <u>three bowls of soup</u> on the table.

③ Emma pasted <u>two sheet of papers</u> together.

④ David put <u>four loaves of bread</u> into the bag.

⑤ I need <u>a few pieces of wood</u> to make a chair.

09 다음 중 어법상 <u>틀린</u> 것은?

① The sun isn't shining today.

② I had breakfast an hour ago.

③ The police station is on the left.

④ Pamela plays tennis every weekend.

⑤ They traveled to Germany by the train.

10 다음 중 어법상 옳은 문장의 개수는?

- I want two sandwiches for lunch.
- Dave came back very late at night.
- They play the soccer on Wednesdays.
- I learned to play the recorder at school.
- Drinking a milk every day is good for you.

① 1개 ② 2개 ③ 3개

④ 4개 ⑤ 5개

11 다음 빈칸에 공통으로 들어갈 알맞은 말을 쓰시오.

- Spain lies in _____ south of Europe.
- Many people search for information on _____ Internet.

→ _____

12 다음 괄호 안의 말을 이용하여 문장을 완성하시오.

My cat caught _____ in the cupboard. (two, mouse)

13 다음 빈칸 ⓐ~ⓒ에 들어갈 말을 [보기]에서 골라 알맞은 형태로 쓰시오.

┌─ 보기 ─┐

bottle   dinner   piece

A: I'm so hungry. What did you order for ⓐ _____ ?

B: I ordered two ⓑ _____ of pizza and two ⓒ _____ of Coke.

14 다음 우리말과 의미가 같도록 [조건]에 맞게 문장을 완성하시오.

중고 시장에는 많은 가구들이 있다.

┌─ 조건 ─┐

1. there, many, piece, furniture를 이용할 것
2. 필요시 단어를 추가하거나 어형을 바꿀 것

→ _____

at the used market.

15 다음 빈칸 ⓐ~ⓔ에 a, an, the 중 알맞은 것을 쓰시오. (단, 필요 <u>없는</u> 경우 ×표)

Last year we went to ⓐ _____ New York. I visited ⓑ _____ Empire State Building. I saw it on ⓒ _____ Internet several times. It was ⓓ _____ familiar landmark. It was ⓔ _____ excellent way to see the whole city.

Practice 01 **지시대명사, 비인칭 주어 it**

01 -1 다음 괄호 안에서 알맞은 것을 고르시오.

1 (It / That) is too dark in your room.
2 (That / Those) man is a football player.
3 (That / Those) are storybooks for children.
4 A: Mina, (this / that) is my brother Junha.
   B: Nice to meet you, Junha.
5 Can I have copies of (this / these) photos?
6 (That / Those) restaurant across the street looks nice.

01 -2 다음 질문에 대한 대답을 괄호 안의 말과 비인칭 주어 it을 이용하여 쓰시오.

1 A: What day is it today?
   B: _____ (Saturday)
2 A: What's the weather like in Jeju?
   B: _____ (windy and cold)
3 A: How far is it from here to the subway station?
   B: _____ (about 700 m)
4 A: What's the date of your birthday?
   B: _____ (December 24)
5 A: What season is it now in Chile?
   B: _____ (summer)
6 A: What time is it by your watch?
   B: _____ (9 o'clock)

01 -3 다음 빈칸에 들어갈 알맞은 말을 [보기]에서 골라 쓰시오. (단, 중복 가능)

보기
this   that   these   those   it

1 Hi, Mike. _____ is my friend James.
2 I don't like this bag. I want _____ bag.
3 Look at _____ kids over there. They are my cousins.
4 _____ is October 11 today. Tomorrow is my birthday.
5 _____ are my shoes. They are comfortable.
6 _____ blue jacket really suits you. You look great.
7 Is _____ boy in front of the gate your cousin?

○ 目目 Answers p.33

01 -4 다음 문장의 밑줄 친 부분을 어법상 알맞은 형태로 고쳐 쓰시오.

1 <u>These</u> is my favorite dessert. _____

2 Are <u>that</u> girls your daughters? _____

3 This baby <u>elephants</u> is very cute. _____

4 Can you move <u>those</u> suitcase for me? _____

5 <u>That</u> takes half an hour to get to Incheon International Airport by car. _____

6 <u>These</u> cat on the wall is not my neighbor's. _____

7 <u>This</u> is very cold at the Arctic Circle all year round. _____

01 -5 다음 우리말과 의미가 같도록 괄호 안의 말을 이용하여 문장을 완성하시오.

1 사진 속의 이 남자아이들 좀 봐. (boys)

→ Look at _____ in the picture.

2 저 식당은 비싸지만 맛이 있다. (restaurant)

→ _____ is expensive but delicious.

3 이 전화번호는 내 것이 아니다. 그것은 보라의 것이다. (phone number)

→ _____ isn't mine. It is Bora's.

4 저 상자들에는 내 예전 교과서들이 들어 있다. (boxes)

→ _____ have my old textbooks.

5 저 모기가 방금 내 다리를 물었다. (mosquito)

→ _____ just bit me in the leg.

6 나는 내 책상과 이 책장의 위치를 바꾸고 싶다. (bookcase)

→ I want to switch the position of my desk with _____.

01 -6 다음 우리말과 의미가 같도록 괄호 안의 말을 바르게 배열하시오.

1 저것들은 노인들을 위한 좌석들이다. (seats, are, for the elderly, those)

→ _____

2 내일 눈이 올지도 모른다. (snowy, tomorrow, be, it, may)

→ _____

3 이것은 멸종된 동물들에 관한 영화이다. (about extinct animals, is, this, the movie)

→ _____

4 나무 밑에 있는 저 벤치에 앉자. (sit, that, under the tree, let's, on, bench)

→ _____

5 너는 창가에 있는 저 여자를 알고 있니? (the window, know, that, do, by, you, woman, ?)

→ _____

6 이 버스는 국립 박물관에 가지 않는다. (the National Museum, go, this, to, doesn't, bus)

→ _____

02-1   다음 괄호 안에서 알맞은 것을 고르시오.

1   Todd wants (some / any) chocolate.

2   There isn't (some / any) water in the bottle.

3   She has an ecobag. She bought (one / ones / it) yesterday.

4   I don't have an eraser. Can you lend me (one / ones / it)?

5   Help (you / yourself) to this delicious *bulgogi*.

6   My little brother makes his bed by (him / himself).

7   It's too hot. Will you have (any / some) cold water?

8   The little girl washes her clothes (itself / herself).

9   Watch out! You will hurt (you / yourself)!

10   I didn't get (some / any) sleep last night.

02-2   다음 빈칸에 들어갈 알맞은 말을 [보기]에서 골라 쓰시오. (단, 중복 가능)

보기		
one	ones	it

1   A: Mom, where is my cell phone?

     B: _____ is on the table.

2   A: Which shoes do you like better?

     B: I like the brown _____ better.

3   A: Do you have a digital camera?

     B: Yes, I have _____. But _____ is broken.

4   A: Excuse me. Is there a book cafe near here?

     B: Yes. There is _____ near the subway station.

5   A: What happened? Did you break this glass?

     B: Yes. I'm so sorry. I dropped _____ on the floor.

6   A: Oh, this pancake is too cold. _____ is terrible.

     B: Wait a minute. I'm going to order another _____.

02-3   다음 빈칸에 some 또는 any 중 알맞은 것을 쓰시오.

1   Do you have _____ books about animals?

2   _____ kids are playing with a ball on the grass.

3   I need _____ colored pencils. Do you have _____?

4   _____ of his words were not true.

5   You don't have to buy _____ shoes. You already have too many.

6   I didn't put _____ salt in the soup yesterday.

7   Judy borrowed _____ magazines from the library.

🔖 Answers p.34

02 -4 다음 문장의 밑줄 친 부분을 어법상 알맞은 형태로 고쳐 쓰시오.

1 Alice makes her children's clothes <u>her</u>. _____

2 Do you see <u>some</u> cats behind the trees? _____

3 My dad seldom does the dishes <u>herself</u>. _____

4 I will drink a cup of coffee. Do you want <u>it</u>? _____

5 This shirt is too colorful. I don't like <u>one</u>. _____

6 These shoes are mine. The <u>one</u> over there are yours. _____

7 They threw away the old sofa. They bought a new <u>ones</u>. _____

02 -5 다음 우리말과 의미가 같도록 빈칸에 들어갈 알맞은 말을 [보기]에서 골라 쓰시오. (단, 중복 가능)

┌─ 보기 ┤
| one | ones | some | any |

1 해변에 몇몇 사람들이 있다.

→ There are _____ people at the beach.

2 저것은 Ted의 컴퓨터이다. 내 것은 왼쪽에 있는 것이다.

→ That is Ted's computer. Mine is the _____ on the left.

3 나의 아버지는 흰색 양말을 안 신으신다. 그는 검정색 양말을 신으신다.

→ My dad doesn't wear white socks. He wears black _____.

4 오렌지 주스 좀 드시겠어요?

→ Would you like _____ orange juice?

5 나는 그 콘서트에서 아무 사진도 찍지 못했다.

→ I couldn't take _____ photos at the concert.

6 스페인어는 어려운 언어이다. 쉬운 것은 없다.

→ Spanish is a difficult language. There isn't an easy _____.

02 -6 다음 우리말과 의미가 같도록 괄호 안의 말을 이용하여 문장을 완성하시오.

1 그들은 여행 동안 즐겁게 보냈다. (enjoy)

→ They _____ during their trip.

2 Kevin은 지갑에 돈이 전혀 없다. (money)

→ Kevin doesn't have _____ in his wallet.

3 나는 장갑을 잃어버렸다. 나는 새것을 사야 한다. (buy, new)

→ I lost my gloves. I have to _____.

4 경찰은 그 용의자에게 몇 가지 질문을 했다. (ask, questions)

→ The police _____ of the suspect.

5 이 잡지는 별로 흥미로워 보이지 않는다. 나는 다른 것을 읽고 싶다. (read, another)

→ This magazine doesn't look so interesting. I want to _____.

01 다음 빈칸에 들어갈 말로 알맞은 것은?

> _____ boxes are filled with used books and toys for the flea market.

① It　　　② This　　　③ That
④ They　　⑤ Those

02 다음 빈칸에 공통으로 들어갈 말로 알맞은 것은?

> · _____ is a nice Korean restaurant.
> · _____ was too dark inside the empty house on the hill.

① It　　　② Any　　　③ One
④ This　　⑤ That

03 다음 빈칸에 들어갈 말로 알맞지 <u>않은</u> 것은?

> Here you are. Is this _____ useful to you?

① map　　　② tools　　　③ book
④ program　⑤ information

04 다음 빈칸에 들어갈 말로 알맞게 짝지어진 것은?

> · I used the computer to read _____ emails.
> · Sue usually doesn't have _____ lunch except for a salad.

① it – some　　② any – it
③ no – some　　④ any – some
⑤ some – any

05 다음 우리말을 어법에 알맞게 영작한 것은?

> 나는 우주 과학에 관한 책을 한 권도 가지고 있지 않다.

① I don't have books on space science.
② I don't have a book on space science.
③ I don't have any books on space science.
④ I don't have some books on space science.
⑤ I don't have a few books on space science.

06 다음 밑줄 친 부분 중 생략할 수 <u>없는</u> 것은?

① I washed the dishes <u>myself</u>.
② We will do the work <u>ourselves</u>.
③ Sue <u>herself</u> was not a great singer.
④ The kids can look after <u>themselves</u>.
⑤ Tony repaired a robot cleaner <u>himself</u>.

07 다음 중 밑줄 친 부분의 쓰임이 나머지와 <u>다른</u> 것은?

① <u>It</u> is Friday today.
② <u>It</u> is going to rain today.
③ <u>It</u> is already past midnight.
④ <u>It</u> is 10 dollars and 35 cents.
⑤ <u>It</u> is fifteen minutes to twelve.

08 다음 중 빈칸에 들어갈 말이 나머지와 <u>다른</u> 것은?

① I have a red pen and a blue _____.
② My tablet PC is old. I need a new _____.
③ Don't drink the milk. _____ smells terrible.
④ This coat is too long for me. Do you have a shorter _____?
⑤ There are many cars in the parking lot. The gray _____ is mine.

09 다음 중 어법상 옳은 것은?

① Do you like that black jeans?

② That is snowing hard in Seoul.

③ We enjoyed us at the dance.

④ These medicine is effective for a headache.

⑤ I don't like math. It is very difficult for me.

10 다음 중 어법상 옳은 문장의 개수는?

· Those sneakers are very good one.

· Would you like some chocolate cake?

· There aren't any people in the square.

· It is five kilometers from here to the station.

· I left my dictionary at home. I have to borrow it from Jane.

① 1개   ② 2개   ③ 3개

④ 4개   ⑤ 5개

11 다음 밑줄 친 부분이 가리키는 바를 영어로 쓰시오.

This cell phone is too expensive. I want to see a cheaper <u>one</u>.

→ _____

12 다음 문장에서 어법상 틀린 부분을 한 군데 찾아 바르게 고쳐 문장을 다시 쓰시오.

These train carries hundreds of passengers to Seoul.

→ _____

13 다음 우리말과 의미가 같도록 괄호 안의 말을 바르게 배열하시오.

그 용감한 남자는 혼자서 다섯 명의 사람들을 구조해 냈다.
(himself, five, the brave man, by, people, rescued)

→ _____

14 다음 우리말과 의미가 같도록 [조건]에 맞게 문장을 완성하시오.

일기예보에 따르면, 내일은 화창할 것이다.

┌ 조건 ┐

1. will, sunny를 이용할 것

2. 필요시 단어를 추가할 것

→ According to the weather forecast, _____ tomorrow.

15 다음 빈칸 ⓐ~ⓓ에 들어갈 알맞은 말을 [보기]에서 골라 글을 완성하시오.

┌ 보기 ┐

any   some   it   one

ⓐ _____ is Friday today. There will be a K-pop concert at the stadium tomorrow. I really want to go there. However, I didn't get ⓑ _____ tickets. I was so depressed. Then, Vanessa called me. She had ⓒ _____ tickets for the concert. She gave me ⓓ _____. I'm so happy now.

Practice 01 **형용사**

01-1 다음 괄호 안에서 알맞은 것을 고르시오.

1 Rachel likes (funny / funnily) movies.
2 The (sleeping / asleep) baby is her child.
3 They thought the man was (diligently / diligent).
4 There were (many / much) people at the market.
5 Can you move (that big box / big that box) for me?
6 My grandparents live in (small a town / a small town).
7 He felt (something strange / strange something) in the bag.
8 I want (a little / a few) more time for myself.
9 We found the homeless dog (health / healthy).
10 (A few / Few) minutes later, he got out of the room.
11 I feel (happy / happily) when I ride my bike across yellow, orange and red leaves.

01-2 다음 우리말과 의미가 같도록 빈칸에 들어갈 알맞은 말을 [보기]에서 골라 쓰시오.

보기					
many	much	few	a few	little	a little

1 Kate는 오늘 밤에 커피를 너무 많이 마셨다.
   → Kate drank too _____ coffee tonight.
2 단지 몇몇 주자들만이 마라톤을 완주할 수 있었다.
   → Only _____ runners could finish the marathon.
3 요즈음 많은 학생들이 시청을 방문한다.
   → _____ students visit City Hall these days.
4 그는 항상 돈을 좀 갖고 다닌다.
   → He always takes _____ money with him.
5 가뭄 때문에 호수에 물이 거의 없다.
   → There is _____ water in the lake because of the drought.
6 우리는 버터 케이크를 만들기 위해 많은 설탕이 필요하다.
   → We need _____ sugar to make a butter cake.
7 이른 아침 공원에는 사람들이 거의 없었다.
   → There were _____ people in the park early in the morning.

01-3 다음 문장에서 밑줄 친 부분의 쓰임이 올바르면 ○표 하고, 올바르지 <u>않으면</u> 바르게 고쳐 쓰시오.

1 Melons are <u>my favorite fruit</u>.   _____
2 Mom, I want <u>delicious something</u>.   _____

3   Michael has <u>few</u> work this morning.   _____

4   Angela is popular. She has <u>a lot of</u> friends.   _____

5   The human document made everyone <u>sadly</u>.   _____

6   Don't do that! You can't lift the piano <u>lonely</u>.   _____

7   During the experiment, he didn't notice <u>anything strange</u>. _____

01 -4   다음 두 문장을 [보기]와 같이 한 문장으로 바꿔 쓰시오.

┌─ 보기 ├─
│
│   He has a computer. It is old. → <u>He has an old computer.</u>
│
└

1   Laura bought a skirt. It is very short.

    → _____

2   Antonio is in a classroom. It is empty.

    → _____

3   There are two monkeys in the cage. They are smart.

    → _____

4   I found a box in that room. It was locked.

    → _____

5   Look at the flowers. They are beautiful.

    → _____

6   I have money to buy a smartphone. It's enough.

    → _____

01 -5   다음 우리말과 의미가 같도록 괄호 안의 말을 바르게 배열하시오.

1   수학은 나에게 어려운 과목이다. (a, me, for, subject, difficult)

    → Math is _____.

2   그는 방학 동안 많은 곳을 방문했다. (a lot of, visited, places)

    → He _____ during the vacation.

3   저 잘생긴 배우는 한국에서 유명하다. (actor, handsome, famous, that, is)

    → _____ in Korea.

4   나의 남동생은 채소를 거의 먹지 않는다. (vegetables, few, eats)

    → My brother _____.

5   그녀는 감동적인 것을 보기를 원한다. (touching, watch, something)

    → She wants to _____.

6   그 두꺼운 겨울 외투가 너를 따뜻하게 해 줄 것이다. (the, coat, keep, winter, will, you, heavy, warm)

    → _____

02-1 다음 괄호 안에서 알맞은 것을 고르시오.

1 Paula arrived at school (late / lately).
2 Clara answered the question (clear / clearly).
3 Judy was a (very beautiful / beautiful very) dancer.
4 The company's new item was (high / highly) successful.
5 I had a (good / well) night's sleep last night.
6 I (usually study / study usually) in the library.
7 Beaches in Jejudo are (bad / badly) affected.

02-2 다음 문장에서 밑줄 친 부사가 꾸며 주는 말에 동그라미 하시오.

1 This exam was <u>pretty</u> difficult.
2 My grandfather snores <u>very</u> loudly.
3 Janet drives a car <u>slowly</u> in the snow.
4 The little boy <u>quickly</u> solved the riddle.
5 <u>Sadly</u>, Mike couldn't come to my birthday party.
6 The kindergarten kids are <u>really</u> cute.
7 I am ready <u>enough</u> to accept his invitation.
8 He makes <u>well</u> over $5,000 a month.

02-3 다음 괄호 안의 말을 알맞은 곳에 넣어 문장을 다시 쓰시오.

1 Jessica speaks in English. (seldom)
   → _____

2 My brother's desk is clean. (sometimes)
   → _____

3 David stays at home on weekends. (never)
   → _____

4 You should treat animals kindly. (always)
   → _____

5 We eat at the Japanese restaurant. (often)
   → _____

6 My younger brother is careful about his communication. (hardly)
   → _____

7 Perfume smells stronger in a warm area. (usually)
   → _____

02-4 다음 문장의 밑줄 친 부분을 어법상 알맞은 형태로 고쳐 쓰시오.

1 He seems busy <u>late</u>.   _____

2 Jinsu plays basketball very <u>good</u>.   _____

3 You <u>always may</u> ride my bicycle.   _____

4 The students listen <u>careful</u> to the teacher.   _____

5 He got into a taxi <u>fastly</u> and went to work.   _____

6 I read the news on the Internet <u>near</u> every day.   _____

7 She is a <u>high</u> educated young woman.   _____

8 Unfortunately, she <u>never will follow</u> your advice.   _____

02-5 다음 빈칸에 괄호 안의 말을 알맞은 형태로 바꿔 쓰시오. (단, 바꿀 필요가 <u>없는</u> 경우 그대로 쓸 것)

1 We have to start _____ tomorrow. (early)

2 The man repaired the printer _____. (easy)

3 George studied _____ to pass the exam. (hard)

4 The burglar climbed _____ up to the window. (quiet)

5 Mr. Kim _____ came into the classroom. (sudden)

6 In the wilderness, camels actually run _____. (fast)

7 I found the mid-term exam _____. (difficult)

02-6 다음 우리말과 의미가 같도록 괄호 안의 말을 바르게 배열하시오.

1 그녀는 오늘 매우 일찍 일어났다. (early, very, got up)

   → She _____ today.

2 그의 사무실은 항상 매우 밝다. (very, is, bright, always)

   → His office _____.

3 너는 저녁 식사 후에는 결코 TV를 볼 수 없다. (TV, watch, can, never)

   → You _____ after dinner.

4 그 동물원은 여기서 꽤 멀다. (far, here, from, quite, is)

   → The zoo _____.

5 너는 너의 가족을 위해 가끔 요리를 하니? (cook, you, sometimes, do)

   → _____ for your family?

6 너는 가끔 주말에 내 재킷을 입어도 돼. (sometimes, may, wear)

   → You _____ my jacket on weekends.

03 -1 다음 괄호 안에서 알맞은 것을 고르시오.

1 My aunt looks (young / younger) than her age.

2 John speaks German as (better / well) as Daniel.

3 The online game is the (most / more) exciting of them all.

4 The safety of the children is the (importantest / most important).

5 This washing machine is as heavy (as / than) that refrigerator.

6 She earns (little / less) money than she spends.

7 Mars is (very / much) colder than Earth.

8 My car isn't (older / oldest) than yours.

03 -2 다음 괄호 안의 말을 알맞은 형태로 바꿔 비교하는 문장을 완성하시오. (단, 바꿀 필요가 없는 경우 그대로 쓸 것)

1 Silver is _____ than gold. (cheap)

2 Billy isn't as _____ as my brother. (funny)

3 I like apples as _____ as mangoes. (much)

4 Dongsu is _____ at math than English. (good)

5 The stew is the _____ in the restaurant. (delicious)

6 This dress is the _____ in the shop. (bad)

7 This restaurant is not so _____ as that new one. (large)

8 Koreans spend the _____ time on leisure. (little)

03 -3 다음 괄호 안의 말을 이용하여 지시대로 비교하는 문장을 완성하시오.

1 Janet is _____ Jennifer. (popular / 원급)

2 The woman walked _____ a turtle. (slowly / 원급)

3 Brown bread is _____ white bread. (healthy / 비교급)

4 The old knife cuts _____ the new one. (well / 비교급)

5 My brother Sam is much _____ me. (old / 비교급)

6 The living room is _____ room in the house. (large / 최상급)

7 That is _____ animal in the zoo. (dangerous / 최상급)

8 *The Starry Night* is _____ of Gogh's paintings. (famous / 최상급)

9 This candy isn't _____ a lemon. (sour / 원급)

10 His condition became _____ around this time last year. (bad / 비교급)

03-4 다음 문장의 밑줄 친 부분을 어법상 알맞은 형태로 고쳐 쓰시오.

1 This year isn't as <u>hotter</u> as last year. _____

2 Paul is more intelligent <u>as</u> his brother. _____

3 This sofa is the most comfortable <u>of</u> the store. _____

4 The east of the country is <u>coldest</u> than the west. _____

5 Christmas should be the <u>happier</u> day of the year. _____

6 My brother enjoys reading comic books as <u>more</u> as I do. _____

7 He is not so clever <u>that</u> he looks. _____

8 The red car looked the <u>worse</u> of the three. _____

03-5 다음 우리말과 의미가 같도록 괄호 안의 말을 바르게 배열하시오.

1 그 건물은 세계에서 가장 높다. (in the world, highest, the, is)

→ The building _____.

2 과학은 수학보다 더 재미있다. (more, math, is, than, interesting)

→ Science _____.

3 그 책은 그것들 모두 중에서 가장 두껍다. (the, of, is, them all, thickest)

→ The book _____.

4 Mike는 그의 아버지만큼 잘생기지 않았다. (as, as, his father, isn't, handsome)

→ Mike _____.

5 그녀는 그녀의 가족 중에서 가장 일찍 일어난다. (the, in, gets up, earliest, her family)

→ She _____.

6 Yao Ming은 우리 중에서 가장 키가 크다. (the, us, tallest, of)

→ Yao Ming is _____.

03-6 다음 표를 보고 괄호 안의 말을 이용하여 지시대로 비교하는 문장을 완성하시오.

	Ace TV	Palace TV	Future TV
Size	40 inch	45 inch	52 inch
Price	$1,500	$1,500	$3,000

1 Palace TV is _____ Ace TV. (large / 비교급)

2 Ace TV is _____ the three TVs. (small / 최상급)

3 Future TV is _____ Palace TV. (small / 원급)

4 Ace TV is _____ Palace TV. (expensive / 원급)

5 Future TV is _____ the three TVs. (expensive / 최상급)

6 Palace TV is _____ Future TV. (cheap / 비교급)

Chapter Test

[01-02] 다음 빈칸에 들어갈 말로 알맞지 <u>않은</u> 것을 고르시오.

01

| Which is _____, this or that? |

① bigger   ② nice

③ heavier   ④ smaller

⑤ more expensive

02

| This house is _____ bigger than that one. |

① very   ② still   ③ even

④ much   ⑤ by far

[03-04] 다음 빈칸에 들어갈 말로 알맞게 짝지어진 것을 고르시오.

03

| • I haven't seen any plays _____. |
| • It is common to be _____ for a party in Peru. |

① late   –   late   ② late   –   lately

③ lately   –   late   ④ lately   –   lately

⑤ lately   –   later

04

| • I need _____ butter for baking. |
| • She went out without _____ money. |
| • How _____ mistakes did you make in the exam? |

① a lot of   –   much   –   much

② a lot of   –   much   –   many

③ many   –   many   –   a lot of

④ many   –   much   –   a lot of

⑤ much   –   many   –   many

05 다음 밑줄 친 부분 중 어법상 틀린 것은?

| This subway station <u>is</u> <u>not</u> <u>as</u> <u>crowded</u>
① ② ③
<u>than</u> <u>usual.</u>
④ ⑤ |

06 다음 중 어법상 틀린 것은?

① Minji is prettiest than Sujin.

② Any other animal is not cuter than dogs.

③ My grandmother is bigger than my father.

④ The book is more interesting than the movie.

⑤ Mt. Baekdu is the highest mountain in Korea.

07 다음 괄호 안의 단어가 들어갈 위치로 알맞은 곳은?

| She ① doesn't ② want ③ anything ④ for dessert. ⑤ (sweet) |

[08-09] 다음 중 어법상 틀린 것을 모두 고르시오.

08

① She buys a few onions.

② My son drinks little milk.

③ I lost a few weight recently.

④ The building has many windows.

⑤ There are many useful information on the Internet.

09 ① I'll never believe you.

② Silver isn't more expensive as gold.

③ My mom works as hardly as my dad.

④ He doesn't speak English as well as I do.

⑤ The amount of water are increasing rapidly.

10 다음 중 어법상 옳은 문장의 개수는?

- I find the movie boring.
- My children are asleep now.
- This potato soup tastes deliciously.
- She sometimes makes me angrily.

① 없음　　② 1개　　③ 2개

④ 3개　　⑤ 4개

[11-12] 다음 우리말과 의미가 같도록 괄호 안의 말을 이용하여 문장을 완성하시오.

11 그 록 콘서트는 매우 성공적이었다.
(high, successful)

→ The rock concert was _____.

12 파리는 프랑스에서 가장 인구가 많은 도시이다.
(populated, city)

→ Paris is _____ in France.

[13-14] 다음 우리말과 의미가 같도록 괄호 안의 단어를 바르게 배열하시오.

13 Molly는 그녀의 부모님에게 좀처럼 거짓말을 하지 않는다.
(tells, seldom, Molly, a lie, to, her parents)

→ _____

14 어떤 사람들은 전기만큼 물을 많이 낭비한다.
(people, much, as, electricity, as, water, some, waste)

→ _____

15 다음 표를 보고, 세 도시의 월별 평균 기온을 비교하는 문장을 완성하시오.

City	April(℃)	May(℃)
Seoul	12	17
Moscow	-1	13
New York	10	17

(1) Moscow is _____ city among three cities in April.

(2) Seoul is _____ than Moscow in May.

(3) New York is _____ Seoul in May.

Practice 01 **보어가 필요한 동사**

01 -1 다음 괄호 안에서 알맞은 것을 고르시오.

1 The weather turned (cold / coldly).
2 The baby tiger looks like (cute / a cat).
3 These rosemaries smell very (love / lovely).
4 Science makes our lives (convenient / conveniently).
5 Good meals will keep you (healthy / healthily).
6 Amy became (famous / famously) in a night.
7 We found the chair quite (comfortable / comfortably).

01 -2 다음 문장에서 밑줄 친 부분이 주격 보어이면 SC, 목적격 보어이면 OC를 쓰시오.

1 The sky looks cloudy.   _____
2 Linda is a famous violinist.   _____
3 He made his son a great scientist.   _____
4 Steve became rich in his twenties.   _____
5 The police officer found his story false.   _____
6 They named their daughter Beyonce.   _____
7 Paul is a middle school student.   _____
8 He always keeps his office clean.   _____

01 -3 다음 우리말과 의미가 같도록 [보기]의 (A), (B)에서 알맞은 말을 각각 한 단어씩 골라 문장을 완성하시오.
(단, 필요하면 형태를 바꿀 것)

┌─ 보기 ┐

(A)	(B)
feel smell look	tired strange sweet
sound taste	pale bitter

1 Sally의 얼굴이 창백해 보인다.
  → Sally's face _____ _____.
2 그들은 쇼핑을 한 후에 피곤함을 느꼈다.
  → They _____ _____ after shopping.
3 그의 목소리가 나에게 이상하게 들렸다.
  → His voice _____ _____ to me.
4 Jane의 새 향수는 나에게 달콤한 냄새가 난다.
  → Jane's new perfume _____ _____ to me.
5 이 소화제는 약간 쓴 맛이 난다.
  → This digestive medicine _____ a little _____.

01 -4 다음 문장에서 밑줄 친 부분의 쓰임이 올바르면 ○표 하고, 올바르지 않으면 바르게 고쳐 쓰시오.

1 The truck is very <u>slowly</u>. _____

2 His brother <u>looks like</u> a model. _____

3 My mother found the jar <u>empty</u>. _____

4 The steak tastes too <u>saltily</u> to me. _____

5 The student made his teacher <u>angrily</u>. _____

6 Her long hair feels <u>softly</u>. _____

7 This soup really smells <u>well</u>. _____

8 They think their son <u>honestly</u>. _____

01 -5 다음 우리말과 의미가 같도록 괄호 안의 말을 이용하여 문장을 완성하시오.

1 미라는 그 인형을 Bobo라고 부른다. (call, Bobo)

→ Mira _____ .

2 Amy의 손은 뜨거운 커피로 인해 따뜻하게 느꼈다. (feel)

→ Amy's hands _____ from the hot coffee.

3 그 사람들은 오늘 매우 행복해 보인다. (look)

→ The people _____ today.

4 Frank는 그의 바지가 짧다는 것을 알았다. (find, his pants)

→ Frank _____ .

5 이것은 중국 음식 같은 맛이 난다. (taste, Chinese food)

→ This _____ .

6 Andrew는 그 문을 연 채로 두었다. (leave, open)

→ Andrew _____ .

01 -6 다음 우리말과 의미가 같도록 괄호 안의 말을 바르게 배열하시오.

1 Kevin의 계획은 흥미롭게 들린다. (interesting, sounds)

→ Kevin's plan _____ .

2 그들은 Jessica를 유명한 가수로 만들 것이다. (Jessica, make, a famous singer, will)

→ They _____ .

3 그 사서는 항상 책장들을 말끔하게 유지한다. (the bookshelves, keeps, neat)

→ The librarian always _____ .

4 그 한국 배우는 전 세계적으로 인기를 얻었다. (popular, all over the world, became)

→ The Korean actor _____ .

5 내 꿈은 언젠가 이루어질 것이다. (come, will, true, someday)

→ My dream _____ .

목적어가 필요한 동사

02 -1 다음 괄호 안에서 알맞은 것을 고르시오.

1 Mary lent some money (to / of) her friend.

2 The doctor didn't ask anything (of / for) me.

3 Mr. Adams teaches (them / to them) English.

4 Betty gave her toy ambulance (Jerry / to Jerry).

5 She made a delicious cake (to / for) her children.

6 My aunt bought (me a pretty dress / a pretty dress me).

7 Tommy passed the football (to / for) Jerry.

8 The teacher told us (his name / to his name).

9 Roger cooked dinner (to / for) his family.

10 The cats will bring good luck (to / for) the people.

02 -2 다음 빈칸에 to, for, of 중 알맞은 것을 쓰시오.

1 Susan found the ruler _____ Fred.

2 Tony lent his history notes _____ me.

3 My mother cooked *galbi* _____ the guests.

4 Joey showed his new bike _____ his friends.

5 Some reporters asked a lot of questions _____ the singer.

6 I got a glass of wine _____ them.

7 She brought some food _____ the cats.

8 This story teaches an important lesson _____ us.

9 My uncle bought this tablet PC _____ me.

02 -3 다음 빈칸에 들어갈 알맞은 말을 [보기]에서 골라 쓰시오. (단, 한 번씩만 쓸 것)

> ┤ 보기 ├
>
> taught   cooked   bought   sent   asked   got   gave

1 Chris _____ a necklace for his wife.

2 His uncle _____ pocket money to him.

3 Ms. Jeong _____ music to us last year.

4 The strange man _____ my name of me.

5 I _____ macaroni and cheese for my friends.

6 The waitress _____ a glass of water for me.

7 Sarah _____ a birthday present to her son.

02-4 다음 문장의 밑줄 친 부분을 어법상 알맞은 형태로 고쳐 쓰시오.

1 Can I ask any questions <u>to you</u>? _____

2 Ben made <u>for his son</u> a bookshelf. _____

3 She brought <u>to him</u> a glass of juice. _____

4 My aunt sends a present <u>for me</u> every Children's Day. _____

5 I would like to order interesting books <u>to you</u>. _____

6 He will demand nothing <u>to you</u>. _____

02-5 다음 문장을 전치사가 포함된 문장으로 바꿔 쓰시오.

1 Hyunju bought her parents a car.

→ Hyunju bought _____.

2 Mr. Wright showed us his office.

→ Mr. Wright showed _____.

3 Kate sent her dad a sports magazine.

→ Kate sent _____.

4 My little brother always asks me many questions.

→ My little brother always _____.

5 The kind policeman found me my purse.

→ The kind policeman _____.

6 I told my best friend the secret.

→ I _____.

02-6 다음 우리말과 의미가 같도록 괄호 안의 말을 바르게 배열하시오.

1 Mike는 그의 여행 계획을 나에게 말해 주었다. (his travel plans, me, told)

→ Mike _____.

2 Sally는 Sue에게 그녀의 라켓을 빌려 주었다. (Sue, her racket, to, lent)

→ Sally _____.

3 Daniel은 Amy에게 꽃을 좀 사 주었다. (Amy, for, bought, some flowers)

→ Daniel _____.

4 그들은 가난한 사람들에게 무료로 점심을 요리해 주었다. (for, lunch, poor people, cooked)

→ They _____ for free.

5 Tina는 그녀가 가장 좋아하는 인형을 그 아이에게 주었다. (her favorite doll, the child, gave, to)

→ Tina _____.

6 그 가난한 남자는 내게 약간의 돈을 달라고 애원했다. (me, of, begged, some, money)

→ The poor man _____.

Chapter Test

[01-02] 다음 빈칸에 들어갈 말로 알맞지 <u>않은</u> 것을 고르시오.

01

Mina looked _____ yesterday.

① free   ② upset

③ busy   ④ an actress

⑤ pretty

02

Her sister _____ a bracelet for her.

① got   ② gave

③ made   ④ found

⑤ bought

[03-04] 다음 중 밑줄 친 부분의 쓰임이 [보기]와 같은 것을 고르시오.

03

┤ 보기 ├
Suji looks just <u>like</u> her mother.

① I <u>like</u> to go out for a walk.

② That sounds <u>like</u> a great idea.

③ Foreign girls <u>like</u> BTS so much.

④ What would you <u>like</u> to have?

⑤ I don't <u>like</u> all kinds of instant food.

04

┤ 보기 ├
Volunteering will <u>make</u> you happy!

① The teacher <u>makes</u> me a better person.

② I'll <u>make</u> you a beautiful ring.

③ She will <u>make</u> a delicious cake.

④ Can you <u>make</u> me some cookies?

⑤ You always <u>make</u> the same mistake.

05 다음 중 밑줄 친 동사의 성격이 나머지와 <u>다른</u> 것은?

① She <u>asked</u> me a favor.

② Jason <u>kept</u> the door open.

③ <u>Give</u> me your best smile.

④ They will <u>find</u> her a job.

⑤ Can you <u>bring</u> me a small box?

06 다음 중 밑줄 친 부분의 문장 성분이 나머지와 <u>다른</u> 것은?

① She cooked me <u>spaghetti</u>.

② Sunshine gives us <u>happiness</u>.

③ She passed her friend <u>an eraser</u>.

④ He will write Betty <u>a love letter</u>.

⑤ I made my daughter <u>a programmer</u>.

07 다음 우리말과 의미가 같도록 괄호 안의 말을 배열할 때 세 번째에 오는 것은?

그는 친구들에게 생일 초대장을 보냈다.
(a birthday invitation, sent, to, his friends, he)

① to   ② his friends

③ he   ④ a birthday invitation

⑤ sent

[08-09] 다음 중 어법상 <u>틀린</u> 것을 모두 고르시오.

08 ① Laura feels sick.

② The pie smells a rose.

③ The lemon tea tastes sour.

④ The old woman looks angry.

⑤ His vacation plan sounds well.

Answers p.37

09
① Everybody calls him Jim.
② I found the book interesting.
③ Gloves keep your hands warmly.
④ They named the new baby Semi.
⑤ The present made me very excitedly all day long.

10 다음 중 어법상 옳은 것으로 알맞게 짝지어진 것은?

> ⓐ He teaches us English.
> ⓑ Ann sent a letter to him.
> ⓒ Kevin showed his picture her.
> ⓓ She made a toy car to her brother.
> ⓔ Her mom gives her some money.

① ⓐ, ⓓ
② ⓑ, ⓒ, ⓓ
③ ⓐ, ⓑ, ⓔ
④ ⓐ, ⓑ, ⓒ, ⓓ
⑤ ⓐ, ⓑ, ⓓ, ⓔ

[11-12] 다음 문장을 같은 의미의 전치사가 포함된 문장으로 바꾸어 쓰시오.

11
> Mom bought me the latest smartphone for my birthday.

→ Mom bought _____
_____ .

12
> He asked me my neighbor's phone number.

→ He asked _____
_____ .

13 다음 우리말과 의미가 같도록 괄호 안의 말을 바르게 배열하시오.

> 일부 박테리아는 우리를 청결하고 건강하게 유지하도록 도와준다.
> (keep, healthy, clean, and, us)

→ Some bacteria help _____
_____ .

[14-15] 다음 우리말과 의미가 같도록 괄호 안의 말을 이용하여 문장을 완성하시오.

14
> 우리는 그 소년이 천재라는 것을 알았다.
> (find, genius)

→ We _____ .

15
> 우리 엄마가 나를 위해 사과 파이를 요리해 주셨다.
> (cook, an apple pie)

→ My mom _____
_____ .

Practice 01 **and, but, or, so**

01-1 다음 괄호 안에서 알맞은 것을 고르시오.

1 The dog is big (but / or) very cute.

2 Is she your sister (and / or) your cousin?

3 Thomas wore a T-shirt (but / and) shorts.

4 The weather became cloudy (and / or) cold.

5 Tom exercised every day, (so / but) his health got better.

6 Will you go home (or / but) play basketball after school?

7 They were busy, (but / so) they couldn't play outside.

8 Kids, be quiet (and / but) just sit down!

9 The museum is between the fire station (and / or) the restaurant.

01-2 다음 우리말과 의미가 같도록 빈칸에 and, but, or, so 중 알맞은 것을 쓰시오.

1 커피나 차 중 어느 것을 더 좋아하세요?

→ Which do you like better, coffee _____ tea?

2 나는 너무 피곤해서 소파에서 잠이 들었다.

→ I was so tired, _____ I fell asleep on the sofa.

3 그녀는 그녀의 사무실에 들어가서 문을 잠갔다.

→ She went into her office _____ locked the door.

4 경찰서는 가깝지만 우체국은 꽤 멀다.

→ The police station is close, _____ the post office is quite far.

5 나는 표지판을 만들어서 학교 도서관에 게시했다.

→ I made signs _____ posted them in the school library.

6 우리는 공공 도서관에 갔지만 그곳은 문을 닫았다.

→ We went to the public library _____ it was closed.

01-3 다음 빈칸에 들어갈 알맞은 말을 [보기]에서 골라 쓰시오. (단, 중복 가능)

보기			
and	but	or	so

1 The book is interesting _____ helpful.

2 My father goes to work by car _____ by subway.

3 Clara had a toothache, _____ she went to the dentist.

4 Arnold passed the math exam, _____ he failed the English exam.

5 He looked for the key _____ he couldn't find it.

6 If it rains, wear a raincoat _____ use an umbrella.

⊟ Answers p.37

01-4 다음 문장이 자연스러운 의미가 되도록 [보기]에서 알맞은 것을 골라 그 기호를 쓰시오.

┌─ 보기 ───┐
│ ⓐ and broke his leg   ⓑ so she went swimming │
│ ⓒ and turned on the light   ⓓ but didn't catch anything │
│ ⓔ or a cup of coffee   ⓕ so she wants to get a blanket │
└──┘

1 It was very hot, _____.

2 Molly stood up _____.

3 They fished all day _____.

4 He fell down the stairs _____.

5 He drinks a glass of milk _____ in the morning.

6 Jane is cold, _____.

01-5 다음 두 문장을 한 문장으로 바꿔 쓸 때, 빈칸에 and, but, or, so 중 알맞은 것을 쓰시오.

1 Do you like blue? Do you like red?

→ Which color do you like better, blue _____ red?

2 Molly learned Japanese. She learned Chinese, too.

→ Molly learned Japanese _____ Chinese.

3 I watched the movie three times. I still can't understand it.

→ I watched the movie three times, _____ I still can't understand it.

4 Clara likes drawing cartoons. She's going to be a webtoon artist.

→ Clara likes drawing cartoons, _____ she's going to be a webtoon artist.

5 We don't have much in common. We are good friends.

→ We don't have much in common, _____ we are good friends.

01-6 다음 우리말과 의미가 같도록 괄호 안의 말을 이용하여 문장을 완성하시오.

1 그들은 신선한 과일과 채소를 판다. (sell, fresh, fruit, vegetables)

→ They _____.

2 어제 눈이 많이 와서 우리는 눈사람을 만들었다. (make, a snowman)

→ It snowed a lot yesterday, _____.

3 Brad나 네가 거실을 청소해야 한다. (must, clean)

→ _____ the living room.

4 그 노부인은 90세이지만 건강하다. (she, be, healthy)

→ The elderly lady is 90 years old, _____.

5 어젯밤에 이웃이 너무 시끄러워서 나는 잠을 잘 못 잤다. (can, sleep well)

→ My neighbor was so loud last night, _____.

02 -1   다음 괄호 안에서 알맞은 것을 고르시오.

1 Look (after / before) you leap.

2 I stayed at a hotel (before / when) I was in France.

3 When I (see / will see) Cathy, I will tell her the news.

4 Harry feeds his dogs (after / before) he goes to school.

5 (After / Before) Monica made a cake, she took a picture of it.

6 You shouldn't drive (when / before) you are sleepy.

7 He drank a lot of water (after / before) he finished the race.

8 (When / After) I was young, I liked to do many things.

9 You should turn off the TV (after / before) you go to bed.

02 -2   다음 우리말과 의미가 같도록 빈칸에 when, before, after 중 알맞은 것을 쓰시오.

1 그녀는 피곤할 때 코코아를 마신다.

   → She drinks hot chocolate _____ she is tired.

2 우리는 숙제를 끝낸 후에 텔레비전을 보았다.

   → We watched TV _____ we finished our homework.

3 그가 결혼할 때 너는 그에게 무엇을 줄 거니?

   → What will you give him _____ he gets married?

4 나는 돈을 모은 후에 그 신발을 살 것이다.

   → I'll buy the shoes _____ I save money.

5 Alice는 너를 방문하기 전에 미리 전화할 거야.

   → _____ Alice visits you, she will call ahead.

02 -3   다음 빈칸에 들어갈 알맞은 말을 [보기]에서 골라 쓰시오. (단, 중복 가능)

┌─ 보기 ┤
│   when   before   after
└

1 I went out _____ I turned off the light.

2 Wipe your shoes on the mat _____ you come in.

3 _____ I was taking a walk at the park, I met my teacher.

4 _____ she goes shopping, she makes out a shopping list.

5 You shouldn't use your phone _____ you are driving a car.

6 _____ he retired in 2021, he tried to enter new fields.

02 -4 다음 문장이 자연스러운 의미가 되도록 알맞게 연결하시오.

1   Go to bed   •   • ⓐ when I saw her.
2   I helped my mom   •   • ⓑ before he went out.
3   Kevin closed all the windows   •   • ⓒ before you answer it.
4   She was wearing a red scarf   •   • ⓓ after you put your toys away.
5   You should read a question carefully   •   • ⓔ when she cooked breakfast.
6   I published her writings   •   • ⓕ when they take pictures.
7   They say cheese   •   • ⓖ three years after she died.

02 -5 다음 두 문장을 접속사를 이용하여 한 문장으로 바꿔 쓸 때, 빈칸에 알맞은 말을 쓰시오.

1   She sings a song. She drinks hot water.
    → Before _____.

2   I entered her room. She was sleeping.
    → When _____.

3   Winter comes. Some animals store food.
    → Before _____.

4   You called me. I was in the bathroom.
    → I was in the bathroom _____.

5   I felt much better. I took some aspirin.
    → I felt much better _____.

02 -6 다음 우리말과 의미가 같도록 괄호 안의 말과 접속사를 이용하여 문장을 완성하시오.

1   나는 삼촌을 찾아뵙기 전에 전화를 드렸다. (visit, him)
    → I called my uncle _____.

2   Ron이 집에 도착한 후에 눈이 오기 시작했다. (arrive, home)
    → _____, it started to snow.

3   우리는 교실을 청소한 후에 야구를 했다. (clean, the classroom)
    → We played baseball _____.

4   Emma가 내 이름을 불렀을 때, 나는 머리를 감고 있었다. (call, my name)
    → I was washing my hair _____.

5   우리는 영화를 보기 전에 함께 저녁을 먹었다. (watch a movie)
    → _____, we had dinner together.

6   여가 시간이 있을 때, 그는 대개 더 많은 아이디어를 위해서 책을 읽는다. (have, free time)
    → _____, he usually reads books for more ideas.

03 -1 다음 괄호 안에서 알맞은 것을 고르시오.

1 It is surprising (that / if) Linda got married to Tom.
2 She felt very cold (if / because) the wind was strong.
3 I think (because / that) he is the best swimmer in Korea.
4 He doesn't clean his room (that / if) it isn't really dirty.
5 If you (won't / don't) chew meat well, you'll have a stomachache.
6 He couldn't go home early (that / because) he had a lot of work.
7 (If / Because) you are tired, you can get some rest in the resting room.
8 I'll visit you if I (will / am) free this weekend.
9 The trouble is (that / if) they don't have enough time.
10 You (will get / get) fat if you eat too much chocolate.

03 -2 다음 우리말과 의미가 같도록 빈칸에 because, if, that 중 알맞은 것을 쓰시오.

1 내가 바쁘지 않으면 너를 데리러 갈게.
   → _____ I am not busy, I will pick you up.
2 가장 큰 문제는 우리 차가 고장 났다는 거야.
   → The biggest problem is _____ our car is broken.
3 Britney는 심한 감기에 걸렸기 때문에 노래를 부를 수 없다.
   → _____ Britney has a bad cold, she can't sing.
4 너에게 에어프라이어가 있다면 쉽게 빵을 구울 수 있다.
   → You can bake bread easily _____ you have an air-fryer oven.
5 그가 다음 주에 내 제안을 받아들일 거라는 것은 확실하다.
   → It is certain _____ he will accept my offer next week.

03 -3 다음 빈칸에 들어갈 알맞은 말을 [보기]에서 골라 쓰시오. (단, 중복 가능)

┌─ 보기 ┤───
│   because   if   that
└───

1 I think _____ the documentary is moving.
2 The door will open _____ you push the button.
3 _____ you take the medicine, you will get better.
4 She couldn't play the cello _____ she hurt her arm.
5 The truth is _____ she didn't graduate from university.
6 My uncle moved to London _____ he got a new job.
7 It is important _____ we share the same vision about the future.

03-4 다음 문장이 자연스러운 의미가 되도록 알맞게 연결하시오.

1 The problem is •

2 You took a taxi •

3 I can't believe you •

4 You'll find the museum •

5 He is very weak •

6 My hope is •

7 It is very dangerous •

• ⓐ if you turn right.

• ⓑ because you got up late.

• ⓒ because he doesn't eat well.

• ⓓ that the painting is a fake.

• ⓔ if you don't tell the truth.

• ⓕ unless you wear a seatbelt.

• ⓖ that my dream will come true.

03-5 다음 두 문장을 접속사를 이용하여 한 문장으로 바꿔 쓸 때, 빈칸에 알맞은 말을 쓰시오.

1 You get a pet. You will feel happy.

→ If _____ .

2 He forgot my phone number. It is clear.

→ It is clear _____ .

3 She has free time. She usually rides a bike.

→ If _____ .

4 I lost my cell phone. I can't send text messages to you.

→ Because _____ .

5 All of you did your best. I know it.

→ I know _____ .

6 Kurt played computer games all day. He didn't finish his homework.

→ Kurt didn't finish _____ .

03-6 다음 우리말과 의미가 같도록 괄호 안의 말과 접속사를 이용하여 문장을 완성하시오.

1 Molly가 그 동아리에 가입했다는 것은 사실이다. (join, the club)

→ _____ is true.

2 내가 나의 숙제를 일찍 끝내면 너를 도와줄게. (finish, homework, early)

→ I will help you _____ .

3 선생님은 Bill이 정직하다는 것을 알고 있다. (honest)

→ The teacher knows _____ .

4 그가 운전면허 시험에 불합격하면, 다시 시험을 볼 것이다. (fail, the driving test)

→ _____ , he will take it again.

5 그녀는 하늘이 더 어두워지고 있었기 때문에 두려움을 느꼈다. (get darker)

→ She felt afraid _____ .

Chapter Test

[01-02] 다음 빈칸에 들어갈 말로 알맞은 것을 고르시오.

01

> A: Which do you like better, online
> _____ offline shopping?
> B: I like online shopping better.

① and   ② or   ③ but
④ if   ⑤ after

02

> He is sometimes very noisy, _____ he
> is a lovely kid.

① so   ② and   ③ but
④ that   ⑤ because

03 다음 빈칸에 공통으로 들어갈 말로 알맞은 것은?

> · Some students tap their feet _____
> they are learning.
> · Janet, _____ did you leave for
> Seoul?

① if   ② that   ③ when
④ before   ⑤ because

04 다음 두 문장의 의미가 같도록 빈칸에 들어갈 말로 알맞은 것은?

> That you take a look back at our history
> is instructive.
> = _____ is instructive that you take a
> look back at our history.

① It   ② When
③ That   ④ What
⑤ This

05 다음 중 빈칸에 들어갈 접속사가 나머지와 <u>다른</u> 것은?

① I was tired _____ I studied more.
② She can sing _____ can't dance well.
③ We tried best, _____ we won the game.
④ I looked for the phone _____ I couldn't find it.
⑤ Mike studied hard _____ he didn't pass the test.

06 다음 밑줄 친 부분 중 생략할 수 있는 것은?

① After <u>that</u>, he finished his homework.
② <u>That</u> she is a famous influencer is true.
③ My son believes <u>that</u> Santa Clause is real.
④ The point is <u>that</u> we need to work together.
⑤ It is a fact <u>that</u> he stole the bag from the store.

07 다음 세 문장이 같은 뜻이 되도록 빈칸에 들어갈 말로 알맞게 짝지어진 것은?

> Junha searched the Internet and then he
> did his homework.
> = _____ Junha searched the Internet,
> he did his homework.
> = _____ Junha did his homework, he
> searched the Internet.

① After   –   Before   ② Before   –   After
③ When   –   After   ④ When   –   Before
⑤ After   –   When

[08-09] 다음 중 어법상 <u>틀린</u> 것을 <u>모두</u> 고르시오.

08 ① He jogs before he has breakfast.
② When I arrived at the bank, it closed.
③ Because he ran fast, he couldn't catch her.
④ We will have a party because of today is Brad's birthday.
⑤ After she washed her dog, she cleaned the bathroom.

09 ① It is important that we recycle paper.
② I hope that she will be a great skater.
③ Please close the window that you go out.
④ If you'll read many books, you'll be smarter.
⑤ You can't do anything unless you have changed.

10 다음 중 어법상 옳은 문장의 개수는?

> ⓐ They couldn't go out because of the bad weather.
> ⓑ I heard math is a useful subject.
> ⓒ When we have problems, we listen to her.
> ⓓ What will you do if you won't go to the concert?

① 없음　　　② 1개　　　③ 2개
④ 3개　　　⑤ 4개

[11-12] 다음 우리말과 의미가 같도록 괄호 안의 말을 이용하여 문장을 완성하시오.

11
> 네가 아플 때는 운동을 하지 마라. (sick)

→ Don't exercise _____.

12
> 나의 아버지는 그의 건강 때문에 담배를 끊으셨다. (health)

→ My father stopped smoking _____
_____.

[13-14] 다음 [보기]에서 알맞은 접속사를 골라 주어진 두 문장을 한 문장으로 바꿔 쓰시오.

> ─ 보기 ─
> so　　if　　because　　that

13
> She had much homework to do. She stayed up late.

→ She stayed up late _____
_____.

14
> He wants to get a good grade in the mid-term exam. His mom will be happy then.

→ _____ he _____
_____, his mom
will be happy.

15 다음 문장과 의미가 같도록 알맞은 접속사를 사용하여 영어로 쓰시오.

> During my childhood, I often visited my grandparents.

= _____
_____

Practice **01**   시간을 나타내는 전치사

01 -1   다음 괄호 안에서 알맞은 것을 고르시오.

1 What do you do (on / at) Sundays?
2 They picked apples and pears (on / in) fall.
3 I slept from eleven (at / to) seven yesterday.
4 They will stay in Seoul (for / during) a week.
5 She usually reads some books (in / at) night.
6 I don't have much free time (for / during) the week.
7 He asked us to wait for him (by / until) 3:00.
8 Can we get to the airport (by / until) 4:00?
9 We had little snow (in / x) this winter.

01 -2   다음 빈칸에 at, on, in 중 알맞은 것을 쓰시오.

1 Banks close _____ weekends.
2 Halloween Day is _____ October 31.
3 His family moved to Tokyo _____ 2012.
4 My brother doesn't exercise _____ night.
5 It snows a lot _____ December in Korea.
6 Mom gets up _____ 6:00 _____ the morning.
7 We have an English class _____ Mondays.
8 The train for Daegu leaves _____ noon.
9 She had a chance to play _____ a theater.
10 The room temperature is warm _____ winter and cool _____ summer.

01 -3   다음 빈칸에 for 또는 during 중 알맞은 것을 쓰시오.

1 I rode a bike _____ an hour.
2 Don't send text messages _____ class.
3 Alisa made some friends _____ the camp.
4 Chris was absent from school _____ three days.
5 My dad slept _____ 30 minutes _____ the movie.
6 Japan ruled Korea by force _____ 36 years.
7 Did you get enough sleep _____ the week?

◦ 🔖 Answers p.39

01 -4 다음 문장에서 밑줄 친 부분의 쓰임이 올바르면 ○표 하고, 올바르지 <u>않으면</u> 알맞게 고쳐 쓰시오.

1 Owls and bats sleep <u>for</u> the day.   _____

2 My parents got married <u>on</u> 2002.   _____

3 Did you call me <u>in</u> the afternoon?   _____

4 Was she staying at home <u>at</u> last night?   _____

5 The lights went off <u>for</u> 30 minutes in the evening.   _____

6 He said that we should come to the party <u>until</u> 7 p.m.   _____

7 The restaurant is open from 11 a.m. <u>to</u> 5 p.m.   _____

8 I need to be back home <u>by</u> the end of the month.   _____

9 Robert is going to arrive <u>at five in this morning</u>.   _____

10 The church was built <u>at</u> the 13th century.   _____

01 -5 다음 우리말과 의미가 같도록 괄호 안의 말과 전치사를 이용하여 문장을 완성하시오.

1 한국에서 학교는 보통 3월에 시작한다. (March)

 → Schools usually start _____ in Korea.

2 나의 삼촌은 휴가 동안 많은 사진을 찍었다. (the holidays)

 → My uncle took a lot of pictures _____.

3 나는 퇴근 후에 양로원에서 자원봉사를 한다. (work)

 → I do volunteer work at a nursing home _____.

4 모두 온종일 열심히 연습했다. 아침에, 점심 시간 동안, 그리고 방과 후에도 말이다! (morning, lunchtime, school)

 → Everyone practiced hard all day: _____!

01 -6 다음 우리말과 의미가 같도록 [보기]에서 알맞은 말을 골라 괄호 안의 말을 이용하여 문장을 완성하시오.

┌─ 보기 ┐
| at   for   before   after   until |
└────────────────┘

1 7시 30분에 만나자. (meet, 7:30)

 → Let's _____.

2 Tom은 점심 식사 후에 농구를 했다. (play basketball, lunch)

 → Tom _____.

3 신데렐라는 자정 전에 돌아와야 한다. (come back, midnight)

 → Cinderella has to _____.

4 우리는 10년 동안 그 아파트에서 살았다. (live, the apartment)

 → We _____.

5 저는 5시까지 직장에서 바쁠 거예요. (busy, at work, five)

 → I'll _____.

장소를 나타내는 전치사

02-1 다음 괄호 안에서 알맞은 것을 고르시오.

1 My classroom is (at / on) the third floor.
2 There was a new bike (in / at) the big box.
3 There is a little concert (at / on) the airport.
4 I will read books (in / at) home this weekend.
5 They had a holiday (in / on) New York.
6 There is a mountain (among / between) the two towns.
7 The sun was rising (over / on) the mountain.
8 I know a nice seafood restaurant (under / near) here.
9 There is a lizard crawling (over / on) the window.
10 I met one of my old friends (at / on) Christmas Eve.

02-2 다음 빈칸에 at, on, in 중 알맞은 것을 쓰시오.

1 There is somebody _____ the kitchen.
2 There are five candles _____ the cake.
3 Michael was _____ Australia last month.
4 Some kids are playing _____ the corner.
5 We spent a lot of time _____ the road because of the traffic jam.
6 Whales live _____ the sea, but they are not fish.
7 The train stops running _____ midnight.

02-3 다음 빈칸에 들어갈 알맞은 말을 [보기]에서 골라 쓰시오. (단, 중복 가능)

┌ 보기 ┐
│ on   at   in   over   behind   among │
└───┘

1 Albert has a ring _____ his pocket.
2 There is a computer _____ his desk.
3 He waited for me _____ the bus stop.
4 The picture is hanging _____ the table.
5 The birds built their nests _____ the trees.
6 Don't step back. There's a child _____ you.
7 The horse is jumping _____ the fence.
8 A Korean man was _____ the survivors.

02 -4 다음 우리말과 의미가 같도록 괄호 안의 말을 이용하여 문장을 완성하시오.

1 그들은 강 근처에 텐트를 쳤다. (the river)

→ They set up a tent _____ .

2 내 파스타 위에서 파리 두 마리가 날고 있다. (my pasta)

→ Two flies are flying _____ .

3 그녀의 강아지는 항상 그녀 옆에 앉는다. (her)

→ Her puppy always sits _____ .

4 여기에서 공원까지 걸어서 20분 걸린다. (here, the park)

→ It takes 20 minutes on foot _____ .

5 자랑스럽게도, 내 여동생이 많은 사람들 앞에서 피아노를 치고 있다. (many people)

→ Proudly, my sister is playing the piano _____ .

02 -5 다음 문장에서 밑줄 친 부분을 어법상 알맞은 형태로 고쳐 쓰시오.

1 I saw the sunset <u>on the horizon</u>. _____

2 The sports center is <u>across my school</u>. _____

3 I dropped my ball <u>among the wall and the door</u>. _____

4 My sister is sleeping deeply <u>behind to a flowery hilltop</u>. _____

5 The band practiced their songs <u>at the garage</u>. _____

02 -6 다음 지도를 보고, 빈칸에 들어갈 알맞은 전치사(구)를 [보기]에서 골라 쓰시오.

┌─ 보기 ─
│   behind   between   next to   in front of   across from
└─

1 The church is _____ the bank.

2 The park is _____ the museum.

3 The bank is _____ the church.

4 The department store is _____ the park.

5 The coffee shop is _____ the museum and the gym.

Chapter Test

[01-02] 다음 빈칸에 들어갈 말로 알맞은 것을 고르시오.

01
> A man sitting _____ me screamed for the entire running time.

① on   ② over   ③ next
④ next to   ⑤ beside to

02
> Bake the cake _____ 40 minutes.

① on   ② over   ③ for
④ during   ⑤ beside

03 다음 중 빈칸에 들어갈 말이 나머지와 <u>다른</u> 것은?

① Christmas is _____ December.
② My son was born _____ 2008.
③ I work best _____ the morning.
④ Will you go shopping _____ Saturday?
⑤ People usually plant trees _____ the spring.

04 다음 두 문장의 의미가 같도록 빈칸에 들어갈 말로 알맞은?

> Mike usually goes to bed at 11 p.m. and sleeps for seven hours.
> = Mike gets up _____ 6 a.m.

① in   ② until   ③ for
④ during   ⑤ at

05 다음 빈칸에 공통으로 들어갈 말로 알맞은 것은?

> · He runs _____ his house to the park.
> · The bank is across _____ the bakery.

① near   ② from   ③ among
④ behind   ⑤ between

06 다음 빈칸 (A), (B), (C)에 들어갈 말로 알맞게 짝지어진 것은?

> · Lizo is ___(A)___ Mexico.
> · It snows a lot ___(B)___ January.
> · The National Bank is ___(C)___ your right.

     (A)   (B)   (C)
① to   –   with   –   for
② at   –   to   –   with
③ from   –   in   –   on
④ from   –   on   –   in
⑤ with   –   at   –   out

07 다음 나열된 인물들을 일렬로 세울 때 다섯 번째로 서게 되는 사람을 고르면?

> · Minji is between Minsu and Suhee.
> · Suhee is in front of Philip.
> · Jacob is first in line.
> · Minsu is behind Jacob.
> · Rebecca is behind Philip.

① Minji   ② Suhee   ③ Philip
④ Minsu   ⑤ Rebecca

[08-09] 다음 중 어법상 <u>틀린</u> 것을 <u>모두</u> 고르시오.

08
① Let's meet at 9:30.
② We'll travel Jeju by Sunday.
③ The students played soccer for two hours.
④ You must finish the essay by next Monday.
⑤ A lot of young people died over the war.

09 ① I lived near the bus stop.

② They are leaving to Sydney.

③ I found my socks under the chair.

④ Ted is walking among his parents.

⑤ Mary is standing next to the copy machine.

10 다음 중 어법상 옳은 것으로 알맞게 짝지어진 것은?

> ⓐ I met him in the concert on July.
> ⓑ I want to visit Hawaii in this summer.
> ⓒ Mike enjoys snowboarding at winter.
> ⓓ She studied in France two years ago.
> ⓔ He watched the scary movie on Halloween.

① ⓐ, ⓓ

② ⓓ, ⓔ

③ ⓐ, ⓑ, ⓔ

④ ⓑ, ⓒ, ⓓ

⑤ ⓐ, ⓑ, ⓓ, ⓔ

[11-12] 다음 우리말과 같도록 괄호 안의 말을 이용하여 문장을 완성하시오.

11
> 우리는 저녁 식사 전에 호텔에 도착했다.
> (hotel, dinner)

→ We arrived _____.

12
> 정오에 구름이 우리 머리 위에 있었다.
> (head, noon)

→ There were the clouds _____
_____.

[13-14] 다음 우리말과 의미가 같도록 괄호 안의 말을 바르게 배열하시오.

13
> Jim은 도서관에서 그의 집까지 걸어갔다.
> (the library, walked, to, from, his house)

→ Jim _____.

14
> 그 편의점은 우체국과 은행 사이에 있다.
> (between, is, and, the post office, the bank)

→ The convenience store _____
_____.

15 다음 글에서 어법상 틀린 부분을 2개 찾아 바르게 고쳐 쓰시오.

> My name is Kim Subin. I was born in August 17, 1998. When I was young, I wanted to be a teacher. I studied very hard to become a teacher. I finally became a teacher at 2021. I like my job because I love children.

(1) _____ → _____

(2) _____ → _____

Practice 01 **to부정사**

01-1 다음 괄호 안에서 알맞은 것을 고르시오.

1 (Play / To play) with my dog is fun.
2 My sister hates (studies / to study) math.
3 (That / It) is fun to learn a new language.
4 He promised (to meet / met) her at the zoo.
5 Janet has no money to (buy / buying) a new bag.
6 My goal is to (graduate / graduates) from college next year.
7 We were pleased (to get / got) a good result.
8 He's saving money (buys / to buy) a gift for his parents.
9 I woke up (find / to find) myself famous.
10 People stick out their tongues (made / to make) fun of others.

01-2 다음 문장에서 밑줄 친 부분의 쓰임으로 알맞은 것에 표시(✓)하시오.

	명사	부사	형용사
1 His job is <u>to catch</u> fish.	☐	☐	☐
2 Many people want <u>to be</u> rich.	☐	☐	☐
3 Harry got up early <u>to cook</u> breakfast.	☐	☐	☐
4 I use a computer <u>to do</u> my homework.	☐	☐	☐
5 <u>To ride</u> a bike on the road is dangerous.	☐	☐	☐
6 The poor boy wanted some bread <u>to eat</u>.	☐	☐	☐
7 I must be a fool <u>to trust</u> him.	☐	☐	☐
8 I know a lot of stories <u>to tell</u> the children.	☐	☐	☐

01-3 다음 밑줄 친 to부정사가 꾸며 주는 말에 동그라미 하시오.

1 There are a lot of dishes <u>to wash</u>.
2 He opened the window <u>to breathe</u> fresh air.
3 We have a good program <u>to watch</u> tonight.
4 Did you buy cola <u>to drink</u> during the movie?
5 Kevin and Kate were excited <u>to go</u> to the amusement park.
6 Does he have anything <u>to do</u> now?
7 My brother went outside <u>to fly</u> his drone.
8 Tom's handwriting is difficult <u>to read</u>.
9 I was surprised <u>to see</u> you play in bare feet.

01-4 다음 문장에서 밑줄 친 부분을 어법상 알맞은 형태로 고쳐 쓰시오.

1 His plan is to <u>helping</u> babies in Africa. _____

2 They recently decided <u>moved</u> to Jeju. _____

3 To have my own room <u>are</u> my dream. _____

4 She went to the bakery <u>meeting</u> her friend. _____

5 I was surprised to <u>saw</u> a snake during the hike. _____

6 I don't have time <u>meet</u> my friends. _____

7 <u>Live</u> in the wild may not be easy. _____

8 He woke up <u>finding</u> his house on fire. _____

9 Please give me <u>to eat something hot</u>. _____

10 <u>That's</u> not easy to write by hand well at first. _____

01-5 다음 빈칸에 들어갈 말을 [보기]에서 골라 알맞은 형태로 고쳐 쓰시오. (단, 한 번씩만 쓸 것)

┌─ 보기 ├─────────────────────────────────────┐
│ see   get   talk   live   drink   run   be │
└──┘

1 It is rude _____ loudly on a bus.

2 My aunt wants _____ in a big city.

3 We ran to the yard _____ the stars.

4 Sally wants fresh orange juice _____.

5 Leo studied hard _____ a good grade.

6 The boy grew up _____ the President of the United States.

7 He earned enough money _____ his own company.

01-6 다음 우리말과 의미가 같도록 괄호 안의 말과 to부정사를 이용하여 문장을 완성하시오.

1 그의 취미는 야구 카드를 모으는 것이다. (collect, baseball cards)

→ His hobby is _____.

2 그녀는 혼자 식사하는 것을 좋아하지 않는다. (eat, alone)

→ She doesn't like _____.

3 좋은 친구를 사귀는 것은 중요하다. (make, good friends)

→ It is important _____.

4 Mary는 Tom에게 보낼 선물을 가지고 있다. (send, a present, Tom)

→ Mary has _____.

5 Amy는 옷을 만들기 위해 재봉틀을 사용한다. (make, a sewing machine, clothes)

→ Amy uses _____.

02-1 다음 문장에서 밑줄 친 부분의 쓰임으로 알맞은 것에 표시(✓)하시오.

	주어	보어	목적어
1 Becoming an actor is his dream.	☐	☐	☐
2 Sujin finished cleaning the table.	☐	☐	☐
3 Hana's hobby is making paper dolls.	☐	☐	☐
4 My sister hates touching dogs or cats.	☐	☐	☐
5 The dolphins practice jumping every day.	☐	☐	☐
6 One of his bad habits is biting his nails.	☐	☐	☐
7 It was really hard to run a meeting.	☐	☐	☐

02-2 다음 괄호 안에서 알맞은 것을 모두 고르시오.

1 Tigers are good at (hunting / to hunt).
2 (Reading / To read) books is a good habit.
3 Did you decide (going / to go) to the concert?
4 His job is (making / to make) bread and cakes.
5 My mom enjoys (cooking / to cook) for my family.
6 Some children started (running / to run) all of a sudden.
7 You should avoid (to make / making) noise late at night.
8 I'm thinking about (going / to go) to Switzerland by myself.
9 The tower seems (being / to be) the symbol of this city.
10 Check what is in front of you before (make / making) a decision.

02-3 다음 빈칸에 괄호 안의 말을 알맞은 형태로 바꿔 쓰시오.

1 Would you mind _____ me? (help)
2 Laura gave up _____ a sweater. (sew)
3 Julie likes _____ along the beach. (walk)
4 He is interested in _____ dinosaurs. (study)
5 Many teenagers enjoy _____ to hiphop music. (listen)
6 I want _____ a toothbrush and some toothpaste. (buy)
7 _____ up early on Sundays is not easy for me. (get)
8 We plan _____ flowers in the backyard. (plant)
9 The baby began _____ her mom's words. (understand)
10 He went out without _____ good-bye to the members. (say)

🔖 Answers p.40

02-4 다음 문장에서 밑줄 친 부분을 어법상 알맞은 형태로 고쳐 쓰시오.

1 The audience began <u>applauded</u>.　　　　　　　＿＿＿＿＿＿＿＿
2 Lisa finished <u>to water</u> the garden.　　　　　＿＿＿＿＿＿＿＿
3 Taking care of babies <u>are</u> very hard.　　　　＿＿＿＿＿＿＿＿
4 Thank you for <u>to fix</u> my smartphone.　　　　＿＿＿＿＿＿＿＿
5 She gave up <u>to climb</u> the mountain.　　　　＿＿＿＿＿＿＿＿
6 <u>Have</u> a big supper makes you fat.　　　　　＿＿＿＿＿＿＿＿
7 She promised <u>coming</u> here by 7:00 p.m.　　＿＿＿＿＿＿＿＿
8 You may not be good at <u>draw</u> pictures with crayon.　　＿＿＿＿＿＿＿＿
9 <u>Giving not up</u> your dream is really important.　　＿＿＿＿＿＿＿＿

02-5 다음 빈칸에 들어갈 말을 [보기]에서 골라 알맞은 형태로 고쳐 쓰시오. (단, 한 번씩만 쓸 것)

┌─ 보기 ───┐
│　play　　write　　take　　watch　　go　　solve　　drive　│
└──┘

1 How about ＿＿＿＿＿＿＿＿＿＿ some medicine?
2 My puppies enjoy ＿＿＿＿＿＿＿＿＿＿ in the garden.
3 Anne likes ＿＿＿＿＿＿＿＿＿＿ out on rainy days.
4 Mom is afraid of ＿＿＿＿＿＿＿＿＿＿ a car alone.
5 ＿＿＿＿＿＿＿＿＿＿ a soccer game is sometimes boring.
6 Why did you stop ＿＿＿＿＿＿＿＿＿＿ novels four years ago?
7 The child continued ＿＿＿＿＿＿＿＿＿＿ difficult puzzles.

02-6 다음 우리말과 의미가 같도록 괄호 안의 말을 이용하여 문장을 완성하시오.

1 나는 밤늦게 커피 마시는 것을 피한다. (drink, coffee)
　→ I avoid ＿＿＿＿＿＿＿＿＿＿＿＿＿＿＿＿＿＿＿＿＿ late at night.
2 Jenny는 냉장고 청소하는 것을 멈추었다. (clean, the refrigerator)
　→ Jenny stopped ＿＿＿＿＿＿＿＿＿＿＿＿＿＿＿＿＿＿＿.
3 그의 재능은 사람들을 행복하게 만드는 것이다. (make, people)
　→ His talent is ＿＿＿＿＿＿＿＿＿＿＿＿＿＿＿＿＿＿ happy.
4 Sally는 발레 연습하는 것에 싫증이 났다. (practice, ballet)
　→ Sally was tired of ＿＿＿＿＿＿＿＿＿＿＿＿＿＿＿＿＿.
5 나는 아프리카의 아이들을 돕는 것에 관심이 있다. (help, children)
　→ I'm interested in ＿＿＿＿＿＿＿＿＿＿＿＿＿＿＿ in Africa.

Chapter Test

01 다음 빈칸에 들어갈 말로 알맞지 <u>않은</u> 것을 <u>모두</u> 고르면?

> She _____ talking to you.

① is fond of
② doesn't want
③ really enjoys
④ is looking forward to
⑤ would like

02 다음 빈칸에 들어갈 말로 알맞은 것은?

> They plan _____ new things and get good grades.

① learn
② to learn
③ learning
④ to learning
⑤ be learned

03 다음 두 문장의 의미가 같도록 빈칸에 들어갈 말로 알맞은 것은?

> You don't have to pay money to send emails.
> = You don't have to pay money _____ emails.

① send
② so as send
③ as so to send
④ in order to send
⑤ in order to sending

04 다음 중 짝지어진 문장이 잘못된 것은?

① To go window shopping is fun.
= It is fun to go window shopping.
② I like to eat out with my family.
= I like eating out with my family.
③ My goal is studying abroad next year.
= My goal is to study abroad next year.
④ He gave up writing a dream.
= He gave up to write a dream.
⑤ To jog in the morning is good for your health.
= Jogging in the morning is good for your health.

[05-06] 다음 중 밑줄 친 부분의 쓰임이 나머지 넷과 <u>다른</u> 것을 고르시오.

05 ① I turned on the light <u>to read</u> a book.
② I went to the bathroom <u>to wash</u> my hair.
③ He reads comic books <u>to learn</u> Korean.
④ He was very glad <u>to see</u> his best friend.
⑤ My brother went to the playground <u>to play</u> basketball.

06 ① The topic is <u>keeping</u> pets at home.
② <u>Reading</u> the webtoon is my hobby.
③ Today we talked about <u>watching</u> TV.
④ He is <u>playing</u> the violin on the stage.
⑤ My job is <u>teaching</u> English in elementary school.

07 다음 중 밑줄 친 It의 쓰임이 나머지와 <u>다른</u> 것은?

① <u>It</u> is difficult to learn how to swim.
② <u>It</u> is not very cold here in winter.
③ <u>It</u> is hard to understand his lecture.
④ <u>It</u> is nice to take a break from classes.
⑤ <u>It</u> is tough to give up sugar for my health.

[08-09] 다음 중 어법상 틀린 것을 모두 고르시오.

08 ① Taking exams aren't exciting.
② Harry's hobby is playing the guitar.
③ Would you mind to mail this letter?
④ Thank you for inviting me to the party.
⑤ They began broadcasting it on television.

09 ① Everybody hopes enjoying life.
② It began to rain in the afternoon.
③ Even washing the dishes was fun.
④ Did you decided going there tomorrow?
⑤ I'm tired of eat hamburgers for lunch.

10 다음 중 어법상 옳은 문장의 개수는?

ⓐ Students should learn about helping others.
ⓑ It is interesting for me to take pictures.
ⓒ Tom went to the library meeting his friend.
ⓓ We kept to speak in English until we arrived in Korea.

① 없음　　　② 1개　　　③ 2개
④ 3개　　　⑤ 4개

[11-12] 다음 우리말과 의미가 같도록 괄호 안의 말을 이용하여 문장을 완성하시오.

11
아픈 동물들을 돌보다니 그녀는 친절한 게 틀림없다.
(kind, take care of)

→ She must _____.

12
나는 어렸을 때 가난한 것을 부끄러워했다.
(ashamed, be, poor)

→ I was _____
when I was young.

[13-14] 다음 우리말과 의미가 같도록 괄호 안의 말을 바르게 배열하시오.

13
밤에 자지 않는 것은 너의 건강에 좋지 않다.
(at night, not, your, sleeping, is, for, good, not, health)

→ _____

14
나는 입을 따뜻한 것이 필요하다.
(I, something, wear, need, to, warm)

→ _____

15 다음 그림을 보고 조건에 맞게 문장을 완성하시오.

Minho	○	X	○
Yuna	X	○	○

(1) Minho enjoys _____.

(2) Yuna doesn't enjoy _____.

(3) They both enjoy _____.

Practice 01 **의문사가 있는 의문문**

01 -1 다음 괄호 안에서 알맞은 것을 고르시오.

1 (Whose / Who) is your cousin?

2 (What / Who) will you do tomorrow?

3 (Where / What) did you go last weekend?

4 (Where / How) do you usually go to school?

5 (Who / Whose) pants are those on the sofa?

6 (Which / What) do you like better, meat or fish?

7 (Why / When) was your father absent from work yesterday?

8 (Who / Why) are you looking for now?

9 (How / What) tall is the tallest building in Korea?

10 (What / How) does he look like?

11 (Why / How) don't you have lunch with your friends tonight?

01 -2 다음 질문에 대한 대답으로 알맞은 것을 서로 연결하시오.

1 Whose car is that? • • ⓐ Last night.

2 What does she do? • • ⓑ It is Jerry's.

3 Who is that woman? • • ⓒ She is my aunt.

4 Where is Jessica's house? • • ⓓ She is a teacher.

5 When did you watch the movie? • • ⓔ It's near the bakery.

6 Which do you want, juice or coffee? • • ⓕ Because I passed my English test.

7 Why are you so happy? • • ⓖ Coffee, please.

01 -3 다음 대화의 빈칸에 들어갈 알맞은 말을 [보기]에서 골라 쓰시오.

> ┌ 보기 ┐
> How often   How tall   How far   How much   How old   How long   How many

1 A: _____ is the ticket? B: It's $25.

2 A: _____ books did you buy? B: Three.

3 A: _____ did your father drive? B: Three hours.

4 A: _____ do you take a shower? B: Every day.

5 A: _____ is her home from yours? B: It's about 2 km.

6 A: _____ is your brother? B: He is about 170 cm tall.

7 A: _____ were you when you B: I was 40 years old.
   invented the program?

01 -4 다음 대화의 빈칸에 알맞은 의문사를 쓰시오.

1 A: _____ was the musical?   B: It was wonderful.
2 A: _____ was the girl crying?   B: Because she lost her mother.
3 A: _____ did she eat for lunch?   B: She ate a hamburger.
4 A: _____ did you call yesterday? B: I called my friend Anna.
5 A: _____ is cheaper, milk or juice? B: Milk is cheaper.
6 A: _____ does the next bus arrive? B: It arrives at 12.
7 A: _____ do you usually go shopping? B: I usually go to the outlets.

01 -5 다음 문장의 밑줄 친 부분을 묻는 의문문을 완성하시오.

1 Susan is <u>12 years old</u>.
   → _____ Susan?

2 The dog is sleeping <u>on the sofa</u> now.
   → _____ now?

3 Kevin borrowed <u>my</u> bike.
   → _____ borrow?

4 I like <u>chicken</u> better than pizza.
   → _____ , chicken or pizza?

5 He visited his aunt in Seoul <u>with his family</u>.
   → _____ did he visit his aunt in Seoul?

01 -6 다음 우리말과 의미가 같도록 괄호 안의 말과 의문사를 이용하여 문장을 완성하시오.

1 그 경기는 언제 시작하니? (the game)
   → _____ begin?

2 Mike는 얼마나 많은 돈을 모았니? (money)
   → _____ did Mike save?

3 그 방에는 얼마나 많은 아이들이 있니? (children)
   → _____ are in the room?

4 너는 생일에 인형과 드레스 중 어느 것을 원하니? (want)
   → _____ for your birthday, a doll or a dress?

5 네 방의 벽을 어떤 색으로 칠하고 싶니? (color, paint)
   → _____ the wall of your room?

02-1   다음 괄호 안에서 알맞은 것을 고르시오.

1 (Are / Be) polite to adults.

2 (Open / Opening) your book.

3 (Not / Don't) ride a bike here.

4 Let's (take / takes) pictures here.

5 (Don't let's / Let's not) eat any candy.

6 Never (make / makes) any noise while in concert.

7 (You start / Start) now, and you will catch the bus.

02-2   다음 문장을 명령문으로 바꿔 쓸 때 빈칸에 알맞은 말을 쓰시오.

1 You should be careful climbing the ladder.

→ _____ the ladder.

2 You should write your name on the paper.

→ _____ on the paper.

3 You shouldn't turn on the computer.

→ _____ the computer.

4 You shouldn't be sure of a bonus this year.

→ _____ a bonus this year.

5 You should keep your room clean all the time.

→ _____ all the time.

6 You shouldn't hold the smartphone near your head.

→ _____ near your head.

02-3   다음 문장을 Let's로 시작하는 청유문으로 바꿔 쓰시오.

1 Why don't we wear seat belts?

→ _____

2 Shall we do volunteer work together?

→ _____

3 Why don't we plant some trees on Arbor Day?

→ _____

4 How about waiting for a few more minutes?

→ _____

5 Shall we go to watch fireworks this weekend?

→ _____

6 What about picking up Laura and bringing her to our house?

→ _____

🔖 Answers p.42

02 -4 다음 문장의 밑줄 친 부분을 어법상 알맞은 형태로 고쳐 쓰시오.

1 <u>Are</u> a good soccer player.　　　　　　　　_____

2 <u>Not</u> fight with your brother.　　　　　　_____

3 <u>To wear</u> a coat because it's cold.　　　_____

4 Let's <u>shares</u> the cake among us.　　　_____

5 Let's <u>don't</u> worry about the future.　　_____

6 Wake <u>never</u> me up tomorrow morning.　_____

7 Never <u>tells</u> the secret by mistake.　　_____

02 -5 다음 우리말과 의미가 같도록 [보기]에서 알맞은 말을 골라 문장을 완성하시오. (단, 중복 가능)

┌─ 보기 ┐

　　watch　　　use　　　go　　　clean　　　sit

1 식사 후에는 식탁을 치워라.

　→ _____ the table after meals.

2 TV로 오디션 프로그램을 보자.

　→ _____ the audition program on TV.

3 이번 주말에 캠핑하러 가지 말자.

　→ _____ camping this weekend.

4 공연 중에는 휴대전화를 사용하지 마세요.

　→ Please _____ your cell phone during the show.

5 기차에서는 이어폰을 사용하라.

　→ _____ your earphones on the train.

6 어딘가 좀 앉아서 쉴까요?

　→ _____ down and rest somewhere?

02 -6 다음 우리말과 의미가 같도록 괄호 안의 말을 바르게 배열하시오.

1 내일까지 그 책을 도서관에 반납해라. (to the library, the book, return)

　→ _____ by tomorrow.

2 밤에 너무 많이 먹지 마라. (at night, don't, too much, eat)

　→ _____

3 걸어서 공원에 가자. (to the park, go, on foot, let's)

　→ _____

4 다 함께 좋은 이웃이 되자. (good, let's, neighbors, be)

　→ _____ together.

5 사람들을 옷으로 판단하지 맙시다. (not, judge, let's, people, their, by, clothes)

　→ _____

03 -1 다음 괄호 안에서 알맞은 것을 고르시오.

1 Your school is big, (is / isn't) it?
2 Jimmy lives with his uncle, (isn't / doesn't) he?
3 She baked the cookies, (wasn't / didn't) she?
4 Let's not waste money, (shall / will) we?
5 (What / How) a pleasant garden it is!
6 (What / How) uncomfortable the bed is!
7 Wash the dog for me, (do / will) you?
8 (What / How) beautiful cars they are!
9 The mouse wasn't afraid of the cat, (was / wasn't) it?
10 (What / How) brave these children are!

03 -2 다음 빈칸에 알맞은 부가의문문을 쓰시오.

1 Your sister can't play the flute, _____?
2 Patrick enjoys swimming, _____?
3 You eat food with chopsticks, _____?
4 Sumi and Nara joined the cooking club, _____?
5 You were tired this morning, _____?
6 Don't be noisy when you play in the park, _____?
7 Let's not waste any more time, _____?

03 -3 다음 문장을 주어진 말로 시작하는 감탄문으로 바꿔 쓰시오.

1 It is a very large airport.
   → What _____!
2 It is a very difficult problem.
   → What _____!
3 They are very cute teddy bears.
   → What _____!
4 The sneakers smell very terrible.
   → How _____!
5 You are a very shy girl.
   → What _____!
6 Cheesecakes are really rich and heavy.
   → How _____!

Answers p.42

03-4 다음 문장의 밑줄 친 부분을 어법상 알맞은 형태로 고쳐 쓰시오.

1 Jenny didn't eat breakfast, <u>was she</u>? _____

2 Don't be late for school, <u>do you</u>? _____

3 Those scissors aren't yours, <u>do they</u>? _____

4 <u>What small</u> the doll is! _____

5 <u>What a delicious cheese</u> it is! _____

6 Let's go abroad during the vacation, <u>will you</u>? _____

7 Turtles can't turn over, <u>aren't they</u>? _____

8 <u>How big</u> eyes your daughter has! _____

9 Don't take pictures here, <u>won't you</u>? _____

10 He'll be much better next year, <u>isn't he</u>? _____

03-5 다음 우리말과 의미가 같도록 괄호 안의 말을 이용하여 문장을 완성하시오.

1 Sam은 한국어를 못하지, 그렇지? (can, speak, Korean)

→ Sam _____, _____?

2 너는 숙제가 많지, 그렇지 않니? (have, a lot of homework)

→ You _____, _____?

3 그 왕자는 정말 행복해 보이는구나! (happy)

→ _____ the prince looks!

4 너는 어젯밤에 Clara를 만났지, 그렇지 않니? (meet, Clara, last night)

→ You _____, _____?

5 그 신발들은 정말 크구나! (big, shoes)

→ _____ they are!

03-6 다음 우리말과 의미가 같도록 괄호 안의 말을 바르게 배열하시오.

1 네 컴퓨터는 고장 났지, 그렇지 않니? (isn't, is, your computer, it, broken, ?)

→ _____

2 그 만화책은 정말 재미있구나! (the comic book, how, is, funny, !)

→ _____

3 그것들은 정말 멋진 사진들이구나! (they, wonderful, what, pictures, are, !)

→ _____

4 Frank는 우리와 함께 머무를 거지, 그렇지 않니? (will, with us, Frank, he, stay, won't, ?)

→ _____

5 날씨가 정말 좋구나! (we, what, lovely, have, weather, !)

→ _____

[01-02] 다음 빈칸에 들어갈 말로 알맞은 것을 고르시오.

01

A: _____ do you like better, the sunset or the sunrise?
B: I like the sunset better.

① How   ② Why   ③ Which
④ Where   ⑤ What

02

A: _____ idea was it?
B: It was Mike's.

① Who   ② Why   ③ Where
④ How   ⑤ Whose

03 다음 빈칸 (A), (B)에 들어갈 말로 알맞게 짝지어진 것은?

· ____(A)____ a wonderful world!
· ____(B)____ useful this web application is!

	(A)	(B)		(A)	(B)
①	How	– How	②	What	– How
③	How	– What	④	What	– What
⑤	What	– Which			

04 다음 빈칸 (A), (B), (C)에 들어갈 말로 알맞게 짝지어진 것은?

· He will send flowers to her, ____(A)____ ?
· Let's not stop in the middle, ____(B)____ ?
· You don't remember meeting me, ____(C)____ ?

	(A)	(B)	(C)
①	will he	– shall we	– don't it
②	won't he	– shall not we	– do you
③	will he	– shouldn't we	– do you
④	won't he	– shall we	– do you
⑤	will he	– will we	– does it

05 다음 중 의미가 나머지와 <u>다른</u> 것은?

① Let's stop for a coffee.
② Shall we stop for a coffee?
③ You must stop for a coffee.
④ How about stopping for a coffee?
⑤ Why don't we stop for a coffee?

06 다음 상황에 알맞은 명령문을 <u>모두</u> 고르면?

① Please be quiet.
② Raise your hands.
③ Don't make a noise.
④ Don't sleep in class.
⑤ Don't watch TV too much.

07 다음 짝지어진 대화 중 <u>어색한</u> 것은?

① A: How old is your father?
   B: He is forty years old.
② A: How much milk do you drink every day?
   B: I drink 500 ml of milk every day.
③ A: How long did you stay in Jeju?
   B: Once a month.
④ A: How far is it from your house to the gym?
   B: It's about 2 km.
⑤ A: How often do you clean your parking lot?
   B: Every weekend.

[08-09] 다음 중 어법상 <u>틀린</u> 문장을 <u>모두</u> 고르시오.

08 ① Be not late for school.
② Listen to the teacher.
③ Don't turn on the TV.
④ Let's ride bikes after school.
⑤ Let's don't doze off during class.

09 ① It's a nice day today, isn't it?
② This place looks nice, doesn't it?
③ You don't have a car, have you?
④ She can play the piano, can't she?
⑤ You must stop and wait, do you?

10 다음 중 어법상 옳은 문장의 개수는?

ⓐ Never tells his secret.
ⓑ What does she look like?
ⓒ Fasten your seatbelt, will you?
ⓓ How hot this chili pepper is!

① 없음　　　② 1개　　　③ 2개
④ 3개　　　⑤ 4개

11 다음 우리말과 의미가 같도록 괄호 안의 말을 이용하여 문장을 완성하시오.

우리의 계획을 포기하지 말자. (give up)

→ ＿＿＿＿＿＿＿＿＿＿＿＿＿＿ our plan.

12 다음 문장에서 어법상 <u>틀린</u> 부분을 찾아 바르게 고쳐 쓰시오.

They won't watch the movie, shall they?

＿＿＿＿＿＿＿＿＿ → ＿＿＿＿＿＿＿＿＿

13 다음 문장을 How 또는 What으로 시작하는 감탄문으로 바꾸어 쓰시오.

Hankuk Middle School is very good.

→ ＿＿＿＿＿＿＿＿＿＿＿＿＿＿＿＿＿

14 다음 표지판을 보고, [보기]에 주어진 단어들을 사용하여 명령문을 만드시오.

┌ 보기 ┐
here　　　　　park

→ ＿＿＿＿＿＿＿＿＿＿＿＿＿＿＿＿＿

15 다음은 각 장소의 주의 사항이다. ⓐ~ⓔ 중 어법상 <u>틀린</u> 것을 2개 찾아 기호를 쓰고 바르게 고쳐 쓰시오.

bus stop	ⓐ Wait in line, please.
museum	ⓑ Not take pictures.
swimming pool	ⓒ Warm up before swimming.
movie theater	ⓓ Please turns off your cellphone.
library	ⓔ Don't make too much noise, please.

(1) ＿＿＿ → ＿＿＿＿＿＿＿＿＿

(2) ＿＿＿ → ＿＿＿＿＿＿＿＿＿

MEMO

MEMO

GRAMMAR
MASTER

GRAMMAR
MASTER